Frederick Watts
and the Founding
of Penn State

Frederick Watts and the Founding of Penn State

Roger L. Williams

The Pennsylvania State University Press
University Park, Pennsylvania

Frontispiece: Frederick Watts (1801–89), Carlisle, Pa., attorney and reporter for the Pennsylvania Supreme Court. Courtesy of the Pennsylvania State University Archives.

Library of Congress Cataloging-in-Publication Data

Names: Williams, Roger L. (Roger Lea), author.
Title: Frederick Watts and the founding of Penn State / Roger L. Williams.
Description: University Park, Pennsylvania : The Pennsylvania State University Press, [2021] | Includes bibliographical references and index.
Summary: "Examines the life and accomplishments of Frederick Watts (1801–1889) in agricultural innovation and his role in the creation of the institution that would grow into Penn State University"—Provided by publisher.
Identifiers: LCCN 2021012462 | ISBN 9780271089898 (cloth)
Subjects: LCSH: Watts, Frederick, 1801–1889. | Agricultural College of Pennsylvania—History. | Farmers' High School of Pennsylvania—History. | College trustees—Pennsylvania—Biography. | Agricultural innovations—Pennsylvania—History—19th century.
Classification: LCC LD4481.P813 W378 2021 | DDC 378.1/011092 [B]—dc23
LC record available at https://lccn.loc.gov/2021012462

Printed in the United States of America
Published by The Pennsylvania State University Press, University Park, PA 16802–1003

The Pennsylvania State University Press is a member of the Association of University Presses.

It is the policy of The Pennsylvania State University Press to use acid-free paper. Publications on uncoated stock satisfy the minimum requirements of American National Standard for Information Sciences—Permanence of Paper for Printed Library Material, ANSI Z39.48–1992.

CONTENTS

ILLUSTRATIONS

PROLOGUE AND ACKNOWLEDGMENTS

It promised to be quite a show: a crowd of five hundred to one thousand rural folk gathered in the late summer of 1840 to witness the first demonstration, in the state of Pennsylvania, of a newfangled farm machine. The impresario: Frederick Watts, age thirty-nine, prominent lawyer and reporter for the Pennsylvania Supreme Court and innovative agriculturalist with an energetic drive for improving the lot of the hardworking farmer. The site: Watts's "Creekside Farm," just outside of Carlisle, in the agriculturally rich Cumberland Valley of the state's south-central region. The machine: the McCormick Reaper, designed by Virginian Cyrus McCormick in 1831 and patented in 1834.

Watts had publicized the event widely, but the crowd he attracted had gathered more for entertainment than edification. They had dubbed the new machine "Watts' Folly," and they expected an embarrassing failure. The horse-drawn McCormick Reaper had got off to a slow, uncertain start during the 1830s, because it could not handle varying conditions and was deemed unreliable. In fact, the first McCormick Reaper wasn't sold until 1840—most likely to Frederick Watts.[1]

On this day, the wheat was ripe and ready for harvest. Watts held the demonstration on a twelve-acre field that yielded about thirty-five bushels to the acre—an expanse designed to put the reaper through its paces. The crowd chortled. Their moment of schadenfreude was at hand.

The demonstration began. The machine worked as intended, but the equally important human factor in the equation failed. The reaper contained a reel to tilt the wheat off the cutter bar and onto the machine's platform. A man was to walk behind the reaper and rake the wheat off the platform and onto the ground, to be bound into bundles. The reaper cut the wheat "quickly and perfectly," but it was blazingly apparent that the hapless raker could not keep up with the job. The crowd broke into laughter.

Then a "well-dressed stranger" came out of the crowd and gave some suggestions to improve the raker's performance. The reaper proceeded to move forward, but after fifty yards or so, the demonstration was halted again because the raker still could not keep up.

Finally, the third time around, the well-dressed gentleman stepped *onto* the machine and raked the wheat off the platform "with perfect ease." This compelled the crowd to reverse its verdict and concede that the machine *could* work as intended. The well-dressed man then introduced himself as none other than Cyrus McCormick. The crowd not only had witnessed the first successful use of the McCormick Reaper in Pennsylvania but also, whether realizing it or not, had just witnessed a giant leap forward for American agriculture.[2] Eventually, the reaper would do more than any other machine "to abolish the famine of the cities and the drudgery of the farm—to feed the hungry and straighten the bent backs of the world."[3]

The demonstration's success established Watts's reputation "not only as an agricultural reformer, but as a recognized leader among the 'independently-minded' Scotch-Irish farmers of the valley."[4] Still, it would be years before the McCormick Reaper would come into wider acceptance in Pennsylvania and elsewhere. For the most part, farmers were bound to traditional practices and reluctant to adopt innovation. In some ways, their aversion smacked of a Luddite-like resistance to new technologies because of the fear that labor-saving machinery would destroy farmwork, farm families, and their entire way of life. The machine made its advent in nearby Lancaster County in 1851 and York County in 1853.[5] What sparked sales of the McCormick Reaper, after the company moved to Chicago in 1849, was the development of another technology—the railroads. The reaper was a heavy, cumbersome device, hard to transport from one place to another until it could be loaded onto railway cars. But what really solidified the McCormick Reaper's reputation was its successful demonstration at London's Crystal Palace Exhibition in 1851, at which a competitor's reaper failed.[6]

Watts's purchase of the reaper and his inaugural demonstration were not his only contributions to Pennsylvania agriculture. The previous year, he introduced so-called Mediterranean wheat to Pennsylvania farmers. This was no small benefaction. From before the Revolution to about 1840, Pennsylvania was the largest wheat-producing state in the nation. In the years after the Revolution, however, the wheat crop was increasingly ravaged by the Hessian fly (*Mayetiola destructor*), an invasive insect thought to have been inadvertently imported to the country via the livestock of Hessian soldiers. By 1790, the fly was causing widespread devastation, particularly in southeastern

Pennsylvania, causing farmers to rethink their heavy reliance on their largest cash crop and diversify their production.[7]

A half century later, visiting the farm of a friend, Watts and his wife, Henrietta, learned of a new variety of wheat. As Watts told the story:

> About the middle of June, 1839, near Trenton, New Jersey, I was met by a former resident of the Carlisle Barracks, Lieut. Wm. Inman, of the United States Navy, who invited us to spend the night at his home on the farm. The next day he showed me a field of beautiful wheat which was ripening for harvest. He told me that two years prior to that time he had procured three bushels of the seed near Leghorn, Italy, and was now raising the second crop. I obtained from him six barrels of the same kind and sowed it on my farm near Carlisle. That was the introduction into the United States of the beautiful variety of wheat which for a long time was very popular and was known as Mediterranean. From the six barrels which I sowed it was spread through the Cumberland Valley and into other parts of the state.[8]

The advantage of Mediterranean wheat was that it matured early, such that it could be harvested before the hatching season of the Hessian fly. Mediterranean wheat quickly began to produce increased yields, ultimately "saving the day" for farmers across Pennsylvania and elsewhere.[9]

A decade later, in the early 1850s, Frederick Watts would use his talents to "save the day" for Pennsylvania farmers in even more profound ways. With like-minded colleagues, he would organize the Pennsylvania farming community into the powerful Pennsylvania State Agricultural Society and serve as its founding president (1851). He wanted to bring farmers together as a self-conscious community to better their social, economic, and political lot in life. Then he would use his presidential platform to advocate urgently for the establishment of an agricultural college (1854 and 1855) that would provide a scientifically based education for farmers' sons. Watts would serve as president of the board of trustees of the new Farmers' High School, later renamed the Agricultural College of Pennsylvania, for nineteen years. Finally, he would cap his career by serving as U.S. commissioner of agriculture (1871–77), appointed by President Ulysses S. Grant.

Although little recognized today, Frederick Watts in earlier decades was acknowledged as "the father of the Pennsylvania State College" (now the

Pennsylvania State University), according to Stevenson W. Fletcher, the historian of Pennsylvania agriculture, and others. Such a claim deserves to be examined again, because for all his accomplishments, that is his most enduring legacy.

There is, however, an ironic arc to Watts's leadership of the fledgling agricultural college. For all of his success in creating and launching the institution in the face of political and financial challenges, he nearly brought it to the brink of closure through a series of disastrous presidential appointments—selecting incapable men—after the unexpected death of its brilliant young founding president, Evan Pugh, in 1864. Furthermore, Watts concurred with the various curricular reforms these presidents recommended, taking the college further away from its original character as the scientific institution Pugh had envisioned and—after the Morrill Act of 1862—as a land-grant college in which agriculture and the mechanic arts (engineering) were to be the "leading object."

Aside from the agricultural college, Watts's work in other agrarian domains deserves reexamination as well. "From 1850 until 1880," Fletcher writes, "he was by far the most outstanding figure in Pennsylvania agriculture."[10] This assertion is especially intriguing in view of the fact that Watts was not a farmer by vocation. In his first fifty years, he rose to eminence as a lawyer, reporter for the state Supreme Court, judge, candidate for political office, private college trustee, railroad company president, and business and civic leader. But concurrent with this work, and beginning about 1820, agriculture, his putative avocation, became far and away his greatest interest in life. And his interest in agriculture coincided with the state's historical dominance in that domain. "For more than a century, from 1725 to 1840, Pennsylvania was foremost among the colonies and states in the production of food," Fletcher says, serving as the "bread-basket of the nation."[11] Long was it known as offering "the best poor man's soil," attracting immigrants in droves, especially from the German states.

Pennsylvania—Watts's "playground," if you will—was regarded as a much different state in the nineteenth century than the Pennsylvania of today, relegated to rust-belt status. According to historian Michael Zuckerman, the state held a reputation for leadership across three centuries of the most profound historical transitions of the Western world. In the seventeenth century, as new ideas of religious freedom emerged, William Penn's "Holy Experiment" stood as a unique beacon of tolerance, a peaceable kingdom for people of all religious faiths. In the eighteenth century came the Democratic Revolution, with Philadelphia the cauldron of rebellion and parent of a new nation enshrining popular participation in government. In the nineteenth century came the Industrial Revolution, nowhere more powerfully than in

Pennsylvania, with its iron, coal, steel, lumber, oil, and gas—the epicenter of the extractive industries and the manufacturing might that ensued.[12] Over this same period, Pennsylvania provided equivalent strength in agriculture, though its salience began to wane about the middle of the nineteenth century as the rich agricultural states of the Midwest began their rise to the fore. Watts stepped into his broader leadership roles at precisely the right time to get Pennsylvania's agrarian community moving in progressive directions.

Frederick Watts has been the subject of a dozen or so biographical sketches over the years, the first completed in 1876 and the last in 2009; for the most part, these accounts are laudatory, some tending toward hagiography. The narrative herein attempts to provide a fuller biographical treatment, with a deeper, more balanced analysis of his life and accomplishments. The focus, however, is on his work in founding, building, and leading Penn State in its formative years; some further detail on the institution's struggles after Watts left the board of trustees in 1873–74 is provided for additional perspective. In addition, Watts's work as U.S. commissioner of agriculture intersected with the new land-grant colleges, and this interaction, as well as his other initiatives with the department, is detailed in the final chapter.

My interest in Frederick Watts grew out of my recent work on the institution's founding president, Evan Pugh.[13] This book on Watts is both prequel and sequel to the Pugh story. I wanted a fuller understanding of the dynamics leading to the school's founding (1850–55) and the four years following, when the institution was located, financed, and built before it could open for instruction in 1859.

As I suspected, and though he had many compatriots in the cause, particularly fellow trustee Hugh N. McAllister, Watts was the indispensable man in getting the institution up and running. The Farmers' High School (1855–62) and then the Agricultural College of Pennsylvania (1862–74) soon flourished under Pugh's adroit leadership (1859–64), in the midst of the greatest crisis in American history. After Pugh, the institution slid into its "era of drift," as Penn State historians have labeled the aftermath (1864–82), eventually devolving into a backwoods classical college and nearly closing for good. Accordingly, Watts, as president of the board of trustees until 1874, must bear the strongest measure of accountability for the appointment of four of the five institutional presidents who floundered and failed during this eighteen-year retrogression. Nonetheless, the institution recovered, stabilized, and reorganized itself for success in the twentieth century under its "second founder," President George W. Atherton (1882–1906).[14]

This book has been greatly aided by the perspective of several colleagues, steeped in both higher education and Penn State history, whose comments were vital to my rethinking and reshaping the manuscript. They are Roger L. Geiger, emeritus distinguished professor of higher education at the Pennsylvania State University and author of numerous influential books, most recently his magisterial two-volume history of American higher education (2015, 2019); Michael Bezilla, former director of research communications at Penn State and university historian, having produced three volumes on the institution's history; Leon J. Stout, emeritus head, Public Services and Outreach, Special Collections in the University Libraries, and author of books and numerous articles on Penn State history; and Jacqueline R. Esposito, former university archivist and head, Records Management, University Libraries, and author of books and articles on Penn State history. I am especially indebted to the Special Collections staff, especially Rachael Dreyer, head of research services, who tracked down and scanned needed photographs in the University Archives during its pandemic-forced closure, and Meredith Weber, research services specialist, who pointed me to useful materials and helped in numerous ways.

At Penn State University Press, I am grateful to director Patrick Alexander for his interest and especially to acquisitions editor Kathryn Yahner for her guidance and support throughout this project, as well as editorial assistant Maddie Caso. I also thank Jennifer Norton, associate director and design and production manager, and Laura Reed-Morrisson, managing editor. And I especially appreciate the anonymous readers commissioned by the press, whose critical comments were so useful to the revision process. Press copyeditor Nicole Wayland was invaluable, as was Sally Heffentreyer, retired assistant director of creative services at Penn State, who provided preliminary editing and other assistance. Billy Toy, webmaster at the Penn State Alumni Association, was particularly helpful in collecting and refining the images herein. My wife, Karen Magnuson, retired assistant director of marketing in the office of strategic communications at Penn State, edited and formatted the manuscript and provided constant encouragement throughout.

Finally, I wish to dedicate this book to my five dear grandchildren: Kaiya N. Weston, Lucy J. Williams, Tommy L. Williams, Kaelan M. Fincham, and Jace A. Fincham. I wish them health, happiness, and meaningful careers in hopes that they may, in ripe old age, see the dawn of the twenty-second century.

CHAPTER I

Frederick Watts's First Fifty Years

For all of his contributions to Pennsylvania and American agriculture, Frederick Watts was not born to the farmstead. Rather, he was highborn, a town dweller, his father a prominent lawyer and his grandfathers officers in the Revolutionary War. Despite his pedigree, he did not inherit wealth; nevertheless, he quickly assumed the mantle of the quintessential nineteenth-century man of affairs and gentleman farmer, amassing power, influence, reputation, prominence, and affluence. Of high intellect, with an innovative, entrepreneurial spirit so well suited to the ambitious nineteenth century, he succeeded famously in his chosen legal profession but also devoted himself to public service in manifold ways. His whole life through, he balanced a variety of significant roles and challenges, with the law certainly, but also with higher education, railroading, civic improvement, and—his interest above all else—the improvement of agriculture, particularly through science and education, and the advancement of the American farmer.

Frederick Watts was born at the dawn of the nineteenth century, on May 9, 1801, in Carlisle, Pennsylvania, a town about eighteen miles west of Harrisburg in the wide and agriculturally rich Cumberland Valley. His father, David Watts, was known as "one of the most distinguished lawyers of his day, whose practice extended through all the middle counties of the state." His mother, Juliana, who married David in 1796, was the daughter of General Henry Miller, who served in the Revolutionary War; in the War of 1812, Miller commanded the U.S. troops at Baltimore.[1]

Frederick's paternal grandfather and namesake was a native of Wales. He immigrated to Pennsylvania in 1760, living first in Chester County, outside Philadelphia. After a few years, he moved to Cumberland County, the second county to be established (1750) west of the Susquehanna River and at the time encompassing all lands in central and western Pennsylvania. Frederick Watts the elder bought a large tract of land at the confluence of the Juniata and Susquehanna Rivers, in what is now Perry County (carved out of Cumberland County in 1820).[2] Today, there remains a vestige of these once-vast holdings, the "Watts Exit" on U.S. Route 322.[3] Grandfather Frederick is said to have been a man "of good education and more than average ability." Prominent in the affairs of the province, and later the state, he became a colonel in the Continental Army. After the Revolution, he was a member of the Supreme Executive Council, the highest governmental authority in Pennsylvania before the adoption of the 1790 Constitution.[4]

His only son, David, was born on the family's holdings on October 29, 1764, four years after his father emigrated from Wales. David was a member of the first graduating class of Carlisle's Dickinson College in 1787 and, like his father and as-yet-unborn son, a man of keen intellect. At Dickinson, he acquired "a taste for and appreciation of the literature of Greece and Rome that he retained throughout his life." After graduation, he read law in the office of a prominent Philadelphia attorney, William Lewis, and passed the bar examination. He returned to Carlisle, was admitted to the bar there, and soon amassed a large clientele. He engaged in politics as well as the looming legal issues of the day. He was described as being "without a superior in the State either on questions of law before the courts, or of facts before the jury."

In certain ways, David Watts was a force of nature. He sired twelve children. He was described as being "a large man, with a powerful voice. His self-confidence was great and of great advantage to him, for his abilities were considerable. He condemned authorities, preferring to argue his cause from first principles, and this he did with great power. He was apt to be violent and overbearing and was in the habit of heaping abuse on his opponents." In addition, he was a spendthrift in "profusion."[5] He also was a freethinker, "an open scoffer against religion and the presbyterian church and clergy," although he attended the Episcopal Church and took part in its liturgical service. Despite his apparent disdain for Presbyterianism, David in 1801 was appointed a trustee of then thoroughly Presbyterian Dickinson College, serving in that role for the rest of his life.[6]

FIGURE 1
David Watts (1764–1819), Carlisle, Pa., attorney and father of Frederick Watts. Courtesy of the Cumberland County Historical Society, Carlisle, Pa.

David's outsize reputation was cemented during the Whiskey Rebellion. Brave and fiercely patriotic, he took a bold public stance in defense of the new federal government when Pennsylvania and New Jersey militias were called to Carlisle in September 1794 to be nationalized by President George Washington in person and commissioned to quell the uprising. The Whiskey Rebellion was fomented by frontier resistance to an excise tax proposed by U.S. Treasury Secretary Alexander Hamilton, in an effort to raise money to pay off the national debt incurred by the Revolutionary War. The tax was levied on whiskey, the literal coin of the realm in the Pennsylvania backcountry, where hard currency was rare. Farmers distilled whiskey and used it like money to barter for goods. But the tax enraged the frontier folk, as it was based not on how much whiskey a farmer actually made but on the maximum capacity his still could produce. The anger grew to the point of violence and talk of secession.[7] At this time, Carlisle, one of the largest centers of white settlement in south-central Pennsylvania, gave rise to anti-government sentiment on the part of its many Scots-Irish citizens. The "Whiskey Boys" in the area erected a "liberty pole" and threatened to shoot anyone who tried to take it down. Ignoring their warning, David Watts "took his axe and rode out to the pole unarmed and alone and chopped it down."[8] No harm befell David Watts. He lived a quarter century more, dying on September 25, 1819, when his son Frederick was eighteen.

Frederick would come to share his father's exceptional legal talent and self-confidence but would be his polar opposite in temperament and fiscal affairs. An 1851 testimonial in the *Carlisle Herald* cited Frederick's cordial relations with young and old members of the bar, his ability to get quickly to the point of a case, and his straightforwardness and lack of vacillation or ambiguity that let an opposing lawyer or judge know exactly where he stood. The testimonial also cited his "fairness, honesty, and impartial administering of justice."[9] Furthermore, Frederick was anything but overbearing and violent. And as will be shown later, his conservative fiscal management and frugality—lessons learned from his father's profligacy—became a hallmark of his organizational leadership.

The town of Carlisle—Frederick Watts's lifelong home—provided a dynamic context for the young man in his formative years. Scots-Irish immigrants had begun filtering into the Cumberland Valley in the 1730s. By 1751, the town, planned by Thomas Penn, was laid out at the intersection of five Native American Indian trails (now the intersection of I-81 and I-76). In 1753, the settlers erected a stockade, upgraded and named Fort Carlisle in 1755. The French and Indian War (1756–63) brought violent resistance from Native American Indians pushing back hard against encroaching white settlement. Carlisle's strategic position at the northern head of the Cumberland Valley enabled the organization of the Forbes Expedition in 1758 and the Bouquet expedition in 1763, just as it provided the mustering ground for federalized troops thirty-one years later to smash the Whiskey Rebellion.[10]

The Scots-Irish settlers were fiercely independent folk and great fighters, providing a profusion of soldiers for the Continental Army. In terms of Pennsylvania's pre-Revolution westward expansion across the Susquehanna, the province's powers-that-be, specifically the Penn family and their agents, encouraged the Scots-Irish to move into the frontier regions of Cumberland County, where they would provide a bulwark against Native American Indian raids. Alternatively, the Penns incentivized the more peaceful German immigrants to settle in York County, contiguous to the southern border of Cumberland County, where the threat was less severe.[11]

Planned by Thomas Penn as one of his six proprietary towns (or county seats) along with York, Reading, Bedford, Easton, and Sunbury, Carlisle quickly grew into "a sizable and significant place" by eighteenth-century standards. As a recent historian has said, it was "a place where things happened: it was a migration gateway to the southern and western interiors, hub of the colonial fur trade, military staging and supply ground during the Seven Years' and Revolutionary Wars, and home to one of the United States' earliest printing presses and colleges."[12]

After the Revolution, Carlisle quickly took on the trappings of civilization. Dickinson College was chartered by the Pennsylvania legislature in 1783, becoming the first college established west of the Susquehanna. The trustees immediately organized themselves at the Philadelphia home of John Dickinson, a founding father of the United States and the noted "Penman of the Revolution." Dickinson, who at the time was serving as president of the state's Supreme Executive Council, made a "very liberal donation" to get the college started and was rewarded with the eponymous naming. The true impetus for the college, however, came from Benjamin Rush, the famous Philadelphia physician and signer of the Declaration of Independence. Rush founded the Carlisle Grammar School in 1773 and in 1782 published his "Hints for Establishing a College at Carlisle in Cumberland County, Pennsylvania." The college was to be Presbyterian to its core, controlled by clergymen.[13]

Dickinson got off to a strong start, led by President Charles Nisbet (1785–1804). Among its early graduates were Roger Brook Taney (Class of 1795), who became U.S. secretary of the treasury and then chief justice of the U.S. Supreme Court from 1836 to 1864, and James Buchanan (Class of 1809), who became president of the United States from 1857 to 1861.[14] Despite its auspicious beginnings, Dickinson would encounter severe existential challenges beginning in the second decade of the nineteenth century—challenges that would eventually engage the talents of Frederick Watts.

In 1815, Frederick Watts, at age fourteen, entered Dickinson College. Although he is listed in the alumni records as a member of the Class of 1819, he did not graduate, albeit through no fault of his own. After his first year, Dickinson closed its doors and entered a half-decade of dormancy (1816–21). Watts took some informal classwork during this time, but the college could do nothing that would lead to the conferral of the baccalaureate degree. There is little documentary evidence of his college days. In 1930, a writer asked the then college president, James Henry Morgan, "whether there is any tradition of anything notable in his college years" and reported that "Dr. Morgan does not know of any such tradition; and found, in an Alumni Record, only the brief statement of things he did in later years."[15]

The source of Dickinson's problems was internal dissension, mainly a long-simmering power struggle between trustees and faculty over control of the institution, a struggle that had finally come to a head. The trustees had inserted themselves aggressively into matters of student discipline and academic programs, especially what should be taught and how it should be taught, domains traditionally the province of faculty. By 1815, the year Watts entered, student enrollment had dwindled to twenty-seven. Then things fell apart. A college historian said, "The lack of harmony in the College, in the Board of Trustees, in the Faculty and between trustees and Faculty—everywhere, in fact, where lack of harmony could exist—had done its work. There appeared to be no hope for the future, and closing the College was the only reasonable thing to do." After nearly four years of closure, the trustees in May 1820 asked the Burgess of Carlisle to call a public meeting to discuss "college conditions." The outcome was a petition to the legislature for an immediate grant of $6,000 to the college for debts and repairs, and to provide an appropriation of $2,000 annually for five years. The legislature agreed and the college reopened in 1821, but its troubles would not end there.[16]

In 1819, after the death of his father, Frederick left Carlisle, embarking on a dramatic life change. He went to live at the farm of his uncle (by marriage), William Miles, a leading lawyer, developer, miller, and farmer in Erie County, in the northwestern corner of Pennsylvania. Watts's main purpose was to read law with his prominent uncle, in preparation for a legal career. Over the two years of his residency, however, something quite unexpected happened. The young "townie," the son of a prominent attorney, fell in love with farm life and cultivated "his taste for agricultural pursuits."[17] Indeed, he felt the stirrings of what would become his lifelong cause—the improvement of agriculture and the advancement of the American farmer.

An Ambitious Legal Career

Despite these stirrings, Watts returned to Carlisle in 1821, determined to follow in the footsteps of his father and begin a legal career. He continued to read law, this time with Andrew Carothers, and was admitted to the Cumberland County Bar in 1824. He then became a partner of Carothers "and soon acquired a large and lucrative practice." Carlisle was fertile ground for an ambitious young lawyer. Watts had rejoined his hometown at a propitious time, at the beginning of what has been described as "the golden age of Carlisle's legal profession." Later historians have maintained that "the legal history of the town is the story of lawyers whose reputations were known throughout the East." These luminaries included James Hamilton; James Willson; Samuel Hepburn; David Watts, later characterized as "father of the brilliant Frederick Watts"; Andrew Carothers; Isaac Brown Parker; and John Reed, who in 1830 published a well-known tome titled *Pennsylvania Blackstone* and a few years later proposed and established what became the Dickinson School of Law under the auspices of the college.[18]

In this milieu, Watts soon became known "as an attorney of superior ability, a reputation he held for his entire life."[19] A contemporary observer described his most prominent characteristics as "force of character and abiding self confidence," though not overbearing like his father. "His temper was completely within control. His equanimity was perfect, and he was ever ready to avail himself of any slip of his adversary." But there was nothing egotistical or mean-spirited in his behavior. "His power with the jury was very great. He knew and was known by every man in the counties where he practiced, and

FIGURE 2
Frederick Watts as a young lawyer in the early 1830s. Painting by Bass Otis. © 2020 Image courtesy of David H. Peiffer: Peiffer Memorial Arboretum and Nature Preserve, Inc., New Cumberland, Pa.

was regarded as a man of large intellect, sterling integrity and unblemished honor . . . he added the impression of perfect belief in the justice his cause . . . always encouraged and treated kindly younger members of the bar . . . when he closed his professional career, he left the bar with the profound respect of all of its members."[20]

No matter how satisfying his law practice, Watts's legal ambitions did not end there. In 1829, he and his fellow attorney Charles B. Penrose won appointments as reporters of the decisions of the Pennsylvania Supreme Court, which met in Harrisburg, the state capital eighteen miles to the east of Carlisle. He and Penrose published three volumes (1829–32), and then Penrose quit; Watts took on the task as the sole court reporter, publishing ten volumes (1832–40). He eventually took on another partner, Henry J. Sergeant, Esq., and together they published an additional nine volumes. Watts ended his reporting in 1845, after sixteen years.[21] Serving as court reporter to the state's Supreme Court was a prodigious task, in and of itself, and Watts did this on top of his ongoing legal practice and other endeavors. Before the introduction of the typewriter, such reporting was a daunting physical as well as intellectual task. At first a nearly illegible writer, Watts had to retrain himself to produce his work in readable cursive. The challenge of the job was described thus:

> In those days paper books were written—not printed—and stenographers and typewriters were unknown. The labor of writing the matter for more than 11,000 pages of his volumes of reports was enormous. The mental work was equally so. It involved a short, comprehensive and clear statement of facts gathered often from a mass of testimony, through comprehension of the Supreme Court's opinion and the formation of syllabi which would give the principles of the opinions in short epigrammatic terms. It was no wonder that while he was doing that work and managing his large practice he had for weeks at a time to snatch but two or three hours sleep a day on a sofa in the room where he did the work. To do it required mental and physical power of a gigantic order and Mr. Watts did it and did it well.[22]

Meanwhile, Watts's continuing work as an attorney involved cases great and small and everything in between. In 1859, shortly before the Civil War, he represented the case of an African American family kidnapped from their home in Cumberland County. The family had been freed by their Maryland master upon his death and subsequently had moved to free-soil Pennsylvania.

Captured by a slaver, they were to be returned to the master's family and used as personal property to erase family debts. The kidnapper was himself captured before crossing into Maryland and brought to Carlisle to stand trial. With Watts and his colleague arguing the case, the kidnapper was found guilty, but, in a compromise, the sentence was suspended in return for the African American family's being allowed to come back to Pennsylvania.[23]

The capstone to Watts's legal career came in 1849, when he was appointed by Governor William F. Johnston, a Whig, to succeed Samuel Hepburn as president judge of the Ninth Judicial District, encompassing Cumberland, Perry, and Juniata Counties. This work had its physically onerous aspect as well. The counties in question, particularly Perry and Juniata, were geographically large, with sparse rural populations and the topographically challenging Allegheny Mountains. As a relative described it: "The judge in discharge of his official duties rode on horseback over the mountains of the three counties . . . carrying the necessary articles in his saddlebags."[24] The term of office was three years, but the Commonwealth changed the rules of the game during Watts's tenure. In 1851, the Office of Common Pleas Judgeships was made elective rather than conferred as a lifetime appointment by the governor. Watts stood for election against another prominent Carlisle attorney, Democrat James H. Graham, but was defeated. Watts carried a majority of voters in his home county. But the rural folk of Perry and Juniata Counties were, in the main, conservative Democrats, and in combination they produced a turnout sufficient to defeat Watts by a margin of four hundred votes.

Politically, Watts was "an ardent Whig."[25] Formerly the alliance of National Republicans and some Anti-Masons, the Whig Party, most conspicuously led by Senators Henry Clay of Kentucky and Daniel Webster of Massachusetts, organized itself in 1833 in opposition to President Andrew Jackson and the Democrats. The Whigs stood for a strong national bank—their anger fueled by Jackson's hatred of and determination to dissolve the (second) Bank of the United States. Whigs also favored protective tariffs to grow domestic industries, governmental support for internal improvements (canals, railroads, turnpikes, etc.) to unify the country, and an expanded system of public education.[26] In 1840, the Whigs elected their first president, William Henry Harrison, who died after only a month in office, his vice president, John Tyler, filling the remainder of his term. In 1848, the Whigs elected another president, Zachary Taylor, who died in July 1850, succeeded by his vice president, Millard Fillmore—the last of the Whig presidents—who filled the remainder of Taylor's term until March 1853. After the deaths of Clay and Webster within months of each other in 1852, "the Whig Party fell to pieces, deprived of the leadership" of these two senatorial giants.[27] The task of putting the pieces back together fell to the new Republican Party, founded in May 1854. The Democrats, electing two one-term presidents from 1852 to 1860, became the party in defense of slavery and its extension during the 1850s; the Republicans emerged as the party of reform, opposing the extension of slavery, though they would not capture the presidency until 1860 with Abraham Lincoln.[28]

The Whig Party is long gone, but the Whig theory of history persists to this day. Irving Kristol defined it as "the record of the struggle between Freedom and Authority, Reason and Prejudice, Left and Right, with the victory of the former assured by the growing preponderance among mankind of rational opinions and rational conduct."[29]

Upon the demise of the Whigs, Watts became a Republican. In 1861, Watts would again run for the same office of president judge, losing to the same James Graham by a margin of five hundred votes.[30] In any event, despite his loss of office in 1851, he would forever after be known as "Judge Watts."

As well respected as he was in Cumberland County, Watts had great difficulty as a Whig in the elective politics of the larger conservative Democratic territory. In 1836, he was the Whig candidate for Congress in his home district, a race he lost, and in 1855, "when there was no chance of his election," he was the unsuccessful Whig candidate for a seat in the Pennsylvania legislature.[31]

During his judgeship, however, Watts had a major opportunity put in front of him. At the Whig state convention on June 24, 1851, he was one of twenty men nominated as candidates for judge of the Pennsylvania Supreme Court. The following day, he declined the nomination, for whatever reason.[32] Perhaps he was consumed with the prospect of running for election to a second term as president judge, or, more likely, he was eyeing an opportunity of an entirely different nature.

For the sake of agriculture, it might be deemed best that his career in the judiciary—whether as a district judge or Supreme Court justice—ended as abruptly as it did. At this same time, he was entering a new phase of life with the founding of the Pennsylvania State Agricultural Society, an organization that in January 1851 elected him as founding president. This new statewide responsibility would enable him to pursue his interest in agricultural improvement in a larger and profoundly different way.

A Man of Many Interests

Beyond his work in the legal profession, Watts engaged himself in other key civic and business initiatives, in which he invariably was tapped for leadership positions. But he also was a family man. In 1827, at age twenty-six, he married Eliza Gold Cranston, of Charleston, South Carolina, whom he met while she was visiting her grandparents in Carlisle. She bore him three daughters but died after five years of marriage, in 1832. Soon after, he married the seventeen-year-old Henrietta Ege of Carlisle, who bore him six children. Watts also was an active member of St. John's Protestant Episcopal Church in Carlisle and a member of its vestry.[33]

FIGURE 3 *Frederick Watts's town house at 20 East High Street, Carlisle, Pa. Courtesy of the Cumberland County Historical Society, Carlisle, Pa.*

FIGURE 4 *Watts's Gothic Revival home at "Creekside," his first farm, northwest of Carlisle, Pa. Photo by author, used by permission of the owners, Ashton and Kimberley Nichols.*

His interest in all things agricultural soon reasserted itself as well. In 1829, while married to his first wife, Eliza, he bought a 140-acre tract of land in North Middleton Township, about three miles northwest of the town center. This was to be the first of three farms he would own over his lifetime. As a "gentleman farmer," he would use these properties for various experiments and innovations.

This first farm he called "Creekside," because its northern edge bordered the Conodoguinet Creek. He built a large Gothic manse that still stands today. His families split their time between their town house at 20 East High Street in Carlisle and Creekside, as seasons and obligations permitted.

He also erected a bank barn, reputed to be the largest such barn in Pennsylvania at the time. This barn contained a radical innovation, the first of several Watts would introduce over his life. This particular innovation was designed to prevent fires caused by lightning strikes. On their roofs, most barns had a cupola, vented to allow the moist, hot air generated by stored hay to rise and escape. This stream of upward-rising moist air also acted as a perfect conductor during electrical storms. Watts solved the problem by eliminating the cupola and instead creating vents along the eaves of the side walls. This innovation allowed the moist air to escape in a diffused mass rather than a concentrated stream.[34]

Another interest extended to iron mining and manufacturing, an industry in which Pennsylvania led the nation. In 1838, Watts and his aforesaid law partner Charles Penrose bought the Pine Grove Iron Works, located along South Mountain in southwestern Cumberland County. Consisting of both a furnace and a forge, the operation produced wrought iron, a bendable metal that could be formed into many shapes. The iron works had gone bankrupt with the Panic of 1837, and Watts and Penrose purchased it for a bargain at a sheriff's sale. Watts did not take a "hands-on" approach to managing the business, however, and the operation was eventually sold to Jay Cooke, the so-called Financier of the Civil War, in 1864.[35]

In 1854, Watts organized the Carlisle Gas and Water Company, another organizational innovation ahead of its time. Individual investors were not able to purchase the amount of stock needed to establish the company, so Watts prevailed on the state legislature to authorize the borough of Carlisle to subscribe to the company's stock. Watts served as president for a brief time but remained on the board of directors until just before his death in 1889. The company bumped along for a number of years, unable to pay dividends, but eventually it turned the corner and gave the borough and its other stockholders double the interest on their original investment.[36] The Carlisle Gas and Water Company was considered a "farsighted move," contributing "heavily to the prosperity and growth of the Cumberland County seat."[37]

Dickinson College Trustee

In the late 1820s and early 1830s, Watts devoted considerable time and energy to serving on the board of trustees of struggling Dickinson College. In 1824, he was named secretary to the board and in 1828 was appointed as a trustee, remaining as such until 1833. His notable contribution was the role he played in ensuring that the on-again, off-again school could find a new denominational sponsor and reemerge from its seventeen years of struggle as a viable institution of higher learning.

After its closure in 1816, Dickinson reopened in 1821, to be sustained entirely by an annual legislative grant of $2,000 over five years. In 1826, the state increased the grant to $3,000 annually over seven years. The new grant was made on the condition of reducing ecclesiastical control, specifying that no more than one-third of the board should be clergymen. In effect, Dickinson became a de facto state institution, though a wobbly one at that.[38] Nonetheless, trustee meddling in the affairs of faculty and students reasserted itself, to the point where the trustees asked the state Senate to investigate the college. Faculty criticism of the board intensified and the tension became intolerable. By 1828, Principal William Neill and his faculty all left at the same time—a near replication of the rebellion that had closed the college a dozen years earlier.[39]

Serving as board secretary during this tumult, Watts and the trustees explored a change in the college's Presbyterian affiliation to one with the German Reformed Church. Their negotiations resulted in a brief, tenuous, and ultimately unsuccessful union between 1825 and 1829.[40]

The college's fortunes continued to sink. A new president, Samuel How, was appointed in 1829. A year later, just as he had organized a new faculty, student enrollment shriveled to fourteen. How saw little hope in keeping the college open under current conditions. The trustees concurred and the college was closed, once again, in March 1832 "for some time to come." Indeed, the legislature refused the last $3,000 payment of its seven-year pledge, terminating the college's main source of income.[41]

The year before the closure, however, Watts and a fellow trustee, the Reverend John Moody, devised a plan—supported by President How—to reform the curriculum and increase student enrollment. In 1831, the student body numbered twenty-two, a slight increase over the fourteen the year before, but hardly enough to sustain the institution. Under the Watts-Moody plan, Latin and Greek would be taught in the first two years only. Juniors and seniors would take only mathematics, with natural and moral philosophy. In fact, boys could actually enter as juniors, forgoing the classics entirely. Clearly, this was a plan to attract young men looking for an education that was more "practical" and less literary. The trustees brought the proposal to the faculty on September 30, 1831, but the two groups were "involved in such a pattern of controversy that no progress was possible." In addition, the faculty feared the new curriculum would cause a loss of academic respectability, and so the measure died.[42]

Salvation was in the offing, however. This was the beginning of an era of denominational college proliferation across the nation. Of the approximately 180 colleges established between 1820 and 1860, only 10 were state controlled; the rest had a denominational affiliation, designed to serve a certain religious community, but generally through preferment rather than exclusivity. By 1830, the nation's largest organized church, the Methodists, realized they were in danger of losing their young college-age members to other denominational schools. The Methodists relinquished their distrust of higher education and quickly began sponsoring colleges. In Pennsylvania, they eyed Allegheny College in the northwest and Dickinson in the south-central region as potential acquisitions. By 1840, the Methodists were supporting sixteen colleges across the country.[43]

In 1833, the Baltimore Conference of the Methodist Episcopal Church asked Dickinson's trustees if they would consider transferring the institution to the conference. The trustees responded affirmatively, and the two groups got together on April 18 to hear the conference's plans. The trustees appointed Watts and two others to confer further with conference representatives and make a recommendation. Watts presented his committee's findings, stating that the college's "depressed conditions" and its recent "history and incidents" dictated that "any effort within the power of the present Board . . . to resuscitate it would prove utterly unavailing." The committee recommended that the college be transferred to the conference, provided that "the literary character of such college should be of high grade" and that the conference "endow the institution so as to insure the preservation of its character."

The final proviso of this transaction required the extant Dickinson trustees to resign as soon as the final document was signed. The Dickinson trustees unanimously adopted Watts's resolution, and the date of June 6, 1833, was set to consummate the transfer. In the meantime, the Baltimore Conference had invited the Philadelphia Conference to partner with it in the venture, but both conferences backed away from promising any money for the endowment. They did offer that they hoped to raise any such funds from "the liberality of an enlightened public" and pledged "their best efforts" in mounting such a campaign. On June 6, 1833, the current trustees resigned, the conferences took control, and the new era began. The new college president, John Price Durbin, was also named president of the board, in hopes of solving the fractious relationship between trustees and faculty that had plagued the college.[44] Under new Methodist auspices, Dickinson began to recover. In the eleven years of the Durbin administration, 367 students went through the college's turnstiles, marking the beginning of gradual enrollment growth.[45]

Frederick Watts's legal and political acumen was instrumental in resolving the Dickinson College crisis of the early 1830s; in fact, he would be asked to return as a trustee on the new Methodist board for the 1841–44 term. Although

Dickinson endured a penurious financial existence through the rest of the nineteenth century, it immediately established, in 1834, what would be known as the nation's fifth-oldest law school. And most important, Dickinson began to build its reputation as a "first-class, small, liberal arts college."[46]

What is especially intriguing is how Watts's Dickinson experience affected his future endeavors in higher education. With Dickinson, Watts and the trustees sought to resurrect a failing denominational college, at first turning to the legislature for life support through annual appropriations. At the eleventh hour, they proposed to reform the curriculum, making it more practical and less literary, which would have changed the college's essential character. In fact, Watts's reform proposal flew in the face of the highly influential Yale Report of 1828. Emanating from the nation's most prestigious institution of higher learning ("Yale, Mother of College Presidents"), the Yale Report sought to defend the classical curriculum against critics who argued for practical or more vocational higher education and the abandonment of the "dead" languages. The Yale report emphasized the two great purposes conferred by the classical curriculum: "the discipline and the furniture of the mind; expanding its powers and storing it with knowledge."[47] Thus the Yale Report helped to keep the classical curriculum at the center of most private, denominational colleges for years to come.

A quarter century after the Yale Report, Watts would embark on a venture to found an entirely different type of higher education institution: an agricultural college, based on science and its practical applications, devoid of the classical languages, and oriented to a social class he felt had been left behind in the American experiment. The "practical" reform curriculum he proposed at Dickinson in 1831—notwithstanding its failure—foreshadowed what he would bring into being in 1855. And, as also had been the case at Dickinson, state financial support would be an essential ingredient for the agricultural college he envisioned.

The Cumberland Valley Railroad

The resurrection of Dickinson College was not the only major development for Carlisle and Cumberland County in the 1830s, a decade characterized as "an economic advance for the town and Valley." In 1831, the Cumberland Valley Railroad (CVRR) was chartered as a sixteen-mile right-of-way from Carlisle east to the Susquehanna River. The railroad would become a critical factor in the valley's growth and development, but not immediately. In 1835, having made little progress, the railroad's directors asked to have its charter revised by the state legislature. Seeking to capitalize itself, the company offered 4,000 shares of stock, followed by an offering of 4,000 additional shares, which were quickly purchased by 375 subscribers. Watts himself bought 100 shares. The revised charter also extended the line southwesterly to Chambersburg, in Franklin County, a distance of thirty-five miles.[48]

In August 1837, the railroad made its first run from Carlisle east to the Susquehanna River, covering the sixteen miles in fifty-seven minutes and prompting great "feasting and rejoicing."[49] That same year, the Panic of 1837 spread to the Cumberland Valley and retarded the railroad's progress—but not entirely.

Shortly after the line had gone into operation, its supervising manager happened to talk to a weary passenger who had just boarded the train at Chambersburg after thirty-six hours of a bumpy stagecoach ride from Pittsburgh. The passenger urged him to provide a car with sleeping facilities. The manager thought the idea worth pursuing. So in the winter of 1837–38, the CVRR retrofitted and placed into service a sleeping car dubbed the "Chambersburg"—very possibly "the first sleeping car in railroading history." About nine months later, a competing line, the Philadelphia, Wilmington, and Baltimore Railroad, introduced a second car. At any rate, these two lines, the CVRR being the first, "had true sleeping cars in operation 20 years before Pullman completed his first car."[50]

By 1840, Watts was appointed as one of five board managers for the railroad. In April 1841, he was elected president. Watts would serve in that capacity for thirty-two years, steadily improving the line and its profitability but confronting a number of serious challenges along the way. A contemporary writer summarized his service thus: "It is to his energy and able management that the people of the valley are indebted for a road which, when he took hold of it, was in debt, out of repair, unproductive, and in dilapidated condition, but which, through his energetic and economical management, has been brought up to a high state of prosperity, having paid all its indebtedness and caused it to yield handsome returns to its stockholders."[51]

Watts could not have assumed the presidency at a more difficult time, however. In his annual report for 1842, he acknowledged the overarching problem: "That depression which so universally pervades the business concerns of the country . . . is visited with peculiar force upon railroad companies, whose source of success is prosperity in trade, commerce and manufacture." Nonetheless, he expressed confidence that the nation would eventually emerge from the depression, at which time, he assured, "the capital stock of the Cumberland Valley will be profitable to its owners."[52]

The Panic of 1837 was a serious, widespread, and long-lasting downturn for the nation. Andrew Jackson's dissolution of the Bank of the United States caused its deposits to be distributed to state banks. Flush with money, these banks expanded credit rapidly, fueling a wild speculative bubble in the value of the federal government's western lands. Before leaving office in March 1837, Jackson tried to end the speculation by requiring that federal lands be paid for in gold or silver—hard currency. The bubble burst. Panic ensued in the nation's financial sector and in a matter of months spread to the larger economy, forcing layoffs, foreclosures, and evictions.[53] The depression persisted for the better part of a decade, up through the Mexican War in the mid-1840s.

In dealing with the depression's effects, Watts's immediate strategy was to reduce operating costs, demonstrating his "ability to pinch each of the company's dollars until the eagle shrieked in agony," as the railroad's historian put it. In 1842, he held operating expenses to $46,0000 against income of $76,000. The $30,000 in savings was consumed by interest on the company's debt, however. And the depression had yet to bottom out; not until the late 1840s, after the Mexican War, would prosperity return in full, as Watts had predicted. In 1846, the CVRR carried twenty-three thousand tons of freight and two years later had increased that tonnage to thirty-five thousand. Passenger service was a key component of the company's fortunes, providing 40 percent of total revenue in 1849. Mail service was a part of the picture, too. In 1844, the CVRR contracted with the U.S. Post Office to carry the "great mails," bringing in new revenue of $8,125 per year and putting the stage lines out of business in that respect.[54]

The 1840s presented other major challenges. The first was the constant maintenance problem caused by the line's wooden rails (capped with an iron strap). Watts wanted to replace them with iron T-rail as early as 1842, but depressed finances precluded his doing so until 1849. In that year, Watts pushed state Senator Robert C. Sterritt to champion legislation authorizing the CVRR to fund its debt into stock, "as all my arrangements to get the iron to relay the road with 'T' rail await the passage of the bill."[55]

The second challenge was the fire destroying the CVRR's new Susquehanna River bridge in 1844. At the time, it was the second-longest railroad bridge in the United States. The loss was valued at $122,000, far beyond the capability of the CVRR to replace it. Watts appealed to the governor and the legislature for help. They responded generously, offering a grant of $60,000 and transferring the state's holdings of $100,000 in CVRR stock back to the company. The new bridge was in operation by 1846.

The third challenge was the most consequential, sealing the CVRR's fate as a regional operation until its eventual merger into the Pennsylvania Railroad (PRR) in 1919. At stake was the pending decision for locating the trans-Pennsylvania mainline route from Philadelphia to Pittsburgh. The CVRR's hope was that the route, from Harrisburg, would utilize the CVRR southwesterly to Chambersburg and then go west across the southern tier of Pennsylvania to Pittsburgh, approximately following the path of today's U.S. Route 30 and the Pennsylvania Turnpike (I-76). Failing that, the CVRR proposed that its line be used to Shippensburg, at which point the line would turn north through Franklin and Huntingdon Counties to the Juniata River. Instead, the PRR determined to go west from Harrisburg through the Juniata River Valley to Altoona, and from there surmount the Allegheny Front to Pittsburgh, approximately paralleling today's U.S. Route 22. The PRR's route through the central tier of the state to Pittsburgh was completed in the early 1850s. The decision halted the CVRR's through traffic and "eliminated the chance of the line to become a link in a trunk route to the West."[56]

Aside from these challenges, Watts searched for ways to improve the CVRR's profitability. In 1842, the CVRR reached an agreement with the nearly bankrupt Franklin Railroad Company to keep that line in operation and extend its link from Chambersburg south to Hagerstown, Maryland. After years of problems, the Franklin was foreclosed in 1850, taken over by the CVRR in 1859 and finally, in 1865, merged into the CVRR, by agreement of the stockholders of both companies. The merger formally extended the CVRR's line from Harrisburg to Hagerstown (a distance of about eighty miles, approximately following today's I-81).[57]

The purchase of the Franklin Railroad marked Watts's efforts to strengthen the CVRR as the Civil War ended. The conflict had brought considerable destruction to the Cumberland Valley. In 1862, a Confederate raid on Chambersburg destroyed the CVRR's buildings, three locomotives, and other equipment, a loss estimated at $50,000. Nonetheless, the CVRR was on such solid financial footing by that time that Watts was able to assure shareholders the loss "will not interfere with the regular payment of interest on our bonds and dividends to the stockholders."[58]

The verdict on Watts's long presidency of the Cumberland Valley Railroad is mainly positive, best summarized by railroad historian Paul Westhaeffer: "In the course of his 32 years in office Watts was to employ his high talent and great versatility to make the company one of the most stable and prosperous in the history of American railroading."[59] With the foundation Watts established beginning in 1841, "the CVRR's success was assured long after his tenure." By the time the CVRR was merged into the PRR in 1919, holders of CVRR stock got three shares of the PRR for one of their own.[60]

There is another important development in regard to Watts's management of the CVRR, however. In 1859, in an effort to foreclose competition from the Reading Railroad, the PRR purchased a controlling interest in the CVRR. This transaction effectively removed the CVRR from the exclusive management of its local proprietors and played an important role in both lines' fortunes thereafter.[61]

For the PRR, this marked the first branch that it gained control of in its expansion into a ten-thousand-mile-long system composed of hundreds of subordinate companies. By 1860, the CVRR's twelve-member board of directors featured six PRR directors or large stockholders. This change in board membership did not force the replacement of any CVRR officers, and Watts continued to serve actively as president. Nor did it cause any significant change in internal company policies. The CVRR "was still operated and regarded as a local Valley institution" and remained as such for many years.[62]

Watts's three decades of leadership with the CVRR was highly successful, advancing it from the brink of bankruptcy in 1841 to "spectacular financial success" by 1873, his last year in the post. A contemporary observer characterized him as "one of the most astute railroad managers of his day."[63] Nevertheless, toward the end, there was some criticism of his administration. After the Civil War, Watts's initiatives were focused on expanding the CVRR's route mileage and enhancing its financial position. Despite the line's impressive annual surpluses, he did little to improve services for passengers and shippers. Watts's parsimonious management philosophy was deemed "no longer appropriate to a secure and highly prosperous corporation." When he was named U.S. commissioner of agriculture in 1871, there was speculation that he would resign and that the PRR would absorb the CVRR totally. But Watts did not resign, prompting two influential members of the CVRR board—PRR president J. Edgar Thomson and prominent Philadelphian Thomas Biddle—to recommend that Watts retire from the presidency "in order that . . . the management of the Company [be] placed in younger and more active hands." The board created the new position of vice president, appointing Thomas Kennedy, who effectively became the line's manager. On October 1, 1873, Watts stepped down, declining to stand for reelection, and Kennedy replaced him as president.[64]

Nevertheless, Watts's experience in guiding the CVRR through the thick and thin of the 1840s, 1850s, and 1860s would yield benefits in other ways. His experience with the rail line would prove instructive as he worked to launch another, but very different, enterprise: the Farmers' High School, a higher education institution that represented a radical departure from the traditional colleges of the day.

Agricultural Experimentation and Innovation

By the late 1830s, Watts had become Carlisle's leading citizen, a prominent man of affairs immersed in substantial activity on many fronts. These roles included his primary professional work of operating an expansive law practice and serving as a case reporter for the Pennsylvania Supreme Court; his contributions as a Dickinson College trustee, with a key role in transitioning the school from failure to viability; his leadership of the CVRR, surmounting numerous challenges and bringing the line into profitability; and, of course, his duties as husband to two successive wives and father of an ever-growing family. He also served on the boards of the York and Cumberland Railroad Company, the South Mountain Railroad and Mining Company, and the Pennsylvania State Lunatic Hospital in Harrisburg.[65]

There were few business and civic enterprises that did not call for his services. In December 1860, as the threat of civil war loomed, the citizens of Carlisle met to discuss "the necessity for some action by which the destruction of our glorious Union may be averted." Watts and a committee had organized the event, and Watts was asked to preside. The assembly passed resolutions recognizing "the existence of Slavery in our Southern Sister States as a Constitutional right" and vowing to return runaway slaves to their owners, as the law of the land dictated. (They did not address the *extension* of slavery to new states, however, which even more than the existence of slavery in the original Southern states was the major source of tension between North and South). Despite their concessions, the citizens drew the line on secession, resolving "that we cannot sanction the attempt of any State to secede from the Union." They construed such an attempt as a "violation of the laws of the United States."[66]

Over the course of his varied activities, Watts did not abandon, or put on hold, his deepest interest: the improvement of agriculture and the betterment

FIGURE 5 *Watts's second farm, adjacent to Creekside, with a barn he designed for aesthetics as well as efficiency. The barn no longer exists, but the farmhouse does. Courtesy of the Cumberland County Historical Society, Carlisle, Pa.*

of the farmer. In 1829, as mentioned previously, he purchased the first of three farms, "Creekside," northwest of town; built a large mansion and bank barn; and began a lifetime of experimentation in farm buildings, fertilizers, soils, crops, agricultural implements, and breeds of stock. The results were made known to the farming community through on-site demonstrations and stories in the agricultural and local press. He also bought a second farm adjoining Creekside and bordering Conodoguinet Creek. In 1857, he bought a third tract, a 116-acre "model farm" about two miles west of town, on the Chambersburg Turnpike.[67]

Like other patricians endowed with high intellect, scientific interest, agricultural concern, financial resources, and ample lands on which to conduct experiments, Watts was a "gentleman farmer," in the argot of the day. He and his class did not have to rely on farming to eke out a living. Their interest in agriculture also had an altruistic motivation: improving livestock, soil fertility, crop yields, and related farm practices for the benefit of their community, state, and nation. Equally important, agricultural experimentation provided a means of satisfying their own intellectual curiosity. Multiply Watts by hundreds if not thousands of empirically minded kinsmen and the collective result is hardly surprising. As the historian of Pennsylvania agriculture put it: "For more than half a century 'gentlemen farmers' were the most potent force for the improvement of Pennsylvania agriculture."[68] In fact, the nine original trustees of the Farmers' High School—exempting the four ex officio members—reflected this lofty stature in varying degrees. Seven were lawyers, most of them graduates of classical or liberal arts colleges. While farming was the primary interest of only three of the nine, "all were ardent patrons of agriculture."[69]

The tradition of the gentleman farmer had its roots in Europe, particularly among the lesser nobility, whose holdings extended not only to land but also to the peasants, crops, and even the village. In 1776, Scotsman Henry Home, Lord Kames wrote a treatise on the subject, praising the transition across the British Isles that was turning gentlemen "hunters" into gentlemen "farmers."

> In former times, hunting was the only business of a gentleman. The practice of blood made him rough and hard-hearted: he led the life of a dog, or of a savage; violently active in the field, supinely indolent at home . . . not a spark of patriotism, nothing done for the public. . . . How delightful the change, from the hunter to the farmer, from the destroyer of animals to the feeder of men! Our gentlemen who live in the country, have become active and industrious farmers. They embellish their fields, improve their lands, and give bread to the thousands. Every new day promotes health and spirits; and every new day brings variety of enjoyment. They are happy at home; and they wish happiness to all.[70]

Forsaking noble birth and lineage in favor of brains and accomplishment, the American experiment relied heavily on its gentlemen farmers for progress in all things agricultural. They founded the Republic's early scientific and philosophical organizations and later begat the early state agricultural associations. They pushed for state fairs and agricultural colleges and championed agricultural experimentation and innovation, hoping to advance the common good as well as satisfying their own intellectual curiosity. Frederick Watts was the exemplar of this ideal. As he told an audience at the Minnesota State Fair in 1872: "For more than forty years have I been engaged in conducting the operations of a farm, not so much with the view of pecuniary profit as for the indulgence of an ardent fondness for the study of the mysteries of the art of farming."[71]

Watts's other motivation as an agriculturalist was the greater good of the farming community. And Cumberland County, the upper half of Pennsylvania's rich, wide "Great Valley" gently curving from northeast to southwest, provided the ideal laboratory for his initiatives and experiments. But local interest in agricultural improvement and organization existed well before Watts became a force to be reckoned with. The Carlisle Fair, an event designed for "the buying and selling of livestock, wares and goods, and merchandise," began in 1806. The fairs were held once a year, basically for "the exchange of personal property." The Agricultural Society of Cumberland County was first organized in 1820—while Watts was at his uncle's farm in Erie County—with something of a political agenda. Members were called upon to "inquire into the propriety of applying for the benefit of the law passed the last session of the Legislature, for the promotion of agriculture, and domestic manufactures." No further documentary evidence of the society can be found until 1827, involving its sponsorship of the annual Carlisle fair. The society evidently went dormant for a time, eventually reemerging and reorganizing in the mid-1840s.[72]

The society's eventual reorganization came through momentum generated by the two profound contributions from Frederick Watts, as outlined in the prologue. His first benefaction, in 1839, was the introduction of Mediterranean wheat. His second, in 1840, was the introduction of the new McCormick Reaper. These two acts generated renewed interest in a local agricultural organization. In January 1844, a large group of farmers met in the courthouse to organize the Cumberland County Agricultural Society. Watts presented the draft of a constitution, which was accepted, and he was elected as the society's president. The new organization met regularly each year on the third Saturday of May and held its annual exhibition on the fourth Thursday of October. Watts was reelected as president every year until 1859, when other ventures demanded his attention.[73]

As the years rolled on, Watts never lost his interest in agricultural experimentation and innovation, and he was always eager to share his results with farmers near and far. In 1857, at the same time he was building the Farmers' High School, he bought his aforementioned third firm of 116 acres for purely experimental purposes. The western half of the farm was devoid of buildings, giving him an ample laboratory for implementing his ideas on the design of farm buildings. Watts quickly got to work on a barn, which was destroyed by arson in 1866. The following year, he designed and built his masterpiece: a tri-gable bank barn that would accommodate the storage of grain and hay, the stabling of animals, and the protection of wagons and machinery, as well as a corn crib, all under one roof.

FIGURE 6 *Aerial view of Watts's model farm (1857–67) outside Carlisle. Courtesy of the Cumberland County Historical Society, Carlisle, Pa. The farm has been replaced by an industrial park.*

The model barn was the realization of a plan Watts had outlined in an earlier essay, "The Pennsylvania Barn," published in the *Report of the Commissioner of Agriculture for the Year 1864*. It featured many innovations: "The usual ramp to the threshing floor was extended and built upon to house corn at each side, with room for storage of the farm machinery in the center. Underneath the ramp there was to be room for additional wagon storage, a root cellar and cistern, a compact design to 'economize the work of the hands, since that business of a farmers consists of bodily labor.' In addition, Watts's barn design created an efficient means to produce manure since farmers believed, 'barnyard manure has no substitute of equal value.'"[74]

Into this scheme Watts included a slew of smaller improvements to expedite the workflow. Gallows in the forebay allowed feeding racks to be raised and lowered according to the height of the accumulated manure. A water trough was situated directly in front of the stables. Particularly innovative was

FIGURE 7 *Innovative barn designed by Watts for his model farm. Courtesy of the Cumberland County Historical Society, Carlisle, Pa.*

"the placement of the hog pen, perpendicular to the forebay, allowing the hogs to root in the manure, a practice beneficial to the hogs and to the manure." Watts also built an innovative tenant house, designed for efficiency and as aesthetically pleasing as the barn.[75]

Watts sold his model tenant farm shortly after he had built the barn and house. It continued to function as a tenant farm for most of the twentieth century. In 1986, the property was bought by Arkansas Best Freight, a nationwide trucking firm. At the same time, the Pennsylvania Historical and Museum Commission was working to nominate the site for the National Register of Historic Places, but ABF ordered the farm destroyed before the final determination could be made.[76] Today, the site is an industrial park, the only reminder of its former life being a state historical marker titled *Frederick Watts (1801–1889)*.[77]

As the nineteenth century approached its midway point, Frederick Watts was approaching his fiftieth year. He was creeping up on the life expectancy (fifty-eight years) for a white male of his time and place who had survived childhood.[78] He had already completed what many would consider to be a full life, achieving much in a wide range of endeavors—law and jurisprudence, higher education, railroading, business, civic life, and agricultural innovation. But his larger roles lay ahead of him, to be performed on the wider stages of his state and nation for many years to come.

CHAPTER 2

The Pennsylvania State Agricultural Society

In January 1851, the Pennsylvania State Agricultural Society was formally established, its members electing Frederick Watts as the inaugural president. The founding did not come as a lightning bolt out of the blue, however. Relative to neighboring states, the Pennsylvania society was late in the making. Its formation came not from some organic impulse from the farming community but from the advocacy of the gentlemen farmers of the renowned and influential Philadelphia Society for Promoting Agriculture. On May 15, 1850, in its "Address to the Farmers of Pennsylvania," the Philadelphia Society called their attention "toward the founding of a State Agricultural Society," asking for their support "in furtherance of the measure."[1]

The Philadelphians' address carried the urgency of a call to arms: "While it is a matter of surprise among the enlightened Farmers of other States, who have formed or projected State Societies, it is a cause of regret to many of our own citizens, that Pennsylvania, essentially Agricultural, cannot yet boast of a State institution, to be made available in diffusing a general knowledge of improved systems of husbandry and tillage, and imparting energy and vigor to the most important of all her industrial pursuits."[2] The first step in moving Pennsylvania agriculture into the dawning scientific age, the Philadelphians averred, was to establish a statewide organization enabling farmers to have "a free interchange of opinion . . . upon the best means of promoting improvement in the theory and practice of Agriculture, and the opportunity of exhibiting annually, at designated localities, their stock and implements, with the products of their fields and orchards."[3]

Neighboring states were racing ahead of Pennsylvania, the Philadelphians pointed out. To the north, the New York State Agricultural Society had been established nearly twenty years earlier, in 1832, although its antecedent organization began as early as 1791 with the founding of the Society for the Promotion of Agriculture, Arts, and Manufactures.[4] To the west, Ohio farmers had organized the Ohio Board of Agriculture in 1845, the state legislature recognizing the group in 1846 as the Ohio State Board of Agriculture. The board established the Ohio State Fair, the first such event being held in Cincinnati in 1850.[5] To the south, the Maryland legislature had chartered the Maryland State Agricultural Society the year previous, as had been the case with Virginia as well. "With such examples before her, and such incentives to action, is it possible that Pennsylvania will not shake off the apathy, that . . . seems to paralyze her energies and her progress?" the Philadelphians asked in frustration.[6]

The problems of organizing a state society in Pennsylvania were twofold, the Philadelphians said: the state legislature and the farmers themselves. "The subject of a State Agricultural Society has . . . for years been . . . discussed by the members of the Philadelphia Society . . . but every effort was checked by forebodings that the Legislature would do nothing in aid of the undertaking." The perceived recalcitrance of the legislature was exacerbated "tenfold" by the lethargy of farmers themselves, "who never, by any combined efforts, attempted to place themselves in the position which of right they should occupy."[7]

The Philadelphians' indictment of a lethargic farming community is intriguing, for in the years before and after the Revolutionary War, agrarian constituents were anything but—particularly in Pennsylvania. The salient example was the Whiskey Rebellion (1791–94) in western Pennsylvania, primarily waged over federal taxation levied on distilled liquors—which farmers sold in profusion—to pay down the national debt incurred by the Revolution. Five years later came the Fries Rebellion, an armed revolt by Pennsylvania German farmers in protest of a 1798 federal law levying taxes on houses, land, and slaves. General social unrest and agrarian revolts over rising taxes were seen from Maine to the Carolinas, the most notable being Shays' Rebellion (1786) in Massachusetts. The strong antiauthoritarian ideal of the independent yeoman farmer revolting against British authority, now replaced by federal authority, provided the political underpinning for agrarian revolt, but other forces were at work as well. Historian Brad Bauerly observed that "as portions of the Eastern U.S. began running out of native lands to confiscate, farmers were forced to specialize to maintain their landholdings when faced with declining commodity prices, rising taxes and advancing industry. For many small farmers in the Northeast, the era witnessed a tightening of the social conditions that allowed them to mostly meet their reproduction needs independently as the forces of the market encroached."[8]

By the middle of the nineteenth century, conditions had changed and agrarian discontent had faded, at least in Pennsylvania. The perception of agrarian lethargy likely derived from farmers' apparent satisfaction with the status quo. Pennsylvania agriculture was still in comparatively healthy shape, which may have retarded the need to self-consciously organize and agitate for change. Pennsylvania still enjoyed something of a halo effect as the "'breadbasket of America' and the most prosperous of colonies," though not without some challenges.[9] At the time of the Revolution, for example, soil exhaustion in Philadelphia and surrounding counties had cut yields from farmers' all-grain regimen in half. But the recovery soon came. Around 1790, the culture of wheat began to accommodate a soil-conserving rotation, including red clover and the use of more manure, to increase yields by roughly 50 percent over the ensuing decades.[10] This change, along with other practices such as the more general use of gypsum and lime, grass and livestock, ushered in the "Great Awakening" or "Golden Age" of Pennsylvania farming—the half century between 1790 and 1840—despite the annual depredations of the Hessian fly and other insect pests.[11] Other factors played an important role as well. The growth of industrial cities and towns increased the demand for farm products, and better transportation facilities such as turnpikes and canals allowed farmers to more easily access these new markets. Laborsaving machinery also made its introduction, although the acceptance of these new devices was often slow and even begrudging.[12]

Nonetheless, for nearly two centuries up until 1840, when hay and corn began to supplant wheat, and dairying took hold, Pennsylvania agriculture "was more prosperous than that of any other colony or state." In that year, the Keystone State produced one-sixth of America's wheat crop, even with the perennial damage to the crop by the Hessian fly. Although few great fortunes were drawn from field and farm as opposed to manufacturing and merchandising, Pennsylvania farmers remained as the "largest and most substantial body of citizens." Their income was more stable and less affected by the periodic economic downturns faced by their urban counterparts, and they remained "the great stable group in the body politic," according to the historian of Pennsylvania agriculture.[13]

Despite its prosperity, by midcentury the state's dominance in agriculture was no longer assured. Thus the call by the Philadelphians to hold a farmers' convention in Harrisburg on the third Tuesday of January 1851. Every county was invited to send delegates to establish the new society and "devise such measures as may best promote and advance the Agriculture of the Commonwealth."[14]

The Philadelphia Society for the Promotion of Agriculture

In 1850, the difference between the Philadelphia Society for Promoting Agriculture and its aborning offspring, the Pennsylvania State Agricultural Society, was, at least initially, the difference between theory and practice, experiment and tradition, wealth and middling prosperity, elite east and democratic west, patrician and plebeian. Nonetheless, that dichotomy was soon to change. Leaders of the Philadelphia Society would overlap on the fledgling State Society, providing leadership to get it up and running while also advocating for an agricultural college. In fact, several Philadelphians would soon be serving on the new school's first board of trustees.

The Philadelphia Society was an organization of "gentlemen farmers," men of affairs, political luminaries, scientists, merchants, lawyers, and physicians—all with an interest in new methods of improving agricultural productivity. The society's members were of the patrician class, men of means with the wealth, discretionary time, and ample country estates on which to experiment, innovate, and make mistakes. Frederick Watts was a classic example, having been admitted to membership on November 1, 1843, a few years after his introduction of Mediterranean wheat and the McCormick Reaper.[15] But far removed from the center of power in southeastern Pennsylvania, Watts never held a leadership post with the organization.

In contrast to the gentlemen, everyday farmers had few resources to devote to experimentation and innovation, given the incessant demands their occupations placed on them and their adherence to traditional farming. Thus it was left to the Philadelphia Society—best thought of as an early scientific organization—to drive agricultural improvement, promote "scientific agriculture," and generally serve as the "fountainhead of progress" in the Keystone State and beyond from the early federal period to the years before the Civil War.

The Philadelphia Society for Promoting Agriculture traced its beginnings to 1785, after the peace treaty with England but before the Constitutional Convention that birthed the United States. There had been earlier efforts at organizing societies in America—in New York, New Jersey, and South Carolina—but they did not last long. The Philadelphia Society was the first to survive and endure to this day. The New York Agricultural Society came into being in 1791 and the Massachusetts Agricultural Society in 1792, but they no longer exist in their original guise.[16] These early societies were private organizations, however, with no state or public funding.

Oddly enough, the impetus for the Philadelphia Society came from a Marylander, John Beale Bordley, who owned large tracts of land on his state's Eastern Shore. By 1784, Bordley had established connections with the Philadelphia aristocracy and become a member of the American Philosophical Society, the country's leading scientific organization based in Philadelphia. Bordley pressed the idea for an agricultural society with his Philadelphia friends and got an enthusiastic response, particularly from Samuel Powell, the last mayor of Philadelphia before the Revolution.[17] By early 1785, many of the city's elite were charter members of the new organization.

"Elite," in fact, may be an understatement. Of the twenty-three founding members, four had signed the Declaration of Independence, four served on the committee to compose the new U.S. Constitution, seven had served as officers in the Revolution, and seven served in Congress. George Washington was elected an honorary member in July 1785, and Benjamin Franklin, upon his return from France, was elected as a resident member. Accordingly, the Philadelphia Society for Promoting Agriculture quickly made its mark as the nation's newest scientific organization and one of its best.[18]

Early on, the Philadelphia Society addressed the problems of insect pestilence and soil exhaustion and recovery. The most pressing challenge was the Hessian fly, as described previously, deemed to be the "principal problem affecting American agriculture at the end of the eighteenth century." The problem was serious enough that by 1788 King George III banned American wheat from entering England. Principally through the research of a Philadelphia Society member, George Morgan, and other society investigators, the organization was able to issue a conclusion the following year. It found that although the fly attacked the plant by depositing its eggs at the base of the wheat stalk, causing destruction, the grain of the plant remained "sound and good."[19] Despite that finding, the pest did not sound retreat. Not until fifty years later, when Watts introduced Mediterranean wheat, was the problem on its way to being remedied.

Meanwhile, another society member, George Logan, was looking into the relationship between crop rotation, the use of clover, and the spreading of manure as a way of regenerating soil nutrients. Clover was known to be beneficial, but clover seed was scarce and expensive to obtain. The solution, as was learned from colleagues in New York State, was to ferment clover tops in water, dry them out, and thresh them. As for (cow) manure, the society knew that it was insufficient by itself to revitalize the nearly exhausted soils of the Philadelphia region. The society advocated for the use of marl, an earthy deposit of clay and calcium carbonate, particularly beneficial for lime-deficient soils and readily found in the Delaware River Valley. The society also promoted the use of gypsum, a common mineral (hydrated calcium sulfate) used to make plaster of Paris as an ornamental material but also quite useful as a fertilizer.[20]

Such were some of the initial concerns and accomplishments of the Philadelphia Society for Promoting Agriculture. In the opening years of the nineteenth century, the society recommended the establishment of a veterinary college in Philadelphia, but the matter rested dormant for decades; the veterinary school did not come into being until 1884, under the auspices of the University of Pennsylvania. The society also had its existential challenges. Philadelphia's two Yellow Fever epidemics of the 1790s disrupted its work. Political squabbles and class resentment took their toll, as did the War of 1812 and the economic panic of 1819, and the society nearly folded by 1825. By the late 1830s, it had renewed itself, investigating and advocating agricultural improvements that benefited Pennsylvania and the nation.[21]

Although the "gentlemen" or "scientific farmers" of the Philadelphia Society were frequently disparaged by the very constituency they were trying to help, they made significant contributions. As the society's historian put it, "if the membership . . . provides us with any guide, it is clear that gentlemen farmers not only carried out extensive experiments on their own farms but also actively sought to create an institutional infrastructure through which these improved methods could be more widely disseminated."[22]

Meanwhile, new county or regional agricultural societies were coming into existence, particularly in southeastern Pennsylvania and environs. In 1836 came the Agricultural Society of nearby New Castle County, Delaware. In 1838, William Darlington, a physician and notable botanist from West Chester,

Pennsylvania, and a member of the Philadelphia Society, initiated with like-minded men the Chester and Delaware County (Pa.) Agricultural Society. The Cumberland County Agricultural Society was permanently organized in 1844, by virtue of Watts's leadership. Other Pennsylvania counties founded their own societies, though the process took many years to accomplish before all were represented.

With this spreading interest in organizing at the local level, it became apparent that a statewide organization could exert greater influence, particularly with the parsimonious state legislature. An agricultural convention was organized in Harrisburg in 1840 but was poorly attended and attracted only a regional constituency.[23] By 1850, the stage was set to give birth to a new organization, of statewide reach, addressing the interests of practicing farmers. Even so, the Philadelphia Society would not fade away, continuing its work into the twenty-first century.[24]

The Pennsylvania State Agricultural Society in Its Early Years

In 1850, Pennsylvania and New York were the nation's leading agricultural states. Within ten years, however, Pennsylvania's position shifted slightly, due to the surging farmsteads of Ohio's flatter landscapes. According to the 1860 U.S. Census, New York had nearly 3.9 million inhabitants, ranking first, with 14.4 million acres of improved farmland with a cash value of $803 million. Pennsylvania, second nationally with 2.9 million inhabitants, now ranked third (after Ohio) on the same agricultural metrics, with 10.5 million acres of improved farmland valued at $662 million.[25] With the quickening development of farming in the Midwest, the imperative of the 1850s was to advance Pennsylvania agriculture through improved farming practices based on science and empirical investigation. Leaders from the Philadelphia Society were especially concerned with keeping Pennsylvania economically competitive. They knew the state could not realize its industrial potential without attendant increases in agricultural productivity.

The competition posed by New York and, more recently, Ohio did not go unnoticed by the Philadelphians. Neither was it coincidental that both states were well ahead of Pennsylvania in establishing publicly funded agricultural societies, New York in 1841 and Ohio in 1846. And in both states, it was the Whigs—the party of internal improvements—who voted overwhelmingly in their respective state houses to support these nascent societies.[26] Sponsored by these same societies, state agricultural fairs got under way on a large scale. Local agricultural societies multiplied as well, such as what occurred in Cumberland County under Watts's leadership in 1844. Independent agricultural newspapers and journals cropped up in profusion, speaking sharply and influentially to the interests of the American farmer. As historian Ariel Ron concluded: "It was, in short, a major social movement, and it was responsible for major policy outcomes"—for starters, the Morrill Land-Grant College Act and the U.S. Department of Agriculture, both in 1862, with more to follow. The agricultural reform movement, as it moved from the 1850s through the 1890s, "ultimately restructured the American state."[27]

In Pennsylvania, then, it was time to get moving. Eight months after the Philadelphia Society issued the call for the formative convention of the state agricultural society, the event took place. On January 21, 1851, the state's agriculturalists converged on Harrisburg en masse, some 262 delegates representing all Pennsylvania counties. Among these inaugural delegates were many who would play roles in the founding and early leadership of the Farmers' High School:

Robert C. Walker of Allegheny County, who would become one of the thirteen original trustees of the Farmers' High School. He would first be elected as one of five secretaries of the convention;

General James Irvin of Centre County, the ironmaster who in 1855 would make the gift of two hundred acres to site the Farmers' High School;

William G. Waring of Centre County, who in 1856 would become superintendent of the building operation at the school, later professor of horticulture and acting principal of the school for a brief time before the arrival of Evan Pugh. Waring also would be elected as one of five secretaries of the convention;

Augustus O. Hiester of Dauphin County, who would become another of the thirteen original trustees;

Thomas H. Burrowes of Lancaster County, who would serve as president of the Agricultural College of Pennsylvania from 1869 until his death in 1871;

Alfred L. Elwyn of Philadelphia, a member of the Philadelphia Society and one of the five coauthors of its call for the farmers' convention. He would become another of the thirteen original trustees of the institution;

Algernon S. Roberts of Philadelphia, another member of the Philadelphia Society and also a coauthor of the call to convention. He too would serve as one of the thirteen original trustees. Both Elwyn and Roberts would be elected as permanent officers of the convention;

Charles B. Trego of Philadelphia, the former state geologist and a scientist at the University of Pennsylvania. He would be courted to become the first president of the Farmers' High School but would decline.[28]

With George Woodward of Luzerne County elected president of the convention, the delegates got down to business on January 22, 1851. They unanimously approved a constitution for the society, its objectives being "to foster and improve Agriculture, Horticulture, and the Domestic Arts." They submitted the constitution as "a basis of legislative action" to the Pennsylvania legislature, requiring both a charter for the Society and the "appropriation of money." They insisted that the undertaking they represented "must be founded on public support." Organizationally, they elected twenty-four vice presidents—one from each of Pennsylvania's twenty-four congressional districts. They appointed Elwyn as corresponding secretary, Walker as recording secretary, and Trego as analytical chemist and geologist.[29]

Frederick Watts was not in attendance, the duties of judgeship keeping him away, his court calendar conflicting with the Harrisburg convention. Nonetheless, the delegates elected him, in absentia, as the first president of the Pennsylvania State Agricultural Society. Politically, it would have been counterproductive for the state society to have elected a Philadelphian to the presidency, and Watts was already one of the most prominent agriculturalists from the Pennsylvania interior. For Watts, the election would mark the beginning of a long arc of agricultural leadership and advocacy on the statewide and national levels. Over the next thirty years, as noted previously, he would come to be regarded as "by far the most outstanding figure in Pennsylvania agriculture."[30]

With Watts as president, the Pennsylvania State Agricultural Society quickly got down to business. And even though it was somewhat late in arriving on the scene, as compared with neighboring states, the society would make up for lost time. Two priorities quickly emerged. The first was to bring working farmers together in an annual exhibition to display their best work and to view and discuss improvements in agricultural practices. Closely allied with this priority was the expansion of agricultural societies to every Pennsylvania county (sixty-four of them at the time). The state society also required the county societies to do a general registry of their agricultural statistics, to be reported annually.

FIGURE 8
Frederick Watts, founding president (1851–55) of the Pennsylvania State Agricultural Society. Courtesy of The Pennsylvania State University Archives.

A second priority was to introduce agricultural education at the highest level, through the founding of an agricultural college that would serve a statewide constituency. Indeed, the most enduring contribution of Watts's four-year presidency (1851–55) would be the chartering of an institution that would, in comparatively short order, emerge as the national model for agricultural higher education.

Priorities such as these would depend upon sufficient means. The society intended to generate its revenue from state fairs and membership fees but also from legislative funding. In little more than two months' time, on March 29, 1851, the Pennsylvania legislature formally incorporated the society and agreed to an appropriation of $2,000 per year. It also authorized the treasurers of every Pennsylvania county to pay $100 to their respective county societies "for the promotion of agriculture knowledge and improvement" on the local level.[31] Thus with legislative incorporation, the promise of state funding, and planned expansion into every county, the Pennsylvania State Agricultural Society was officially up and running.

The first year of operation, 1851, generated substantial results. Working to mount a statewide agricultural exhibition in a matter of months, Watts's executive committee tasked smaller committees with visiting the annual exhibitions of the New York State and Maryland agricultural societies to see how things were done. Watts himself was one of the four-member committee assembled to visit the expansive New York State Fair.[32]

The inaugural Pennsylvania exhibition was set for October 29–31 in Harrisburg. The city was, of course, the state capital, but it was also removed from Philadelphia and more conveniently located at the junction of the rolling piedmont and the mountainous ridge-and-valley section of Pennsylvania. Harrisburg was much more accessible to the vibrant farming communities from the adjacent Cumberland and Lebanon Valleys, the nearby Lancaster and York Counties to the south, and the farther reaches of central, northeastern, and western Pennsylvania. The Harrisburg site also made it easier for state legislators and government officials to visit and see for themselves what the new state society could do.

The October 1851 exhibition went forward without incident and was deemed a success, with more than twenty thousand in attendance. "It exceeded far the general interest it excited," the society crowed in its first annual report. "The large attendance of Farmers, and grand display of Agricultural products, implements and stock, met the most extravagant expectations of the most enthusiastic friend of the project, and they found themselves now with all expenses paid and several thousand dollars in the treasury."[33]

Society communications were addressed that first year, too. Watts's executive committee deemed "the establishment and success of an Agricultural Journal, published in Pennsylvania, as essential to the proper exposition of the principles of agriculture as practiced in this State." Thus the committee endorsed the *Pennsylvania Farm Journal*, edited by S. S. Haldeman and published by A. M. Spangler, for that purpose. The committee also resolved that the proceedings of the society's annual meetings be printed in the German-language *American Farmer and Agriculture Journal*, published in Harrisburg. This was not a sop to a minor constituency. Beginning in the late 1720s and continuing up to the American Revolution, German-speaking peoples immigrated in vast numbers to Pennsylvania. Fleeing the political and religious turmoil of the German principalities, they were drawn to the Keystone State because of its rich limestone soils, similar landforms, and the promise of tolerance inherent to William Penn's "Holy Experiment." By the time of the American Revolution, there were between sixty-five thousand and seventy-five thousand ethnically German residents in Pennsylvania, and some historians put the number as high as one hundred thousand. Benjamin Franklin wrote that more than one-third of the province's population were German. Further, contemporary observers, and the later historiographical consensus, held that the Pennsylvania Germans, soon to be called the "Pennsylvania Dutch" (a variant of "Deutsch"), made for highly efficient farmers, far surpassing the agricultural practices of Pennsylvania's other ethnic groups.[34] More recent scholarship has shown that German agricultural superiority was more myth and lore than fact. Historian Sally McMurry unearthed accounts of earlier Lancaster County historians who examined records and found no real differences between English and German farmers in terms of crop choice, livestock ownership, farming techniques, and, most importantly, productivity.[35]

Nevertheless, Germans were in profusion in the fourteen "distinctively German Pennsylvania counties" in the populous southeast quadrant of the state.[36] As such, they were an important source of new members for the state agricultural society. And membership growth, a vital source of revenue and a reflection of political muscle, was a major priority. During that first year, 1851, the society enrolled 2,090 dues-paying members. Dues were $1 per annum, but $10 for life membership, for which thirteen individuals signed up. Watts, of course, became a life member, as did five vice presidents of the society who would later serve on the inaugural Board of Trustees of the Farmers' High School: Algernon Roberts of Philadelphia, John Strom of Lancaster, Hugh McAllister of Centre County, William Jessup of Susquehanna County, and James Miles of Erie County.[37] Total income that first year was $4,900.29, with a majority of it supplied by admission tickets to the state exhibition. Expenses amounted to $4,321.75, leaving a balance at the end of 1851 of $578.54 in the treasury.

Perhaps most significant, the new society sought to extend its influence beyond the borders of Pennsylvania and prod the federal government into taking action to advance American agriculture. At its second annual meeting, on January 20, 1852, the society charged President Watts and Secretary Robert Walker with petitioning the U.S. Congress to establish a national agricultural bureau. "Agriculture is the only firm and stable foundation of national greatness," the society proclaimed, "and the various State societies have already full demonstrated the fact that in no way can this great and valuable science be so substantially and rapidly improved, as by organized and concerted action, and it is therefore a self-evident fact, that the formation of a National Agricultural Society is, at this time, a matter of great moment and importance." The society then called for a "Convention of Agriculturalists of the United States" to meet in Washington, D.C., "as soon as it is ascertained that a sufficient number of

States . . . have approved of the plan to warrant its undertaking." When that number is reached," the resolution continued, "the President of this Society [Watts] shall immediately . . . fix on a time for the meeting of said Convention." The society was unwilling to wait forever, as it resolved that only five states needed to signal their assent for the convention to be called.[38]

In sum, in its first year under Watts's leadership, the society had enrolled a substantial membership; endorsed key communications media, held its inaugural agricultural exposition in Harrisburg, attracting twenty thousand attendees; and pushed aggressively for a national organization. Not surprisingly, Watts was reelected president of the Pennsylvania State Agricultural Society for 1852.

In its second year of operation, the society accomplished more. The organization doubled its membership to 4,200. Its second annual exhibition was moved to Lancaster, in the heart of Pennsylvania German farm country. Although the society reported no attendance statistics, the fair was said to be "far more extensive than the one of the previous year, and for a *second* exhibition, was probably unprecedented in the history of State Agricultural Societies." In the event's aftermath, however, the society determined that the annual exhibitions were being held too late in the season (at the end of October) and thus set the dates for the third annual fair at the end of September 1853, expanding the fair's length to four rather than three days.[39]

The society was now publishing in its annual reports the extensive lists of premiums won at its exhibitions in every conceivable aspect of agricultural endeavor. It also required, in its act of incorporation, that county societies submit their own annual reports of their local exhibitions to the state society, so that a comprehensive statewide compendium could be published, showing the breadth and depth of agriculture in the Keystone State. In 1852, however, only nineteen county societies existed, and none of them submitted a report.[40] That would change as the years rolled on, although the quality and detail of the county reports would vary widely.

The society's initiative in calling for a national convention to establish a U.S. Agricultural Society also came to fruition, although seven other state societies joined in the call. The first step in this process was correspondence initiated in January 1851 by Marshall P. Wilder, president of the Massachusetts Board of Agriculture, to state societies across the country. In responding, only Pennsylvania (in January 1852) and Maryland went further in recommending that the convention be used to establish a national society. Wilder issued the call in May 1852 and 123 delegates from twenty-three states and territories came together in Washington, D.C., in June to form the United States Agricultural Society. The national society's constitution called for the establishment of a Board of Agriculture within the national society, to be appointed by the respective state agricultural societies. The board was broadly charged with watching over the "interests of agriculture." The Executive Committee of the Pennsylvania Society appointed Watts, Hugh McAllister, and John Ewing to serve as members of the board, but this internal body never came into active existence and the society proper instead carried out the organization's mission.

The United States Agricultural Society enjoyed a brief but influential life. It flourished from 1852 to 1860 and, with the onset of the Civil War, eventually passed out of active existence. A powerful body with the ability to influence Congress, it joined forces with Congressman Justin S. Morrill in his first attempt to enact agricultural college legislation (passed by Congress in 1859 but vetoed by President James Buchanan). It also pushed hard during the 1850s for the creation of a U.S. Department of Agriculture, finally authorized by Congress in 1862 and signed into law by President Abraham Lincoln. As early as 1853, the U.S. Agricultural Society called on Congress to establish a federal agriculture department with a cabinet officer at its head.[41] The U.S. Agricultural Society also encouraged the establishment of agricultural societies across the country. When the national society was established in 1852, there were some three hundred active farm organizations in thirty-one states and five territories; by 1860, that number had grown to nearly one thousand.[42]

In January 1853, at the second annual meeting of the Pennsylvania State Agricultural Society in Harrisburg, the fast-growing scope of the statewide organization was evident. In its 1853 report, forty typeset pages were devoted to the thousands of judges and premiums awarded at the society's Lancaster exhibition in October 1852—in such categories as cattle, sheep, stallions and brood mares, quick draught and saddle horses, heavy draught mules and teams, poultry, tobacco, fruit, agricultural implements, fireproof chests, dairy and honey, vegetables, flowers, household manufactures, silk, domestic wines, bacon hams, plowing matches, mechanic arts and enumerated articles, and so on.[43] By year's end, the reports of the county societies would begin to roll in. Most of them recounted the premiums from their county fairs; thus their reports would be submitted in the October–December 1853 time frame, after fair season. But at least they were beginning to comply with the state society's mandate for the submittal of annual county reports. The first wave came from twenty-three counties: Allegheny, Beaver, Bucks, Bedford, Bradford, Chester and Delaware (jointly), Centre, Dauphin, Fayette, Franklin, Juniata,

Lancaster, Lawrence, Mercer, Northampton, Northumberland, Susquehanna, Union, Warren, Wayne, Westmoreland, and York.[44]

For its third annual exhibition, the society opted to demonstrate its statewide reach by moving from the east to the west. Watts and his committee selected Pittsburgh as the site, with the event being held at the end of September 1853. It was reported to be the biggest yet, "excelling by far either of those [Harrisburg and Lancaster] preceding it." Contemporary estimates placed attendance at one hundred thousand on Thursday, the fair's biggest day.[45] The state's agricultural papers were extremely complimentary. "It is doubtful whether a more successful exhibition has ever been held in the United States," crowed the *Pennsylvania Farm Journal*, congratulating the society "upon the complete success which has attended their efforts to establish the agricultural reputation of our great state."[46] The society's secretary waxed equally enthusiastic: "People were there by scores of thousands, and the railroads and steamboats which conveyed them, were in want of capacity to carry many thousands more who wished to attend this great gathering in the west. . . . Thus in the space of three short years, has the Pennsylvania State Agricultural Society, placed itself side by side with institutions of an older growth, with which it can vie with equal merit in dispensing those benefits, which will redound to their honor and credit."[47]

The annual exhibitions had become by far the biggest moneymakers for the society. The Pittsburgh fair brought in $13,428.83 from receipts and tickets, with the city of Pittsburgh providing an additional $2,500 to support the event. Together, those two revenue streams provided nearly 70 percent of the society's $23,024.82 income for the year.[48] The society's secretary, in his 1854 report, characterized 1853 as a year of "unprecedented prosperity" for the organization.[49]

Planning Begins for a State Agricultural School

In January 1853, there was something even more important than annual exhibitions on the society's agenda: an educational institution. A committee of five was hastily appointed to report on the "expediency of adopting measures for the establishing of a State Agricultural School, to be called 'The Farmers' High School of the State of Pennsylvania.'" Again, Watts was not in attendance at this meeting (but was reelected president for 1853). And so the president pro tem, Charles B. Trego, appointed Algernon Roberts, Augustus Hiester, Jonas Konigmacher, James Carothers, and David Mellinger to meet and report out during the evening session. Their brief resolution set in motion the chain of events that would soon lead to the chartering of the Farmers' High School.

Roberts's committee believed it was "an auspicious period for the introduction into . . . Pennsylvania of a scientific and practical system of education, particularly adapted to the improvement and extension of Agricultural knowledge," the advantages being "so obvious, that the committee do not deem it necessary to enlarge on them at this time." The first step in galvanizing the state's agricultural constituency in this venture was to call a general convention of delegates to gauge the "full expression of public sentiment" and, "if favorably entertained," to adopt the means of bringing such a school into being. The committee maintained that "a large sum of money would not be necessary." The convention would have to figure out how to raise an amount the society might contribute, coupled with "a moderate appropriation from the State." Whatever might accrue from these two sources would be "ample" for the "establishment and maintenance of an Agricultural School and Farm."

The committee then called for an agricultural convention to be held in Harrisburg on March 8, 1853, to adopt measures "for the establishment of an Agricultural institution, to be styled 'The Farmers' High School of Pennsylvania,' with a model farm attached thereto." The delegates to the convention would be drawn from every House and Senate district as well as the county agricultural societies. The resolution passed unanimously.[50] (The convention and resultant activity to charter the institution will be addressed in the next chapter.)

In 1854, Watts was reelected for the fourth time as president of the state society. It would be the final year of his presidency. He would resign the post in January 1855 to devote more time and energy to getting the Farmers' High School off the ground. Meanwhile, the society continued to prosper in his final year, becoming one of the largest and most active of its kind. "A great end has been accomplished in a short time," the Executive Committee observed, "and a period has arrived when your society can step forth untrammelled from the pecuniary embarrassment which has retarded other state societies, and render material aid in fostering institutions for the benefit of the farmer and the promotion of agriculture."[51] Membership exceeded eight thousand in 1854, and twenty-four county agricultural societies filed annual reports, many of them lengthy, detailing county fair premiums.[52] Nonetheless, the society was distressed at the greater number of counties that still had not formed their societies. The twenty-four counties reporting represented only 37 percent of the state's sixty-five counties then in existence.

The crowning achievement of 1854, however, was the society's annual exhibition, held in Philadelphia, the nation's second most populous city. Attendance far exceeded the one hundred thousand estimated in Pittsburgh the year before. The Philadelphia Society for Promoting Agriculture suspended its own annual exhibition to concentrate on supporting the state society's fair. The Pennsylvania Horticultural Society and the City of Philadelphia also dedicated their resources to supporting the event. The Philadelphia Fair "was one of unusual attraction, and in amount of numbers of attendance, it exceeded any other exhibition probably ever held in the United States." Ticket revenue amounted to nearly $25,000—some $12,000 more than the Pittsburgh Fair generated—and alone provided 60 percent of the society's $41,782 in revenue for 1854. Ticket sales would suggest attendance hovering around two hundred thousand visitors, but the majority were "city-folk"—curiosity-seekers and tourists far outnumbering practicing farmers.[53]

The experience of the society's annual agricultural exhibitions—growing in attendance tenfold, from twenty thousand to two hundred thousand, in four years—would serve Watts two decades later as he prepared for an exhibition on a much grander scale: the United States' Centennial Exhibition in Philadelphia in 1876. As commissioner of agriculture, Watts would oversee the many exhibits and events of the U.S. Department of Agriculture at that exposition, visited by ten million people.

Watts's last year as president of the state society was notable for an additional development: philanthropy was introduced for the first time in the society's annals. At its January 1855 annual meeting, the society gratefully acknowledged a substantial bequest from the estate of Elliott Cresson, a long-standing member of the Philadelphia society as well as the state society. Cresson had died on February 20, 1854, leaving a bequest of $5,000 "towards the erection and support of an agricultural college."[54] This gift—valued at $154,929 in 2020 dollars[55]—marked the first act of philanthropy to the as-yet-unborn institution, a gift of faith in the future, made before the school had been chartered, located, and built.

The Pennsylvania State Agricultural Society's rapid rise under Watts's leadership provides an insightful case study of how these societies filled a critical lacuna in the absence of an activist federal government in mid-nineteenth-century America. State agricultural societies played the central but oft-overlooked role in accelerating the development of the modern bureaucratic state—which emerged in the 1870s through the 1890s largely in response to the pressure exerted by agricultural organizations and constituencies. Certainly politics at state and national levels played an important role in that process, but that role was *supportive rather than leading*. And that support came mainly from Northern Whigs and later Republicans, in the face of opposition from conservative Democrats—the salient example being the veto of Representative Justin Morrill's first agricultural college bill (1859) by Democratic president James Buchanan largely on "constitutional" grounds. As historian Nathan M. Sorber has posited, Morrill's "land-grant college act was another internal improvement program in the Whig tradition, aimed at developing a modern capitalist economy in an upstart nation."[56]

Historians are devoting increased attention to the role of voluntary agricultural associations and their leaders in influencing the politics and economy of nineteenth-century America and the subsequent emergence—again, largely in response to agricultural concerns—of the twentieth-century bureaucratic state. The initiatives exerted by agricultural organizations, historian Ariel Ron observes, "suggest a reappraisal of farming in the North and especially the Northeast, which remained two-thirds rural on the eve of the Civil War and where agricultural fairs and the societies that sponsored them originated. Such a reappraisal reveals a massive yet largely unrecognized agricultural reform movement that altered the day-to-day practices of numberless farmers, shaped contemporary understandings of political economy, contributed to the hardening of sectional lines, and ultimately restructured the American state."[57]

Such considerations put Frederick Watts, as leader of one of the most powerful state agricultural societies, into sharper perspective. From the first, these societies were dynamic, progressive organizations striving to improve the situation of the nation's largest constituency. The societies pushed hard, not only for a stronger political, social, and economic position for American farmers—an especial concern of Watts—but also for science, invention, measurement, statistics, reporting mechanisms, standardization, and modernized, *responsive* bureaucratic structures across federal and state governments, structures that would be largely in place by the dawn of the twentieth century. For agricultural societies, "government" was not seen as the "problem." Rather, it was viewed as the eventual *solution* to addressing the increasingly complex challenges of American agriculture.

CHAPTER 3

Chartering and Locating the New School

As president of the Pennsylvania State Agricultural Society, Frederick Watts sent forth a resolution in January 1853 calling for an agricultural convention in Harrisburg on March 8 to "adopt measures for the establishment" of the Farmers' High School. The society asked for delegates from each Pennsylvania House and Senate district. These delegates were to be selected by each extant county agricultural society and, in those counties where no such society existed, "by the friends of agricultural education."[1]

And so they came, meeting in the Senate Chamber in Harrisburg and called to order by Simon Cameron of Dauphin County, a Pennsylvania political luminary who had served a term as a U.S. senator, would serve another term in the late 1850s, and would then be chosen by Lincoln to serve as secretary of war. Thirty-six counties were represented, more than half the state. The Philadelphia Society for Promoting Agriculture showed up in force, with nine delegates, including several who would go on to play a larger role in the founding of the institution—Alfred L. Elwyn, Algernon S. Roberts, and Charles B. Trego. The more than two dozen officers of the state society, including Watts, attended as well. The convention's permanent chairman, John Strohm of Lancaster County, had appointed a committee to prepare the agenda. Strohm's committee included the leading lights of progressive agriculture: Elwyn, Roberts, and John S. Hart of Philadelphia; Simon Cameron of Dauphin County; G. Blight Browne of Montgomery County; Benjamin Herr of Lancaster County; Hugh McAllister of Centre County; and, of course, President Frederick Watts of Cumberland County.

Watts read the committee's report, which signaled a philosophical shift from farming by tradition to farming by science: "agriculture, which . . . was regarded as a kind of tranquil retirement for dull minds, has passed to the crucible of the chemist, the closet of the philosopher, under the close and deep examination of the man of science, and entered among the profound speculations of the political economist. . . . It is now a progressive art, and rapidly assuming the form and condition of a science." Watts added that the purpose of the convention was not only to "keep pace with the general movement" but also to prevent Pennsylvania from "falling behind other states, which are already commencing the establishment of Schools and Professorships of Agriculture."[2]

The report addressed the particulars for the Farmers' High School. Despite the name, it was to be of collegiate grade, award baccalaureate degrees, and have a prescribed curriculum geared to scientific and practical agriculture. Manual labor on the part of students would be required, as much as three hours per day. The buildings, facilities, and equipment were to be substantial, encompassing all that was necessary to meet the needs of the state's largest constituency. The school's location, as yet undetermined, needed to be accessible to markets but not be near a large town or city, where the distractions and temptations of urban life would be inimical to the education of students. Other desiderata addressed by Watts included the quality of land, the school's organization, students, teachers, assistants, and other resources. But much was still uncertain. "Our view is to let this project have a beginning, and we all have confidence, that, under the general influence of enlightened minds, it will work itself into public favor."[3]

The convention appointed a committee to draft a bill "in accordance with the principles of this report" for consideration by the Pennsylvania legislature. The committee of five included Watts, who with his legal talents drafted the bill. Their "Act to Establish an Agricultural School" was introduced to the Senate on March 11. On March 23, the bill was reported out of the Senate's Committee on Agriculture and Domestic Manufacturers as "An Act to incorporate the Farmers' High School." On April 7, it was considered by the Senate in a Committee of the Whole, but the bill failed to pass. Its introduction came too close to the Senate's adjournment for the year. In addition, objections were raised regarding a section of the bill that called for "free scholars," whose attendance would not require tuition. It was thought that "free scholars" would place a financial burden upon the institution while introducing a select number of pupils—perhaps one from each congressional district—whose presence would represent "favoritism" and stir resentment among the others.[4] In his report to Governor William Bigler, Watts blamed the bill's failure on its late introduction to the legislature but vowed that "it yet remains to be done."[5]

Indeed, the fire had been lit. The state's agricultural journals fanned the flames and the agricultural community called for passage of the bill in the next session. Watts himself had sent epistles to the state's newspapers, bewailing the manner in which the merchant class, the learned class, and the mechanic class had advanced their standing in society "whilst the farmer stands to gaze with mingled feelings of doubt and astonishment, that all the other pursuits of life whirl so rapidly past him." The remedy for this "evil," Watts averred, was "the education of farmers' sons through the medium of an agricultural school." If the act of incorporation were to fail, he concluded: "Let the farmers of the State look to it that it does not fail again."[6] With public opinion now growing quickly, the school's establishment would be just a matter of time.

Outlining the Plan for the Farmers' High School

Shortly after its annual meeting in January 1854, the Pennsylvania State Agricultural Society published, for the first time, and in one 481-page volume, its transactions from 1850 to 1854. Included were the minutes of the society's meetings, its premium winners from the annual exhibitions that had been held in Harrisburg, Lancaster, and Pittsburgh, as well as reports from those county agricultural societies that had formed and could submit a report. Also included were the Philadelphia Society's 1850 address to the farmers of Pennsylvania, as well as the society's constitution and the subsequent legislative act of incorporation. Watts was pleased to introduce the volume, *Annual Report of the Transactions of the Pennsylvania State Agricultural Society*, published February 18, 1854, by the state printer. It was, Watts said, "a brief of all the transactions of the society, from its origin to this time, so that no part of its history shall be lost."[7]

Prefacing the volume was Watts's four-page report, dated January 20, 1854, to Governor William Bigler (1852–55), a staunch advocate for Pennsylvania agriculture. Watts's report culminated in a précis of how the Farmers' High

School would function educationally and what would be required financially to bring the institution into being and maintain it thereafter.

"That farmers require education to place them in that rank of society where they are entitled to stand, as well as to give effect to the important business of their life, is a point which needs no discussion," Watts wrote. "But *how* they shall be educated is a subject not so well understood." Watts noted that existing classical colleges were not adapted "to the education of young men for the business of agriculture." Further, such colleges would "unfit" young men for agricultural pursuits. With their focus on "the uninterrupted application to books," these colleges would render the body "incapable of labor" and the mind "ill adapted to the practical operations of the farm." Watts proposed to prepare agriculture students not so much "for the professional pursuit of scientific subjects, but to teach them that which is valuable for a farmer to know." The subjects to be covered would include English, mathematics, geography, chemistry, botany, astronomy, and other related subjects that are "practically useful," along with the "art of farming." Manual labor would be required, toward making the model farm "productive" and the school to some degree self-sustaining from the sale of produce. "Such an institution is loudly called for—Many farmers throughout the State would be glad to educate a son, if it were not at the risk of destroying his usefulness for active life," he declared.

Watts then outlined the estimated costs of building the school and maintaining it thereafter. The basic component, of course, was a farm of substantial acreage on which to locate the school. Watts thought three hundred acres (at $60 an acre) would be suitable, at a cost of $18,000. Additional buildings to accommodate the students would run $10,000; livestock and implements would cost $3,000; furniture, books, and scientific instruments, $5,000; and contingencies, $2,000. In all, the total cost would be $38,000. This could be financed, Watts recommended, by a $20,000 appropriation from the state legislature, a $10,000 subvention from the state agricultural society, and an $8,000 mortgage on the property.

Annual operating costs would total $16,000. Some $10,000 would be needed for the "support of the professors and pupils." The salary of the "principal professor" would be $2,000. Two other faculty members would command a salary of $1,500, or $3,000 together. The fourth faculty member would earn $1,000 per year.

Operating costs would be borne mainly by tuition revenue, estimated at $15,000 annually, based on two hundred students paying $75 per year. The state agricultural society would provide another $5,000 annually, and the sale of farm produce would bring in $2,000 per year. Total annual income would thus be $22,000, the additional $6,000 over and above the projected annual expenses of $16,000 being used "to expand the capacity of the institution for the accommodation of a greater number."

Watts anticipated criticism that the plan "is too limited and parsimonious for the great State of Pennsylvania." He foresaw that demand for admission would soon outstrip capacity but had faith that the institution would succeed immediately and grow accordingly.[8]

In Governor Bigler (1814–1880), Watts had a sympathetic ally, though Bigler was a Democrat and not a Whig like Watts. Governor of Pennsylvania from 1852 to 1855, Bigler, like Watts, was born in Cumberland County. Apprenticed as a printer, he moved to Clearfield, Pennsylvania, in 1833, where he established the *Clearfield Democrat* newspaper. He was elected to the state Senate for two terms in the 1840s and in 1851 was elected governor. In March 1855, Bigler was appointed to the U.S. Senate to fill an unexpired term and in 1856 was elected to the office for a six-year term.[9]

After his governorship and as Pennsylvania's newest U.S. senator, Bigler was invited to address the Philadelphia Society for Promoting Agriculture on September 15, 1855. It also was a gesture of appreciation for his role in supporting the Farmers' High School, which, by the time of his address, had been chartered by his own hand and then rechartered by his successor. "I am for the establishment of farm schools, in which may be blended both the theory and practice of agriculture, so that the student may have the opportunity of reducing the science to practice and at once testing its utility," Bigler said. "And why should not such a system of education be regularly established? Why should the means of instruction, so fully provided in every other branch of industry, be neglected in this, the greatest of all? . . . I am aware that some right-minded citizens have had strong prejudice against these views, and what they term 'book farming,' or 'fancy agriculture.' But I have never been able to see the force of the objection," he concluded. "If agriculture be not a proper field for the operation of intellect, where else shall one be found?"[10]

The First Act of Incorporation

After the state society's annual meeting in January 1854, Watts and his committee lost no time in getting a draft of a new bill incorporating the Farmers' High School of Pennsylvania to the legislature. Written mainly by Watts, the bill quickly passed both chambers and was signed into law by Governor Bigler on April 13. The act established a board of trustees, charged with managing and governing the school. The board consisted of more than sixty individuals, theoretically, including the president and vice presidents (twenty-five in all) of the Pennsylvania State Agricultural Society and the presidents of those county agricultural societies with at least one year of organization under their belts. All that was needed for a quorum, however, were thirteen trustees.

The act (section 5) required that the Board of Trustees meet in Harrisburg on the second Tuesday of June 1854 to "organize the institution" and select "the most eligible site" for its location. The tract of land, to be obtained through purchase or gift, must be at least two hundred acres. They were also to select a principal for the school who, "with such scientific attainments and capacity to teach . . . shall be a good practical farmer." The principal and faculty were to "control the immediate management of the institution" and the "instruction of all the youth committed to its care."

The trustees were to meet quarterly at the school, and more often if necessary. The trustees were empowered to "pass all such by-laws, ordinances and rules, as the good government of the institution shall require. And therein to prescribe what shall be taught to, and what labor performed by the pupils." The trustees were urged to employ a qualified faculty as soon as possible, to provide students with knowledge of "English language, grammar, geography, history, mathematics, chemistry, and such other natural and exact sciences as will conduce to the proper education of a farmer"—a course of study quite similar to what Watts had outlined to the governor in January. The students, in turn, would be required to do "all the labor necessary in the cultivation of the farm." Finally, the board was required to make a "full and detailed account" of the school's operations annually, including a full financial report, to be submitted to the state agricultural society, which in turn had to submit it to the legislature before the first Monday of each new year. The act also allowed the state agricultural society to appropriate to the school up to $10,000 annually out of its own funds.[11]

But the bill as passed had been amended from the original draft, and the changes incensed Watts. Its flaws were twofold: The act of incorporation included no state financial support whatsoever while creating a governing board with far too many members to be manageable. "Of the millions that are appropriated to other objects, it is not even proposed to appropriate one farthing to so important an object," Watts complained. The act of incorporation was "stupid and senseless in every feature, having a board of trustees of twenty-five or seventy-five, as the case may be, so situate that they never can be got together, and if so convened once the same persons would probably never be got together again."[12]

Watts was right. The trustees did try to meet in Harrisburg on June 13, as the act required, but the members present did not constitute the needed quorum of thirteen. Nonetheless, George Woodward, a vice president of the state agricultural society from Wilkes-Barre and thus an ex officio member of the board, appointed a committee of three to formulate "a plan of organization" for the school, "with such modifications of the charter and such legislative appropriations as may be deemed advisable to apply for next winter." The committee consisted of Watts as chairman, plus James Gowen and John Strohm. Those trustees agreed to hold another meeting in a month, on July 13, also in Harrisburg, making sure that each member of the board "should have personal notice" of the upcoming conclave.[13]

July 13 came and went, with only six trustees present, Watts and five others. Watts's committee did, however, submit its report, recommending that the April 1854 charter be abolished and a new one introduced. Watts again cited the two deficiencies: "First, in providing for a board of trustees composed of fifty or sixty members . . . that there could be no hope of getting them together to act at any time." Instead it recommended that the board "should not consist of more than thirteen members." The governor, secretary of the Commonwealth, attorney general, and president of the state agricultural society were to be ex officio members. The remaining nine were to be named individually in the new charter, each serving a three-year term and, in staggered fashion, ending their terms in cohorts of threes after each year.

The second deficiency was financial. The 1854 charter made no state appropriation "in aid of the project." This was doubly important in view of the belief that the nation's "literary institutions" educated their students to a state of "total unfitness" not only for the pursuit of farming but also "as a companion to his family, leading into a profession for which he has little capacity, and where he is subjected to all the temptations of an idle life." By contrast, the Farmers' High School would do quite the opposite, providing an education "appropriate to a farmer" and which would make the institution "so nearly self-sustaining as to bring education . . . within the reach of every man who desires to make his son an educated farmer."

The report then enumerated the proposed costs to build and maintain the school, the estimates having risen slightly from Watts's January 1854 letter to Governor Bigler. The cost of starting the school was pegged at $40,000 rather than $38,000, the increase accounted for by a mortgage of $10,000 instead of $8,000. The cost of annual operation had risen to $16,700, the additional $700 to be used for a principal's salary of $2,500 rather than $2,000, with the additional $200 being used for the lowest-paid faculty member (whose salary would increase from $1,000 to $1,200). Embedded in the start-up cost was a $20,000 appropriation from the state, which the committee decreed could be paid out in five annual installments of $4,000. Farm produce was also estimated to bring in $4,000 per year rather than $2,000. Tuition was held at $75 per year, in hopes of attracting an enrollment of two hundred students, generating $15,000 per year. Then, as now, the institution was to be heavily tuition dependent.[14]

Watts's committee called on the legislature to sanction the revisions and issue a new charter at its next session, beginning in January 1855. The committee expressed "the most entire confidence in the ultimate success of the work," expecting "more applicants for admission to such an institution than should be brought together at one point."

One final item of business remained: The committee's report was to be referred to Watts, George Woodward, and Alfred Elwyn, who would be charged with addressing "the people of the State" on the matter and asking the legislature to amend the bill. This same committee should "make all necessary inquiries where the Farmers' High School . . . may be most advantageously located, and . . . invite propositions from all parts of the State, for its location."[15]

Their brief "Address to the People of Pennsylvania" came out a week later, on July 21, 1854. They pointed out that farmers "have never derived any advantage from the large appropriations which have been made by the Legislature to the several colleges of the State." The Farmers' High School, by contrast, would be a place where "practical farming and all knowledge which pertains to a right understanding of the subject be taught," where the profits from the products of the students' labor would be applied to the cost of education, so as "to bring the price of learning" within their reach. "How many are there, who, knowing the value of an education, feel desirous that their sons should have its benefit, and yet look around in vain for an institution whose teachings are so practical as to prepare youth for the pursuit of agriculture?" they asked. "How many, too, fear the dissipations of a town—the temptations of a period devoted alone to study—the conviction that the son will be educated in mind and habituated in body, to a state of entire unfitness for practical and active life?"

The establishment of the Farmers' High School would represent an act of altruism by men "who have no feelings to gratify, beyond the mere desire to do good," and who "are willing to devote their time and their money to the organization of such an institution." These same individuals, representing the state agricultural society, vowed to appropriate more money for this purpose than would be asked of the legislature (even though the legislature was being asked for $20,000). They then turned their attention to where the school should be located. "It is very certain that its location will confer great advantages on the community around it." The committee asked for proposals from all parts of state, which the board of trustees would consider as soon as the institution was organized.[16]

The New Charter for the Farmers' High School

Carrying the "Address to the People of Pennsylvania," the state's agricultural press advocated enthusiastically for the new Farmers' High School. By late autumn 1854, Watts expressed confidence that public sentiment was such that lawmakers would issue a new, revised charter for the institution when the 1855 legislative session opened in January. He also was becoming concerned with how much work would be required to get the school sited, funded, built, and staffed—all of this to be completed before the first class of students could be invited to apply. Therefore he resigned his presidency of the Pennsylvania State Agricultural Society on January 15, 1855, during its annual meeting in Harrisburg, in order to devote more time and effort to the academic enterprise.

In his letter of resignation to society secretary Robert C. Walker, Watts said his interest in agricultural matters would not abate and that he would continue to serve the society "in any subordinate position" to any cause the society deemed necessary. In fact, he would continue to serve on the executive board. Watts acknowledged his regret that he could never attend the society's annual meetings because they were held of necessity during the winter lull in the agricultural cycle, but at a time that fell "when professional duty commands my attention elsewhere." He expressed his wishful interest in meeting with farmers all over the state to help them "devise plans and means to promote their interest" and said he would be "especially pleased" to urge upon them their right to establish a school "where their sons may be taught the science, as well as the practical operations of agriculture, at a cost commensurate with the profits of their business." Acknowledging the demands of his busy life, he lamented that "this opportunity is denied me."[17]

Nevertheless, it was to this end—the school's establishment—that Watts's energies would now be devoted. As he stepped down, James Gowen of Mount Airy, Philadelphia County, was elected president of the state society. Hugh McAllister of Bellefonte, Centre County, who would become Watts's closest ally in the new educational venture, was reelected as a society vice president representing the Centre County congressional district.

In early 1855, things happened as expected. The legislature repealed the 1854 act of incorporation and passed the new one overwhelmingly. It was signed into law on February 22, 1855, by Governor James Pollock, who had succeeded William Bigler. A Princeton graduate and a lawyer, Pollock was elected to the U.S. House in 1844 from Pennsylvania's Thirteenth District. As a freshman congressman, Pollock lived in the same rooming house as another new congressman, Abraham Lincoln. Pollock was an early supporter of internal improvements such as the telegraph and the transcontinental railroad. After three terms in Congress, he served as a judge and was nominated by the Whig Party to run for governor in 1854. He was a strong supporter of agriculture, education (he later served as president of Lafayette College), and the movement for an agricultural college in Pennsylvania. His concurrence with the new charter was never in doubt.[18]

The 1855 charter was not substantially different from the earlier one, except in one crucial respect: the membership of the board of trustees was reduced from sixty-plus to thirteen. There were four ex officio members: the governor, the secretary of the Commonwealth, the president of the Pennsylvania State Agricultural Society, and the principal of the institution. The charter specified that nine additional members be appointed by name: Alfred L. Elwyn and Algernon S. Roberts of Philadelphia; Hugh McAllister of Centre County; Robert C. Walker of Allegheny County; James Miles of Erie County; John Strohm of Lancaster County; August O. Hiester of Dauphin County; William Jessup of Susquehanna County; and Frederick Watts of Cumberland County. The act directed these nine members to divide themselves into classes of three, the first class terminating after one year in 1856, the second after two years in 1857, and the third after three years in 1858. A slate of three candidates would be elected every year by votes of the executive board of the Pennsylvania State Agricultural Society and votes of three representatives from every county agricultural society.[19]

These nine original trustees were a veritable Who's Who of Pennsylvania agriculture. All were members of the Philadelphia Society for Promoting Agriculture as well as the Pennsylvania State Agricultural Society. Furthermore, these men represented broad statewide support for the Farmers' High School—from Erie to Philadelphia, from northeastern Pennsylvania to Pittsburgh—as opposed to the local and parochial interests that characterized Pennsylvania's "literary colleges." Politically, these trustees tended to be Whigs—in favor of internal improvements and public education, among other things (described in the preceding chapters) designed to develop and unify the state and nation. As the national Whig Party fell apart in the mid-1850s, most of the Pennsylvania Whigs, including these trustees, moved to the Republican Party and became strong Lincoln supporters.[20]

One of the four original ex officio trustees was especially energetic in his advocacy for the Farmers' High School: James Gowen, president of the state agricultural society. On March 28, 1855, little more than a month after the new charter had been enacted, Gowen addressed the Pennsylvania legislature, maintaining that the school needed a $20,000 appropriation from the state to become operational. "The Legislature, in 1851, chartered the State Agricultural Society, and appropriated to its use two thousand dollars annually. Had this grant been withheld, the charter, in all probability, would have remained to this day a dead letter upon the statute book," Gowen pointed out. "So in like manner . . . that without adequate pecuniary aid, the charter of the Farmers' High School may remain inoperative."[21]

Gowen's plea was ignored by the legislature. Eight months later, in November 1855, he appealed to the twenty-five vice presidents of the state agricultural society for their help in mounting a drive for new life members. He asked them to solicit their "fellow-citizens" toward that end. "If one thousand could be found throughout the State, to enrol themselves at ten dollars each, it would cover the first instalment to the Farmers' High School."[22] The membership campaign did not come close to yielding the projected $10,000 amount, however.

Selecting the Site

The act of February 22, 1855, mandated that the Board of Trustees meet at Harrisburg on the second Sunday of June 1855 to begin organizing the school and selecting its site. The trustees were to procure a tract of land of not less than two hundred or more than one thousand acres and attend to the business of selecting a principal and hiring faculty. Following the legislative directive, the new board met in Harrisburg on June 14. Watts nominated Governor Pollock as chair, and Elwyn nominated Robert C. Walker as secretary, both being elected. The board then began to consider the various proposals that had come in from the earlier solicitation.[23]

Offers to *donate* two hundred acres came from: (1) James Miles, in Girard Township near Erie, a Great Lakes seaport. Miles, a newly appointed member of the school's board of trustees, was a lawyer, judge, and businessman, and the son of William Miles, on whose farm Watts lived and read law from 1819 to 1821; (2) James Irvin, the prominent ironmaster of Centre County, a remote locale in the geographic center of the state; and (3) Elias Baker, the prominent ironmaster of Blair County, near Altoona, a fast-growing railroad city also in central Pennsylvania.

Offers to *sell* land came from: (4) Joseph Bailey of Perry County, two thousand acres "upon liberal terms." Bailey was an ironmaster, state senator, and state treasurer, and later a U.S. House representative; and (5) George Bayard, of Allegheny County, near Pittsburgh, six hundred acres. Bayard was a businessman with interests in real estate.

The board formed a three-man committee consisting of Watts, Elwyn, and Governor Pollock, and instructed them to quickly "view the lands" of the offers. The same directive permitted the committee to examine "such other situations as to them shall seem advisable" and encouraged the other trustees to accompany the committee on its site visits. Four more trustees decided to do so: Walker, McAllister, Jessup, and Hiester. The seven-man entourage was to gather in two weeks at Harrisburg, and the committee was to make its report at the board's meeting in July.[24] The visits took ten days. The sites offered by Centre and Erie Counties were visited first, followed by those of Allegheny and Blair Counties.

In addition to his donation of two hundred acres, Irvin of Centre County later proposed another two hundred acres to be rented "at a reasonable rate" and eventually purchased, if needed, at $60 per acre. Miles, who also had proposed two hundred acres of donated land, matched Irvin's offer by including two hundred acres of additional land to be purchased at $60 per acre. The Bayard estate in Allegheny County would provide six hundred acres to be purchased at $35 per acre. The two-hundred-acre donation from Elias Baker of Blair County also included an additional two hundred acres that could be purchased at $25 per acre. In the meantime, another proposal donating two hundred acres had come in from W. H. Easton of Franklin County, which the committee visited much later, on September 12.

The trustees convened again in Harrisburg on July 17, electing Watts as chair. The selection committee noted that it had wanted to make a site decision quickly but also wanted to do it fairly and impartially. Thus it chose to postpone any decision. "One [site] already offered we have had no opportunity to see, and doubtless others will be presented," Watts reported. Indeed, that was already happening. Simon Cameron of Harrisburg appeared before the board and said that if a decision could not be reached "at once," he was confident that $10,000 could be raised in Dauphin County to purchase a farm, and that he would donate $1,000 himself. Meanwhile, a delegation from Blair County offered to sweeten the proposal of Elias Baker by purchasing an additional two hundred acres of his land to provide a four-hundred-acre donation.

The trustees set a deadline for additional proposals to be submitted for consideration by its deadline of September 12, when it would next meet in Harrisburg.[25] Meanwhile, on July 17, the executive board of the state agricultural society appropriated $10,000 for the establishment of the Farmers' High School.[26]

At the trustees' September 12 meeting, chaired by Governor Pollock, Watts made the committee's final report. He noted the committee had visited the Franklin County farms of W. H. Easton, who had proposed to donate two farms, with a third, more developed than the others, being offered for sale. To make the Franklin County site more compelling, the citizens of Mercersburg agreed to raise the funds needed to buy the third property that would also be donated.

Another bid had come from David Blair of Huntingdon County offering to donate a 200-acre farm near Shade Gap. And from Union County came an offer from trustees of an estate proposing to sell 265 acres. Meanwhile, the Blair County offer of Elias Baker had become even sweeter. In addition to providing an additional 200 acres of land on a farm adjoining the Bakers' original offer, the citizens now proposed to provide $10,000 for the school, to be raised by subscription.

The Centre County offer also had been sweetened. In addition to his original offer of two hundred acres, Irvin proposed to include an additional two hundred acres in adjoining farmland, to be leased at $600 per year and then to sell it to the institution for $60 per acre, or $12,000 in all, half of that sum to be paid upon the sale with the remaining $6,000 to be paid in two annual payments thereafter. That was followed by a guarantee to provide an additional $10,000, signed by Irvin, McAllister, and Andrew Curtin, an ex officio trustee serving as secretary of the Commonwealth. The text: "Gentlemen: Whereas the citizens of Centre and Huntingdon Counties have subscribed ten thousand dollars to the Farmers' High School of Pennsylvania on the condition the institution be located on the lands offered by General James Irvin of Centre County, and Whereas the subscription and standing of many of the subscribers are unknown to the Trustees, we do hereby guarantee that the sum of ten thousand dollars shall be collected and paid upon subscription to the Farmers' High School of Pennsylvania agreeable to the terms and conditions thereof."

Watts moved to adopt "the proposition of General James Irvin," noting that the Centre County site would "best promote the interests of the Institution." Then things got more interesting. James Gowen and Alfred Elwyn made substitute motions for two other sites, for the offers of Baker of Blair County and Easton of Franklin County, respectively, but both motions failed. Watts then moved for postponement of the vote, recommending instead a new selection committee of James Gowen, Augustus Hiester, and John Strohm to examine sites and propose a final location. Watts's fair-handed motion was voted down, however. Then another motion was made to select the offer from George Bayard of Allegheny County, but it, too, was defeated. Finally, Watts's original motion to accept the Centre County site was approved.[27]

All of these proposals came from counties in central and western Pennsylvania, regions west of the Susquehanna (except for Simon Cameron's eleventh-hour offer for Dauphin County, which did not materialize into a formal proposal). Oddly, no proposal came from southeastern Pennsylvania, the region where agricultural practice was most advanced. The Philadelphia vicinity, Chester County in particular but also Lancaster and York Counties, and parts of the Great Valley, were rapidly shifting from the wheat monoculture to farming practice based on more diversification: an integrated grain and livestock regimen, systematic crop rotation, and systematic manuring, with successful results.[28] Southeastern Pennsylvania boasted numerous progressive agricultural societies but apparently lacked interest in vying for an agricultural college.

In Centre County, the sentiment was quite the opposite. The groundwork for the successful Centre County bid had been laid months before. In the wake of the January 1855 annual meeting of the state agricultural society in Harrisburg (to which Centre County had sent delegates), the Centre County Agricultural Society met on January 24. The Centre Countians passed a resolution endorsing the establishment of the Farmers' High School and urging the legislature to issue the second charter, which the lawmakers did on February 22. Irvin spoke vigorously in support of the resolution. To demonstrate

FIGURE 9
General James Irvin (1800–1862), Centre County ironmaster and benefactor of land for the Farmers' High School. Courtesy of The Pennsylvania State University Archives.

Centre County's interest in the new school, Irvin offered to donate two hundred acres of Centre Furnace land. The same day the institution was chartered, Irvin made his offer official to the executive committee of the state agricultural society, which in turn passed it on to the new Board of Trustees of the Farmers' High School.[29] Noting the value of the school to the state at large, Irvin stated that "it would be especially beneficial to the particular district in which it shall be established, and I therefore desire its location in Centre County—If we would add dignity to manual labor, if we should have it held in honor by the community, we must associate it with Science, and if we would lessen the expense of acquiring Scientific Knowledge so as to bring the cost within the means of the farming community, we must connect its acquisition with manual labor."[30]

The site selection committee—Watts, Elwyn, and Governor Pollock—and four other trustees visited Irvin's lands on June 26, 1855. The Centre County Agricultural Society, headed by President George Boal, had arranged a gala welcome for the committee. Irvin offered them the choice of three farms, which the committee inspected. Afterward, "the Trustees and all the company repaired to the dwelling house of Moses Thompson at Centre Furnace where one hundred and fifty persons were entertained by a sumptuous dinner prepared by Mrs. Thompson."[31] The large turnout of local folk was complemented by the presence of such luminaries as ex officio trustee Andrew Curtin, serving both as secretary of the Commonwealth and superintendent of public instruction; James T. Hale, president judge of Centre County's twentieth judicial district; Moses Thompson, Irvin's son-in-law who owned one-third of the Centre Furnace operation; and William Waring, a local horticulturalist who would soon be hired to superintend the school's farm.

Not that the dinner, per se, swayed the committee's decision, as demonstrated by the competing motions for other sites at the trustees' September 12 meeting and Watts's impartiality in proposing a new site selection committee after his initial motion in favor of Centre County had been defeated. But the offer from Irvin, who had been talking about a "Farm School" for Centre County since 1850, carried considerable weight. He was a prominent Whig and one of the wealthiest men in Pennsylvania. He also was general of a state militia division. As a former two-term congressman (1841–45) and unsuccessful candidate for governor (1847), he was well connected in state politics, his connections influencing the decision to select his offer. His site also offered some political safety, being far removed from the power centers of Philadelphia, Pittsburgh, and Harrisburg.[32]

After Watts's motion of September 12 for the Centre County site was approved on the second go-around, critics began to sound the alarm. They cited the school's remote location, inaccessibility by rail, poor soil, and lack of running water as major drawbacks. The criticism would continue through the 1850s and metastasize during the 1860s, when various "literary colleges" would conspire with their legislative allies to wrest the Morrill Land-Grant endowment from the school and claim the funds for themselves.

The September 12, 1855, trustee meeting was notable for other reasons beyond the selection of a site. As for the matter of a principal for the school, Elwyn reported that his selection committee would recommend Charles B. Trego. Watts, McAllister, and Miles were appointed to a committee to work with the new principal to begin the preparations for a college building. Moses Thompson of Centre Furnace, a partner of James Irvin and living in the ironmaster's mansion that adjoined the site selected for the Farmers' High School, was requested to work with the committee and the principal in getting the enterprise into operation. And, certainly not least, Watts was unanimously elected president of the Farmers' High School Board of Trustees, a post he would hold for nineteen years.[33]

The Charles Trego Affair

As for a school president or principal, the trustees decided to appoint an eminently qualified candidate: Charles B. Trego, a member of the Philadelphia Society for Promoting Agriculture, an officer of the Pennsylvania State Agricultural Society, and a practicing scientist.

In 1855, Trego was professor of geology at the University of Pennsylvania in the newly established (1852) School of Mines, Arts, and Manufactures. Around that time, Trego had been pushed by the state agricultural society for the proposed new post of state agricultural chemist, a post favored by then governor William Bigler but never established by the legislature. Trego grew up on a farm in Bucks County and was largely self-educated but lacked a college degree. He taught school in Philadelphia from 1821 to 1834. Elected to the state House of Representatives in 1835, Trego took the initiative to promote a bill authorizing the first geological survey of Pennsylvania. Trego then served as assistant state geologist from 1837 to 1841, conducting that survey and afterward producing the four-hundred-page *Geography of Pennsylvania*. He then returned to the state House, serving from 1841 to 1847. He also studied science and technology through the Franklin Institute, was elected to the American Philosophical Society, and later served on Philadelphia's city council, including a term as president. He began researching and writing a history of Philadelphia but never finished the project. Over sixteen years, he arranged and catalogued, on a part-time basis, the American Philosophical Society's collection of the papers of Benjamin Franklin into sixty folio volumes.[34]

Thus Trego was well known to the trustees and the obvious choice for the post. The selection committee for a "principal" recommended Trego on September 12 and was instructed by the board to approach him about the position.[35]

Shortly after the meeting, trustees Elwyn and Watts arranged to meet Trego in Harrisburg to discuss the offer, but Trego did not show up. "The Doctor [Elwyn] has decided to communicate to you the information that you had been chosen the Principal of the proposed Farm School, to consult with you about it and advise me of the result," Watts told Trego. "I am therefore quite disappointed in not hearing from him any information on your disposition on the subject, and as I had supposed that you would communicate with him . . . did not deem it necessary . . . to make any communication to you myself. Will you do me the favor to say what you think about it?"[36]

Trego quickly responded to Watts, seeking more information about what the position might entail. He offered that he had been examining the plans and curricula of "a considerable number of agricultural schools" in Great Britain and Europe, finding "many features that I think should be advantageously adopted in ours," though none that he would be "willing to follow entirely as a model." Nonetheless, he expressed concern about his ability to satisfy a board of trustees entertaining a variety of opinions about the new institution and, "not agreeing among themselves, will expect and require more from the Principal than he will be able to perform."[37]

Watts conceded that he could not speak for the board but offered his own assessment of what would be required. "The subject of this 'Farm School' is so entirely new and so little consideration has been given to the plan of organization by the Board of Trustees that I can but express my individual opinion about it," Watts replied. The board would require the principal to "devise an entire plan and with the concurrence of their committee (who is McAllister of Centre and myself) make all arrangements without delay to carry it into effect so that they may take possession of their property in the spring to erect their buildings during the next summer." The immediate imperative, Watts added, was "to lay out the grounds and buildings and invite proposals for their erection, arrange a proper plan for Scientific and Literary instruction, determine at what periods the Institution can be made ready for the reception of pupils, how the farm is to be managed during the next summer to be." Watts said the salary had not yet been set but added that the principal would be expected to live at the school.[38]

Trego voiced concerns about the proposed salary ($1,500); the full-time nature of the job; the expectations for residency and the extent to which it would detract from his other interests and pursuits; the trustees' vague and uncertain plans for the school, as Watts himself had suggested; the lack of a firm financial foundation for the school; and, finally, the school's remote location, lack of running water and fertility of soil, and inaccessibility by rail. "I have serious apprehensions that the successful accomplishment of the design of the institution will, unhappily, be rendered much more difficult if a more accessible and better adapted site had been selected."[39]

But there was more. Trego was especially upset over the mixed signals he had received from the trustees. Elwyn told him he had been selected while another trustee said the board had only favorably received the nomination but had not yet acted upon it. "I believe it is usual for a person who is actually appointed to any station of trust and responsibility to have some official notice of the fact," Trego wrote to Watts.[40]

Thus the ideal candidate turned the job down. Trego opted to stay in Philadelphia, pursuing his career at the University of Pennsylvania, remaining as the only faculty member in the School of Mines, Arts, and Manufactures until its operations were suspended with the start of the Civil War. With Trego's refusal, the presidency of the Farmers' High School would go unfilled for nearly four years.[41]

Watts Speaks to the State's Farming Community

Two weeks after the trustees' September 1855 meeting, the state agricultural society's fifth annual exhibition took place in Harrisburg. After four years of successively larger fairs, the crowning feature of the 1855 event was the visit of U.S. President Franklin Pierce (1853–57)—a vivid testament to the society's stature. A Democrat, Pierce at the time of his visit was embroiled in the raging sectional controversies over the Kansas-Nebraska Act (1854), which he had championed. The act effectively repealed the Missouri Compromise of 1850 by allowing popular sovereignty to determine whether slavery would be allowed in these two new states. Ultimately, Pierce's handling of the situation would deny him the Democratic nomination for a second term in 1856, in favor of James Buchanan. But September 26, 1855, was a day for other, more celebratory activities. Watts, new U.S. Senator William Bigler, and three others were appointed by state agricultural society president James Gowen to greet President Pierce and accompany him to the grounds.

Pierce's remarks were what might be expected: praise for Pennsylvania's historical role in the building of the United States, for the farmer, for the exhibition, and for the type of organization that brought him to Harrisburg. "The science of agriculture is doubtless better understood, and the art more skillfully practiced in some parts of the old world than in this, the new, but we are on the march, impelled by the energies of a young and free people, with State agricultural societies leading the way," Pierce observed.[42]

Watts, who had resigned as president of the society the previous January, was invited to give the annual address for the exhibition, on September 28. Although the trustees had settled on Centre County as the site for the Farmers' High School only sixteen days earlier, he made no explicit mention of the Farmers' High School or the selection of the site. Rather, Watts took a broader philosophical approach that he hoped would result in widespread support for the new school. Thus he championed the awakening of Pennsylvania's previously isolated farmers as a self-conscious agricultural constituency that needed to take its place among the other economic, political, and social sectors of American life. And he emphasized that higher education specifically designed for the sons of farmers was an essential element of advancement for the agricultural class. In sum, he called vigorously for a new class consciousness on the part of farmers.

"The last few years have given birth to a new era," Watts declared. "Our attention has been arrested and our minds suddenly called to contemplate the importance of agriculture. Cultivators of the earth have been . . . pressed to take their place in the race which is now being run in the world's progress." Isolated and largely ignored, farmers had left too much to chance, to fate, and must now unite to advance their common cause: "That farmers . . . are not as truly aware of and united to defend their real interests, we mean to proclaim."

Watts sought to disabuse his rural audience of the idea that farmers and their organizations should have nothing to do with politics. "Have you ever given yourselves the trouble to inquire whether the existing laws give sufficient protection to your rights and property?" he asked, adding that "your interests are nowhere." He talked about laws to advance the merchant, tariffs to protect the mechanic and manufacturer, government funds to teach military science and engineering but asked, "Have you ever heard of a department of agriculture?" He urged farmers "to assert boldly and fearlessly your rights and your wants, and to stand together and by your numbers command respect."

Aside from political action, Watts offered, the best way to promote agricultural progress was through the *study* of agriculture. "We should put our hands to the noble work of education, and . . . direct that education to that . . . subject in which you are engaged and for which the world has done so little." He criticized the existing colleges—"literary institutions"—for offering a curriculum that "is unprofitable for you."

Farmers should demand a new form of education suited to their needs and interests, he urged. "Whilst schools, academies and colleges receive the fostering care and bountiful endowments of the government, the farmers' school demands the like support." Accordingly, Watts appealed to the "merchant and mechanic . . . to look with favor upon any project which shall have for its object the education of the farmer." He asked the "professor and student" to add their "influence . . . into the scale of agricultural progress," as he did the statesman, lawyer, and minister. He even appealed to mothers to work their influence as well.

Finally, Watts praised the annual exhibitions of the state agricultural society for their role in bringing farmers together and demonstrating their potential for influencing the political process. "Here, too, you learn to realize the force of numbers, of intelligence, of strength, of which you are composed, and that power which may be wielded by your will."[43] Thus on that late September day did Watts once again plant the seeds of class consciousness, of political advocacy and agitation, as well as the necessity for advanced agricultural education among Pennsylvania's farming citizenry.

Defending the Centre County Site

Although support for the *idea* of the Farmers' High School had materialized broadly across the state by 1855, its new Centre County location would draw criticism throughout the remainder of the 1850s. Perhaps Watts sensed the potential for controversy as he refrained from talking about the newly selected site in his speech to the state agricultural exhibition.

As the first Penn State historian put it: "Visiting committees deplored an adequate Baedeker to guide them to the institution which was located in Centre County near Boalsburg, Spruce Creek, Lewistown, or Bellefonte, but where were they?" In 1859, an editorial in Philadelphia's *Public Ledger* lamented the school's location. "To call it 'near Boalsburg' is not very clear, till one knows where Boalsburg is. It is in Centre County, twelve miles from Bellefonte, but the school is not so near even Boalsburg, we believe that it has been necessary to establish a 'Farm School Post-Office' for its special accommodation. It is a central position, and anticipated railroads will ultimately bring it more within reach. Till then, in these days of rapid travel, twenty-five miles by stage over the 'seven mountains' from the nearest station, is a serious thing."[44]

Without question, the school *was* hard to find. In 1861, a large, detailed map of Centre County was produced "from actual surveys" directed by H. F. Walden and published in New York City. The largest nearby settlements—all of them hamlets or villages—were identified as Boalsburg, Linden Hall, Oak Hall, Dale's Mills, Houser's Mills, and Centre Furnace. Adjacent to the latter was "Farmers' High School of Pa." Along with other notable county buildings, an architectural drawing of the school's main "College Building" was featured in a corner of the map, although the edifice would not be completed until early 1864.

The school's trustees fought hard to defend the Centre County site. In his address to the sixth annual exhibition of the state agricultural society on October 3, 1856, in Pittsburgh, society president George Woodward, an ex officio trustee of the school, explained the board's reasoning: "Centre county contains some of the best farm land and some of the best Farmers in Pennsylvania. No where are better crops of wheat and corn produced than in Nittany and Penn's valleys; and in one of the most healthful and beautiful portions of the latter is the Farm School to be planted. It was the generosity of the donor [Irvin] which determined the location. The objections have reference principally to the want of water and the distance from railroad communication," Woodward said. "The School will be some twenty miles from the Central railroad, and, in my judgment, that is near enough. Boys had better be away from the temptations and annoyances peculiar to railroads, whilst acquiring education. And surely they can travel twenty miles without steam, in pursuit of such advantages as this school is to offer." Then Woodward called for the addition of similar agricultural colleges in other parts of the state, particularly in Philadelphia and Pittsburgh.[45]

Watts made an even tighter case for the school's location at his "Barn Speech" delivered at the school on September 2, 1857:

> Let there be no adverse feelings founded on local preference. What motive could there be to induce those who examined and determined the locality of this school to do else than right? With the approval of my associates, I could gladly have taken it into my own dear valley of Cumberland, but in the exercise of a sound and clear judgment (I speak for all as an inconsiderable one only), the Board having looked over all proposed lands and considered all circumstances, believed the one chosen to be best. It is possible that we were in fault, yet I have ever believed the selection made combined more advantages than any other offered, and I ask for myself and associates the credit at least of honest motives, and of all to consider how many of the most essential advantages of soil, surface, exposure, healthfulness, and centrality are combined in the ground we have met upon.[46]

Nevertheless, criticism of the school's location would not abate during Watts's tenure as board president.

CHAPTER 4

Building the School and Preparing to Open

Having chartered and located the Farmers' High School, although absent a principal, Frederick Watts and the board of trustees now could get on with the business of building the physical plant and securing the finances needed to support the new institution. At the September 1855 meeting, the board's building and business committee had been appointed, consisting of Watts, McAllister, and James Miles. Their charge was to "make preparations for buildings and for other purposes."[1]

At its first meeting of the new year, on January 4, 1856, in Harrisburg, the full board addressed those matters. McAllister moved to appoint a three-person committee, which he would head, to request a $50,000 appropriation from the Pennsylvania legislature. The board then approved "the general features of the plan of the College as presented by H. N. McAllister and of the plan of the Barn presented by Frederick Watts."[2] The board hired William Waring, a local nurseryman and farmer, to lay out the plan and plant the grounds with trees and shrubs. Edward C. Humes of Bellefonte was appointed as the board's treasurer and authorized to accept the $10,000 appropriation granted to the school the previous July from the Pennsylvania State Agricultural Society. Finally, the board expressed its intention to accept the additional two hundred acres of land offered by James Irvin, renting the land for five years and eventually purchasing it within that timeframe at $60 per acre or $12,000 in all.[3]

Watts's business and building committee lost no time in getting things moving. In mid-May 1856, they contracted with the Carlisle, Pennsylvania, firm of Turner and Natcher to construct the main building—hereafter called the "College Building"—for $55,000. Watts was familiar with his hometown construction firm and quickly secured its services. Another contractor was hired for $3,500 to build Watts's large barn. Other facilities such as corn cribs, wagon sheds, cisterns, a farmhouse, and the like were under way as well. Construction for the College Building began on June 24, with brickmakers and excavators doing the preliminary work. The first stones of the foundation were laid on August 18, 1856.[4]

The trustees met again, for the second and last time in 1856, on October 6, convening at the school to see for themselves what was being done. Watts reported on the progress made on the College Building, barn, and farmhouse. The board reviewed the work and conferred its approval. James Irvin, the local ironmaster who gifted the two hundred acres of land, was appointed board secretary. By virtue of its own members and a handful of county agricultural society delegates who had ventured from points distant to the meeting, the board elected three individuals to a three-year term (1856–59): Alfred L. Elwyn and Augustus O. Hiester, both reelected, and J. W. K. Snodgrass of Allegheny County, a newcomer. Finally, Watts was asked to write to the officers of all county agricultural societies, asking their cooperation in raising funds for the Farmers' High School.[5]

Progress on the buildings and grounds continued apace. A year later, in 1857, Watts could report that the "walls of the west wing are up three storeys and are plainly but very substantially built of superior, gray lime stone. They are four feet thick at the base, and are founded entirely upon solid rock." The wing, when finished, was to contain a suite of rooms for a private residence on the first and second floors, four recitation rooms on the first floor and two on the second, a "society hall" on the third floor, five storerooms, and sixty-nine dormitory rooms. The hope was to have the wing completed and ready for occupancy by November 1858, Watts said.[6]

Meanwhile, the effort to secure an appropriation from the state had finally come to fruition. On May 20, 1857, the legislature appropriated $25,000 free and clear and promised an additional $25,000 if an equal amount could be raised through a private subscription campaign. This would be the first state appropriation in the institution's history; the second would be a long time coming, not until 1861.

The high-water mark of those early years came in September 1857, as construction continued, roads leading to the school were laid out, and petitions for a mail route to the school were submitted. The board of trustees met at the school, the major business at hand being to elect three individuals to three-year terms (1857–60). For this purpose, the trustees were joined by a large number of delegates—forty-five in all—from twenty county agricultural societies. Watts was reelected to the board, and then reelected as its president; James Miles was reelected, and newcomer Joshua P. Eyre Jr. of Delaware County was elected.

Others had been invited as well to view the proceedings and the progress at the Farm School, including "distinguished guests, friends, and enemies of the new movement"—about two hundred in all. The only place suitable for the gathering was the large barn of Watts's design, completed in 1856. After the election of trustees, a "collation [a light meal] was served by the Ladies of

FIGURE 10 *Farmers' High School Campus Barn of Watts's design, built in 1856 on the site of the present-day Carnegie Building. It was moved to West Campus in 1889 and was burned to the ground in 1891. Courtesy of The Pennsylvania State University Archives.*

the neighborhood." After dinner, President Judge James Tracy Hale of Bellefonte spoke briefly and then introduced Watts.[7]

In what thereafter would be called his "Barn Speech of 1857," Watts characterized the new agricultural education offered by the Farmers' High School as the lever that would lift the farming community into parity with the more powerful industrial and mercantile sectors of the state. Although the state was rapidly industrializing, Pennsylvania's wealth in the 1850s was still generated largely by agriculture. Yet the farming community, Watts strongly believed, had received nothing in return, having been ignored by the state's power brokers for far too long.

"We must combine the cultivated intelligence and social amenities of mental refinement with the strong practical usefulness and sound virtues of the agriculturalist," Watts said. "If these be not thus wedded, this great agricultural State of Pennsylvania must remain as now, with the balance of influence and power in the hands of comparatively few." He further lamented that "the great body of citizens . . . the great agricultural body, have not the power and influence which they ought to have, for the proper balance and benefit of society." The power of that "great body" could be increased only through education. "Education will impart influence," Watts emphasized, but it had to be the right kind of education combining science, art, and labor. The Farmers' High School, he added, "is intended to supply this great social, political, moral and economic want, and while it improves the agricultural mind, and trains the hands, it will do both at less expense than the purely literary training can be obtained for." Watts urged his audience to do everything in their power to help raise the $25,000 needed through private contributions to match the additional $25,000 promised by the state legislature (beyond the sum already appropriated). Watts then pledged to "be one of ten, to give a thousand dollars each, toward making up that amount."[8] Others stood up and made pledges in amounts ranging from $500 to $1,000. It seemed as if about $10,000 was "raised" that evening, either through the personal resources of the trustees and delegates or through fundraising efforts to be conducted in their home counties. If only $15,000 more could be raised, the school could match the state's additional $25,000.[9]

Despite criticism of its location, the aborning school attracted rhetorical if not political support. A month later, after the trustees' September 1857 meeting, Edwin C. Wilson gave the annual address before the Pennsylvania State Agricultural Society at its seventh annual exhibition in Philadelphia, endorsing the school thus: "Your Farmers' High School, established by your

Legislature, aided by private donations, and largely aided by this society, both deserves and needs your fostering care. . . . This school is yet in its infancy; the Farmers must nurse the child a little while, until its youth is fairly passed, and manhood begins, then will be seen a giant out of whose hands shall be scattered far and wide the seeds of peace and plenty."[10]

The Panic of 1857 and Its Effects on the School

September 1857 was notable for another reason, this one ominous, foreshadowing tougher times ahead. The Panic of 1857, a national financial crisis, began that same month. It crippled the nation's economy and severely impacted Pennsylvania's iron industry. The fundamental causes were a declining international economy and an overexpanding domestic economy. In the years before the Panic, the American economy was prosperous, allowing merchants, banks, and farmers to take risks with their investments. As the money supply contracted, and prices began to fall, the effects were felt quickly and sharply. The Northern economy would not begin to recover until the advent of the Civil War in 1861.[11]

The trustees met again in December 1857 and March 1858 but in both instances could not muster a quorum and conduct official business. The board would not meet again until June 16, 1858. By then, the effects of the national economic malaise were evident, prompting Watts and his fellow trustees to address the situation.

Before that, however, Watts had issued the first annual report of the Farmers' High School to the House and Senate of Pennsylvania. Dated January 19, 1858, the report was designed to "detail its beginning and progress to the present time." Watts reminded the legislators that the institution began to build itself with $45,000—$10,000 contributed by the citizens of Centre County, $10,000 from the state agricultural society, and $25,000 appropriated by the legislature in May 1857.

The college barn, a farmhouse, and various outbuildings had been constructed, he said. The main college building, "two hundred and thirty-three feet in front and five stories high, with wings at either end . . . is in a state forwardness, and will be completed during the ensuing summer," Watts projected rosily. Waxing even more optimistic, he anticipated receiving an additional $5,000 from the estate of Elliott Cresson, $25,000 from individual subscriptions, and the additional $25,000 the legislature had promised in matching funds. Anticipating success from the fundraising campaign, Watts said the board had "received such assurances that the individual subscriptions will be made." Watts ended his first annual report by praising William Waring, the general superintendent of the school's farm, for his progress in "making the necessary preparations for the future operations of the institution."[12]

Waring was born in England in 1806 but immigrated to America in 1833. In Centre County, he was the founder of the first teachers' institute in Pennsylvania at Linden Hall in 1851 and also began a nursery with his brother on the farm he had purchased in nearby Oak Hall. He wrote numerous articles for journals, served as horticultural editor for the *New York Tribune*, and authored the *Fruit Growers Hand Book* (1851). Waring was hired by the trustees' business committee to lay out the buildings, grounds, and agricultural plots and manage all of it. Although he held no college degree, he was named acting principal of the faculty as the school opened for instruction in February 1859 and remained as such until President Evan Pugh arrived in October 1859. Fairly or not, Waring endured criticism from the faculty, students, and others, and resigned on September 30, 1862.[13]

Contained in Watts's 1858 annual report was Waring's twenty-page report detailing every imaginable aspect of the school's farm. He accounted for every

FIGURE 11
William Waring (1816–1906), hired in 1856 as general superintendent of the Farmers' High School. Courtesy of The Pennsylvania State University Archives.

hour of work from April through December 1857 in such operations as plowing and harrowing, experimentation, manuring, horticulture, seeding and planting, cultivating, harvesting, threshing, and storage—thousands of hours of labor performed by Waring and his assistant. He even reported that forty-three hours had been expended in August preparing for the meeting and election of trustees in September 1857.

Waring prefaced his report thus: "The barn [of Watts's design] west of the farm house was finished late in 1856. In January and February, 1857, arrangements were made and stocks prepared for the nursery plantations, and at the opening of spring Mr. John Herman moved into one of the shanties; implements were purchased; six mules, three horses and a cart were hired, and on the 31st March, the ground thawed sufficiently to enable us to commence work in the orchard and corn ground."[14] Such were the beginnings of operations at the Farmers' High School, two years before students would arrive.

Even so, the eventual arrival of students was uppermost on Watts's mind. At the end of his report, he provided an ambitious list of thirty-four "subjects proposed to be taught"—mathematics, natural philosophy [physics], agricultural engineering and mechanics, implements and machinery, drawing, conveyancing [titles, deeds, etc.], language and literature, principles of government, accounts, farm economy, hydraulics, drainage, agricultural chemistry, geology, geography, astronomy, meteorology, mineralogy, botany, vegetable physiology, animal physiology, health, veterinary practice, entomology, breeds of stock and poultry, feeding, training of animals, culture of the soil, manures, produce, agricultural history, horticulture, experiments, and "malpractice—what to avoid doing."[15]

A few months later, by late spring 1858, the situation had shifted dramatically, and not for the better. At their June 16 meeting at the school, Watts and the trustees had to pivot quickly to keep things moving forward. The pressing issue was a threatened halt to the completion of the College Building. Watts's business and building committee reported the "embarrassment" of Turner and Natcher, the Carlisle construction company, that "they may fail" from completing the project. The company's bills for materials and supplies were overdue, and liens upon buildings for materials and labor were looming large.[16] In fact, work on the building would stop altogether just three weeks later, on July 7, 1858.[17] In its contract for $55,000, the firm of Turner and Natcher had severely underestimated the cost of the building; it was becoming evident that the project likely would require $100,000 to complete.[18] The drain on the school's resources was causing problems large and small. Watts was worried about a potential lawsuit filed by Turner and Natcher for a remaining debt of $885.46 that they claimed was still owed them. Watts told McAllister that $700 should be reduced from that total because of an allowance for "bad brick" that the contractor had used.[19] The matter was settled without a lawsuit.

In September 1857, as Watts had reported, the building's west wing was about 60 percent complete; three stories had been built, but two more stories plus the roof remained to be added. It would be impossible to enroll students and begin operations until the west wing—representing one-third of the envisioned building—was finished. Although substantial progress on the remaining two stories had been made by the summer of 1858, the trustees now needed to complete the wing and have it ready for occupancy by winter 1859. With the help of architect C. B. Callahan, directing construction for the remainder of the project, they completed the task on time.[20]

Meanwhile, upon McAllister's initiative, the board authorized a new campaign for subscriptions, in hopes of reaching the full $25,000 that the state had promised to match. The state agricultural society was having trouble raising money and the earlier appeals to the citizens of the state fell short of expectations as well. McAllister himself donated $500 to help pay down bills and soon after advanced several thousand dollars out of his funds to cover pressing construction bills. He personally solicited his fellow Centre Countians, but only $5,700 was realized, the drag of the declining national economy being felt. The trustees also committed $5,000 of their personal funds to the cause, but it would not be enough to trigger the release of the state's match.[21]

Meeting again at the school on September 1, 1858, the board conducted its annual election of trustees. Three were to be elected to three-year terms while a fourth was to be elected to serve the remaining year for Alfred Elwyn, who had resigned. Thirty-eight delegates representing seventeen county agricultural societies joined seven electors from the Pennsylvania State Agricultural Society to reelect Hugh McAllister and elect George Browne of Montgomery County and Archibald McAllister of Blair County, all to three-year terms. Centre County president judge James T. Hale—who in November would be elected to Congress—was elected to fill the remaining one-year term of the seat vacated by Elwyn. In addition, the U.S. Post Office address for the institution was changed from Boalsburg, Penna., to Farm School P.O., Centre County, Penna.[22]

The annual meeting of September 1858 was notable in other respects, chiefly for its spirit of positivity in the face of serious financial problems. In the manner of his predecessors, governors William Bigler and James Pollock, the state's new Democratic governor, William F. Packer (1858–61), took an interest in the new school and attended the meeting. "My sympathies were altogether with this institution before I left home, and I had some knowledge of the plan before I came here," Packer offered, "but I must now say, like the queen of Sheba: 'The half had not been told me.'" He maintained that "it is for the interest of all, that the great agricultural basis of society should be amply educated to a full equality with any and every other clan. . . . I shall be glad of opportunities to forward the interests of the Farmers' High School of Pennsylvania."[23] Also in attendance was the nation's highest agricultural official: D. J. Brown, chief of the Agricultural Department of the U.S. Patent Office. Brown "evidenced his approval of the system of culture and registry pursued on the School Farm" and donated three sets of wheat, each set containing one hundred varieties of the plant.[24]

After the business meeting, it was time for dinner, at an eighty-five-foot-long table in the college barn. After dinner, at the request of Governor Packer, the group reconvened. It was now time for speeches and a particularly proud evening for Watts. The Farmers' High School, he boasted, "is an institution of which there is no counterpart in full operation on our continent." Without disparaging the nation's "present scholastic institutions," he lamented their inability to provide practical education, especially for farmers. "Our school is founded on a scale that will afford complete instruction, equal to that of our leading colleges, for should not the education of Farmers' sons be *superior*, rather than less than equal to that of any other class?"

"We wish to make the standard high enough to secure such results," Watts added. "It is a matter for future determination whether we shall admit all the studies prosecuted in our colleges. We may discard the dead languages, but shall certainly cultivate and practically exercise all the sciences and arts that can aid in accomplishing the full education of a country gentleman—an American citizen."

He acknowledged the difficulty ahead in finding "competent professors willing to undertake the new and untried system of training which will be necessary here" but vowed the board's untiring efforts to secure "the best men." As for an academic leader of the institution, "We want a practical man at the head, a man not endowed with learning alone, but with tact, familiar with the transactions and habits of every day business and business men, a man possessed of both engaging manners and of controlling administrative talent and energy."[25] He knew it not then, but in six months' time Watts would find arguably the best young scientist-administrator in the English-speaking world to lead the institution.

Trustee McAllister also spoke that night, urging the audience to contribute as much as they could to the subscription campaign, which, if it reached the $25,000 goal, would release an equal amount from the state legislature. But aside from the educational value of the Farmers' High School, McAllister stressed the benefits to be derived from its disinterested research and experimentation. "The Farmer who desires to know whether he may wisely grow a particular variety of grass, or root, or grain, or fruit, or breed of stock, or use a particular instrument, implement or a certain manure, comes here and finds on the registers of the experimental department, the annual and final results of full trials, on the soil of the school farm. . . . As an institution for supplying chemical analysis to the Farmers of the State, this will furnish what in other States is secured by the appointment of scientific salaried analysts."[26] Here, McAllister was presciently outlining the school's research and public service missions.

Preparing to Open for Instruction

As the year drew to a close, the trustees' sense of urgency was on full display as they convened in Harrisburg on December 8, 1858. Although financial problems and the interruption of construction had weighed heavily on them since the summer, they nevertheless resolved to recruit students and open the school in early 1859. The west wing of the College Building was now complete, so the trustees empowered the business and building committee to hire the faculty, buy furniture, and otherwise do everything necessary to get the school into operation. The start of classes was scheduled for Wednesday, February 16, 1859.

The trustees set sixteen years as the minimal age for students, all of them male. Their goal was to begin the inaugural academic year with one hundred Pennsylvania students, each to be recommended by their county agricultural societies; students applying from counties where no such society existed would be judged for admission by a special committee of trustees. The quota for admitted students from the various counties would vary, weighted by the number of taxable citizens in that county. With hopes of generating $10,000 that first year, the trustees set tuition at $100, which included room and board. Following the rhythm of the agricultural calendar, the school year was scheduled to begin in mid-February and end ten months later, in mid-December, with no vacations in between. William Waring, the school's general superintendent, was instructed to receive contributions of books, animals, implements, and the like from individuals and societies, and to maintain a record of "observations and experiments" on the farm.[27]

The trustees also refined the criteria for admission, requiring "a good knowledge of reading, writing, geography, arithmetic, and grammar"; those with a grounding in natural philosophy, geometry, and algebra would be given extra consideration. Furthermore, they needed to present evidence of "good moral character and industrious habits." Students would be required to perform three hours of labor daily, on the farm, in the shops, or at or about the college buildings. The deadline for applications was set for January 15, 1859, but later extended to February 1.

As a stratagem to raise more money, the trustees devised an incentive for individuals with the means to contribute $500 to the school. The donor, and his heirs, would retain the lifetime right to nominate a student of their choosing for admission, although that student would be subject to the standards required of all students. The number of those $500 contributors was capped at twenty.

Finally, they thought it wise to purchase the additional two hundred acres of land offered by Irvin—land that they had been renting on a five-year lease with the option to buy at any time within that period for $60 an acre, or $12,000 in all. In addition, the trustees authorized the mortgaging of two hundred acres of the original college property to secure a $20,000 loan to finance the school's operation.[28]

"A new light is about to break upon the agricultural community," Watts wrote in his second annual report to the president of the state agricultural society in early 1859. "This institution will afford a place where their sons may be educated to a fitness for a high position in any of the walks of life; as well to enable them to conduct the operations of the farm with the aid of scientific attainment."

On a more prosaic note, Watts explained the somewhat tangled situation with the admission of students. On February 1, 1859, the board's executive committee had met to determine who should be admitted. Many counties were prepared to present candidates "far beyond their ratio of representation," but other counties had done nothing. The committee deemed it wise to extend the time of application to the actual start of classes, "so as to afford those who were not represented an opportunity to make presentations." Watts said that eighty students already had been admitted but predicted the school would open with one hundred—"which is about the number that can be comfortably accommodated in the building as yet finished."[29]

Despite the trustees' stipulation that the students have "a good knowledge" of basic subjects and be of "good moral character and industrious habits," the quality of the students did not uniformly match the sought-after ideal. Withdrawals and expulsions were not uncommon. Early in his presidency, Pugh remarked that "experience soon proved that this flock was not without its black sheep."[30] Waring characterized the students as "many of them the worst sort expelled from other schools."[31]

As for the faculty, Watts noted the trustees had not yet appointed "a principal" for the school but projected that one would be hired in "the early part of the summer." The trustees had, however, completed the hiring of faculty. Operations "for the present" would be conducted under the direction of William Waring, professor of agriculture and horticulture; J. S. Whitman, professor of natural sciences; Samuel Baird, professor of mathematics; and R. C. Allison, professor of English literature.

And so on February 16, 1859, with sixty-nine students present, four faculty members but no president, and a building one-third complete in an

FIGURE 12 *Students in front of the College Building, 1859. The central figure is Frederick Watts's son (1843–1915), eponymously named, of the Class of 1862. Courtesy of The Pennsylvania State University Archives.*

improbable location but with well-defined purpose and lofty ambition, the Farmers' High School of Pennsylvania opened its doors and went to work.[32]

Finding a President

Although a president had yet to be appointed, the wheels were in motion, as Watts had suggested. The matter had been long deferred, as building and financing the institution had taken precedence. More than three years had passed since the trustees had approached Charles Trego, who, though eminently qualified, declined the offer. In the meantime, William Waring filled the lacuna of leadership, building out the plan for the school, overseeing the planting and construction of the farm and its appurtenances, and beginning experimental field crops—and keeping meticulous records about everything. As the school opened, Waring was assigned the additional responsibilities of acting principal until a new president could be hired.

For some time, the trustees, or at least a few of them, had their eye on a young man who in 1853 left his Chester County, Pennsylvania, home to pursue an advanced scientific education in Europe. The man was Evan Pugh, who in February 1859 had just turned thirty-one years of age.

In 1855, while the Trego affair was in play, the trustees were casting about not only for a president but also for faculty members, particularly a professor of chemistry. Trustee Alfred Elwyn had written to Samuel Johnson, the young Yale- and European-educated chemist, for a recommendation about any possible candidates for the professorship of chemistry. Johnson had studied for a time with Evan Pugh at Leipzig University, and the two chemists formed a fast friendship. After two years, while Pugh remained in Europe, Johnson returned to Yale and in 1858 also became the chemist for the Connecticut State Agricultural Society.

Elwyn, who lived in Chester County, was a colleague and friend of William Darlington of West Chester, the seat of Chester County. In fact, Elwyn and Darlington had both earned M.D. degrees at the University of Pennsylvania, though about twenty years apart. Darlington had taken young Evan Pugh under his wing and encouraged him to go to Europe for advanced training in the sciences (graduate study was, as yet, unavailable in American colleges). It is likely that Elwyn might have heard about Pugh from Darlington, who held the young scientist in high esteem. And, too, he very likely would have read Pugh's numerous dispatches about agriculture and science as practiced in Europe, as these epistles were published in the *Pennsylvania Farm Journal*, headquartered in West Chester, beginning in 1853, and other papers.

In any case, Elwyn was well qualified to look for promising faculty members. Before receiving his M.D. from Penn, he had earned his bachelor's degree from Harvard in 1823. A gentleman farmer, he never practiced as a physician, preferring rural life and his scientific interests. He was one of the oldest members of the American Association for the Advancement of Science and of the Academy of Natural Sciences, and a member of the Philadelphia Society for Promoting Agriculture and the Pennsylvania State Agricultural Society. His interest in agriculture was experimental as well as practical. In fact, he was the first agriculturalist in Chester County to apply guano (a natural manure composed mainly of the excrement of sea birds) on his lands.[33]

In any event, Johnson soon responded to Elwyn, strongly recommending Pugh for the professorship. Elwyn did not offer the position outright to Pugh but was certainly gauging his interest. Pugh took advantage of the opportunity and responded to Elwyn at great length. Pugh observed that farmers were poorly served in terms of education and that *scientific* agriculture, in comparison with Europe, was virtually nonexistent in America. "When agricultural science is properly developed its subjects will be such as can only be understood by *Study*," Pugh wrote.

Pugh informed Elwyn that the development and introduction of agricultural science to farmers would have to be done carefully, as their skepticism was already high because of the surfeit of "quack" solutions that hucksters, under the guise of science, had foisted on them. He felt that "an earnest effort in proper hands" could get things moving in the right direction, and Pugh wanted Pennsylvania to take the lead in this effort by "founding an agricultural college with the necessary appendages." He observed that the "character" of the first such college would be paramount, as new institutions emulating the model would begin to sprout up across the country. Pugh expressed his interest in the professorship but not immediately. He wanted more information about the plans for the Farmers' High School so that, during his last year of study, he could purchase books and apparatus accordingly.

Then Pugh proffered his recommendations for the new school. He wanted it to be financially self-sustaining. He wanted it to be free to do research and experimentation "without any regard to pecuniary loss or gain by the individual results." He wanted the faculty to be researchers of international reputation and that the school be in the process of continually collecting various "soils, Minerals, manures, plants, etc.," for investigation. Additionally, the school should establish a newspaper to publish the results of its research for the benefit of farmers.[34] Writing to Elwyn in 1855, at age twenty-seven, Pugh knew what agricultural colleges needed to be and to do to win the confidence of both scientists, the generators of knowledge, and farmers, the end users of that knowledge.

In the ensuing years, Pugh continued to express his interest in returning to Pennsylvania as professor of chemistry and even as president of its new agricultural college. Following up on his letter to Elwyn, Pugh wrote Johnson that he "would be willing to accept the position of Principal in the School," and that he would "take it *gladly* at the end of two years," when he expected to be finished with his education. Pugh asked if Johnson would "be good enough" to inform Elwyn "of my intentions."[35] Pugh believed that if he could gain either post, he could wield great influence over the direction of the school. "One must first gain the confidence of interested persons, and then *influence* over them follows."[36]

Three years later, Pugh wrote to his Chester County mentor, Dr. William Darlington, to recommend a colleague for a post at another institution. He also took the opportunity to let Darlington know of his continuing interest in the Farmers' High School. Pugh was concerned that he might have made the wrong impression in his earlier response to Elwyn.

> Dr. Elwyn wrote to me through Prof. Johnston . . . over a year ago to know if I would accept the professorship of chemistry in the college. I replied at some length, stating what I thought should be kept in mind as of fundamental importance in starting his college. In Dr. Elwyn's reply he did not disguise the fact that he thought I was too theoretical and that to 'run a straight furrow' was of more importance than he thought I supposed. I had dwelt upon the importance of our lack of *Agricultural principles* rather than Ag. practice which the student could learn at home and I am happy to say that I have no one who has had anything to do with agricultural teaching who does not agree with me upon the point at issue. And I have talked upon this subject with all the great teachers of Ag. Chemistry in Germany, France & England and I cannot think that Dr. Elwyn would be of different opinion could we talk the matter over.[37]

This exchange reveals a fundamental philosophical difference between Pugh and his future employers, the trustees of the Farmers' High School. Watts and Elwyn wanted the emphasis to be weighted toward the practical education of farmers. Certainly science courses would be part of that education (as would manual labor), but the goal was to produce graduates who would be well equipped and predisposed to going back to the farm and operating it at the highest level of efficiency and effectiveness. In ever-growing numbers, the thinking went, such graduates would elevate the practice of farming across the Commonwealth.

On the other hand, the *science* of agriculture was paramount for Pugh. Although chemistry was making great strides in Europe during the first half of the nineteenth century, its application to American agriculture was inchoate and in the initial stages of experimentation. While Pugh was realistic enough to know that graduates of Farmers' High School would not, in every case, go on to be practicing agricultural scientists, he nevertheless wanted them to be steeped in science above all else. Scientific theory and principles needed to be the centerpiece of agricultural higher education, Pugh maintained. The practical aspects of farming—such as "running a straight furrow"—could be learned at home, on the farm.

Pugh's reputation grew ever stronger during his six years abroad. He earned a Ph.D. in chemistry at the University of Göttingen, summa cum laude. After sojourns to Heidelberg and then Paris, he accepted a post at the famous Rothamsted Agricultural Experimental Station in England, led by the chemists John B. Lawes and Joseph Gilbert. Rothamsted had been established in 1838, some fourteen years before the first agricultural experiment facility appeared in the German states. There, over sixteen months, Pugh devised and conducted an elaborate experiment that settled a raging controversy over how plants assimilate nitrogen: through the soil, rather than from the air. The achievement earned him a fellowship in the London Chemical Society and established the foundation for the modern ammonium nitrate fertilizer industry. A twenty-first-century scientist observed that "if research of such significance were published today, the author would likely get a Nobel Prize."[38]

As 1858 drew to a close, Watts and the trustees were resolved to bringing Pugh back to Pennsylvania to lead the fledgling school. In early February 1859, Watts extended to Pugh the offer to serve not only as professor of chemistry but also as president of the institution. Responding to Watts on March 3, 1859, Pugh accepted the offer, though he negotiated for a delay in his arrival so as to complete his work at Rothamsted. Pugh was thrilled to accept "a position . . . to which I had hoped to devote the labors of my life." That was no exaggeration. Before leaving for Germany in 1853, Pugh said that his goal was to "fit" himself as a scientist in order to invent and lead a scientifically based agricultural college—of which, in America at least, none existed at the time. Pugh told Watts he wanted to make the institution "a central point to which the farmers of the whole country could look with confidence for advice" on all things agricultural. He further suggested that if the trustees agreed to invest $500 to $1,000 for the purchase of scientific equipment, he would be willing to acquire the best that Europe had to offer.[39]

Watts was delighted with Pugh's acceptance. He approved his request to be allowed to complete his research at Rothamsted and agreed to refer to the trustees Pugh's offer to buy apparatus. "Ours is among the first indeed . . . the very first that has gone into operation; for whilst there is an Ag. School in Michigan it differs from ours in what we deem essential features," Watts said. He congratulated Pugh for the opportunity now before him "of so moulding the Farmers' High School . . . as to make it do perfect work."[40] Eventually, Pugh did receive the requested funds and the president-elect traveled to laboratories in England and Germany to pick up the best equipment money could buy. "Can the money say $800 be sent to him for the purchase of apparatus of which he speaks?" Watts asked McAllister in early July. "It would be desirable if we have the means—I like the tone of his letter very much. If it be acceptable to write to him and send him a draft it must be done soon as there is little time to lose."[41] McAllister said the school did not have the means to spare the money. Watts then proposed to McAllister that they each contribute $400 out of their personal funds to send Pugh $800. As it finally turned out, Watts took out a loan for $800, returned McAllister's $400, and purchased a draft for the amount in London to be "forwarded to Prof. Pugh without delay."[42]

Notwithstanding their correspondence, Pugh was hired sight unseen, without interviews, formal search-and-selection committees, or the other trappings of the modern presidential search. Watts and Elwyn (who resigned as trustee in 1858) had never met Pugh. Watts's first meeting with him did not occur until late September 1859, in Philadelphia, where Watts "received favorable impressions of him," as he wrote to Waring, the acting principal.[43]

Evan Pugh finally arrived on the grounds of the Farmers' High School on a snowy, blustery October 26, 1859, more than eight months after classes had begun. He had taken the train to the depot at Spruce Creek, twenty-two miles west of campus, where he was met by McAllister and driven by buggy to his destination. As Watts had proclaimed in early 1859: "A new light is about to break upon the agricultural community." With Pugh's arrival, that light would break brilliant indeed.

CHAPTER 5

The Presidency of Evan Pugh

WATTS'S "NEW LIGHT" BREAKING upon the agricultural community alluded to the new school proper, but it just as well could have been the perfect metaphor for its new president, Evan Pugh. His six years of education and research in Europe now over, Pugh could get on with his true purpose in life: "to develop upon the soil of Penna. the best Ag. College in the world for the ag. student of America."[1] In just four and a half years, before his untimely death in 1864, Pugh would do exactly that. It would be anything but easy, however.

In mid-nineteenth-century America, it was difficult to establish and sustain a college of any sort, much less a new, scientifically based institution such as an agricultural college, a college for farmers, which to many Americans sounded oxymoronic. In 1860 America, some 209 colleges were operating. Although the number of institutions had essentially doubled from 107 since 1840, they remained relatively small in the number of students, the average institutional attendance being 79.[2]

In addition, nearly all of these institutions were private, affiliated with a religious denomination and often led by a minister in the presidency. Of the 180 or so colleges founded between 1820 and 1860, only ten were state controlled, as the new Pennsylvania institution repeatedly characterized itself.[3] "The Agricultural College of Pennsylvania is a State Institution," Pugh wrote in 1864. "The State has appropriated $100,000, and the people of the State have donated nearly an equal sum to bring it into existence. It belongs to the

State: its property is held by a Board of Trustees elected by delegates from the County Agricultural Societies of the State."[4]

Although the older historiography of American higher education characterized these private colleges—variously called literary, denominational, classical, or antebellum institutions—as being resistant to science in their curricula, newer scholarship has shown that to be not quite the case. The numbers of science and mathematics professors grew from about sixty in 1828 to more than three hundred in 1850.[5] By midcentury, most practicing scientists were, in fact, on college faculties. But their ability to advance their disciplines was another thing. They manned lonely outposts, isolated from one another, overburdened by the demands of teaching and student discipline, and heavily constrained to do any kind of research or otherwise keep up with advancements of the larger scientific world.[6] And American science lagged far behind that of Europe. As historian Roger Geiger has observed: "The United States in the first half of the nineteenth century was a provincial outpost in the world of science, and American scientists knew it too."[7]

In returning to America as one of the best-educated young scientists in the western world, Pugh faced a daunting challenge: He sought to invent, in concert with Watts and trustees, a new kind of educational institution designed, through science and its applications, to improve the state of American agriculture. Yet at that time in the United States, there existed very little agricultural science, per se; no curriculum for teaching the subject; and virtually no institutions of higher learning devoted to the task. All this and more would Pugh take on, developing the model agricultural college for America as the central challenge of his presidency.

A few attempts were made to establish agricultural colleges in midcentury America, but nothing took hold or endured. The Farmers' College, a private institution founded in 1846 near Cincinnati, presaged the land-grant college in trying to offer education to farmers and mechanics, in addition to the traditional classical curriculum. It peaked in the mid-1850s with an enrollment of 350 students but an inchoate agriculture curriculum. As one Farmers' College faculty member wrote to Pugh during the Civil War, asking for his guidance in teaching agricultural science: "From my amateur Stand point the only embarrassing feature is to know where to enter, upon the vast field of instruction which has remained all untouched thus far."[8] Beset by financial problems, the institution was in sharp decline by the Civil War and by 1884 was reorganized and renamed Belmont College. In his 1862 report on the nascent agricultural college movement, Pugh noted that the Farmers' College "course of instruction does not differ essentially from that of an ordinary literary college."[9]

Two purported agricultural colleges were chartered in New York State in 1853, but one floundered and folded shortly after it opened in 1860 and the other never operated. Agricultural colleges were chartered in Massachusetts (1856), Iowa (1858), and Minnesota (1858), but they could not begin operations until after the Civil War. The Maryland Agricultural College was chartered in 1856 and opened for instruction in October 1859. But it was founded by and oriented to the wealthy planter class and, as Pugh described it, was more aristocratic and literary than agricultural.

The most curious case was that of Michigan. The Michigan Agricultural College in East Lansing was chartered ten days before the Farmers' High School in February 1855. It opened for instruction in May 1857, becoming the first state-sponsored agricultural college in the United States to begin operations. But then strange things began to happen. The curriculum was oriented to the liberal arts as well as agriculture—and, oddly enough, nearly all of the students opted for the liberal arts. The college's president, a former newspaper editor, resigned in March 1859. The state superintendent of public instruction was then appointed as president, underspending the budget and reducing the curriculum from a four-year course to a two-year program designed to teach farm management. The faculty and students demanded a return to the four-year course, and the students especially wanted the liberal arts curriculum back in place. "There is probably not one young man that has come here for the sole purpose of studying the science of agriculture," wrote a contemporary faculty member. The Michigan legislature concurred and the dual four-year program was restored in 1861, the liberal arts curriculum again proving far more popular than the agricultural one. The college did manage to produce seven bachelor of science graduates in absentia in November 1861, however.[10]

And so it would be left to Pugh, Watts, and the trustees to develop the *model* agricultural college for America—the template for those that would follow. Pugh had impressed Watts from the beginning, but he also succeeded in forging a strong relationship with trustee Hugh McAllister of Bellefonte, who had greeted Pugh at the Spruce Creek train station and driven him to campus in October 1859. An 1833 graduate of Jefferson College in southwestern Pennsylvania, McAllister was an attorney who in 1859 went into law partnership with James A. Beaver. In 1874, Beaver—by then McAllister's son-in-law—would succeed Watts as president of the college's board of trustees and later become governor of Pennsylvania. Like Watts, McAllister had been a strong champion of moving Pennsylvania agriculture ahead scientifically and in establishing an agricultural college for that purpose. McAllister was a founding member and a vice president of the Pennsylvania State Agricultural Society and a founding trustee of the Farmers' High School, a role in which he would serve until his death in 1873. He was one of the three trustees, along with Watts, charged with planning the school's physical plant. It was McAllister who would design the main College Building, as it was called, based largely on Princeton's Nassau Hall. Conveniently living eleven miles northeast of the school, McAllister was asked by Watts to oversee the construction of everything. As the "local trustee," McAllister was in frequent contact with Watts and Pugh on matters large and small. And McAllister helped with fundraising for the school, providing his own money when the situation so demanded. As the original Penn State historian wrote: "There was scarcely a day which did not have some task for the college which demanded his thought and counsel."[11]

From the start of his presidency in October 1859, Pugh proved himself to be a force of nature, quickly vindicating Watts's faith in his abilities to build

FIGURE 13
Hugh McAllister (1809–1873), Bellefonte, Pa., attorney and member of the Board of Trustees, 1855–73. Watts's closest friend and colleague. Courtesy of The Pennsylvania State University Archives.

an experimental college predicated on science. As the 1860 school year got under way in mid-February, Pugh's first order of business was to set standards and expectations for student discipline. His inaugural address to the student body was published as a twenty-six-page pamphlet, titled "On the Mutual Relations of the Teacher and the Taught." He first focused on the problems caused by student "insubordination," but then appealed to their better natures: "We are here with the eyes of the friends of agricultural education, in every civilized country in the world . . . to demonstrate the practicability of combining agriculture practice with the study of agricultural principles in an educational institution. . . . We owe it to the friends of the Institution, and to the people of our great Keystone State . . . not to let this great experiment fail."[12]

Pugh then sought to expand the institution's mission and reorganize the curriculum. The overarching goal would be "to associate a high degree of intelligence with the practice of Agriculture and the industrial arts, and to seek to make use of this intelligence in developing the agricultural and industrial resources of the country and protecting its interests." With the trustees' concurrence, Pugh would develop four "objects" (or "mission" in modern parlance) for the college: (1) teaching all the natural sciences, since "more scientific knowledge is required [for agriculture] than for all other industrial arts combined"; (2) ensuring that a large part of students' education be devoted to practical application, "in the field and laboratory," with manual labor deemed essential "for the preservation of health, and the maintenance of habits of industry"; (3) conducting research and experimentation so as to contribute to the development of the agricultural sciences and yield practical benefits for farmers; and (4) protecting the industrial interests of the state, "particularly the agricultural interest." In all respects, Pugh's "objects" presaged the teaching, research, and service mission of the modern land-grant university.[13]

The revised four-year curriculum, a lockstep progression leading to the bachelor of *scientific* agriculture degree (B.S.A.), the first such degree offered in America, was ordered as follows:

First Year: Arithmetic, Elementary Algebra, Botany, Elementary Anatomy and Physiology, Geography and Elementary Astronomy, English Grammar and Composition, Elocution, History, Practical Agriculture, and the details of management on the College Farm

Second Year: Advanced Algebra and Geometry, General Chemistry, Vegetable Anatomy and Physiology, Zoology and Veterinary, Geology, Paleontology, Physical Geography, Practical Agriculture and Horticulture, Logic and Rhetoric

Third Year: Surveying, Leveling, Drafting, the use of instruments, Analytical Geometry, Elementary Calculus, Natural Philosophy, Qualitative Chemical Analysis, Veterinary Surgery, Entomology, Agricultural Botany, Practical Agriculture and Pomology, Political and Social Economy

Fourth Year: Analytical Geometry, Differential and Integral Calculus, Engineering, Drafting, Mechanical Drawing, Quantitative Chemical Analysis, Veterinary Pharmacy, Gardening, Agricultural Accounts and Farm Management, Moral and Intellectual Philosophy[14]

Finances would be a preoccupation of Pugh, Watts, and the trustees. In the 1859 and 1860 school years, total income was $12,912.39 and $12,938.85, respectively. With no money coming from the state and very little being provided by the state agricultural society, the institution was heavily dependent on tuition at $100 per year. In fact, tuition accounted for 86 percent of total revenue in those first two years.[15] In the first year (1859), 119 students had matriculated, though there were never more than 100 in residence at any time; in the second year (1860), enrollment dipped slightly to 110. Observing the decline, Pugh, Watts, and the trustees were concerned that enrollment needed to grow substantially if the school were to succeed. "It requires nearly as much expenditure in Professors' Salaries, and in Farm and Garden Superintendence, with 110 students as it would with three times this number," Pugh said.[16] In fact, the College Building was designed to hold 165 dormitory rooms, accommodating 330 students upon completion, but completion was still several years away. Ultimately, Pugh wanted to enroll between 400 and 800 students—big numbers for the era.

In October 1860, Watts encouraged Pugh to take the institution's message on the road. He invited Pugh to address the fall meeting of the Cumberland County Agricultural Society, important constituents of Watts's home county. Pugh's address—"What Science Has Done and May Do for Agriculture"—was published as a thirty-nine-page booklet and sent to influential persons and organizations across Pennsylvania and the nation.

Pugh's address did not center on local interests in Cumberland County. Rather, it was a manifesto for a system of agricultural science and education

FIGURE 14
Evan Pugh (1828–1864), president of the Farmers' High School and Agricultural College of Pennsylvania, 1859–64. Courtesy of The Pennsylvania State University Archives.

in the United States that should, he asserted, surpass similar systems in Europe and the British Isles. The United States was lagging substantially, he said, and so he laid out a grand plan for how the nation could move ahead of Europe in agricultural productivity. He wanted nothing less than a national system of agricultural science and education, the apex of which would be American agricultural colleges, with the Farmers' High School as the national model. He wanted a national system of agricultural research and investigation, and a concomitant system for collecting agricultural statistics on a national scale. He also called for a "National Agricultural Bureau" that would serve as a kind of union between "all the isolated agricultural interests of the country." Although castigating the nation for its lack of progress, Pugh waxed optimistic about the potential for leadership offered by the Farmers' High School. "If this Institution is sustained as it should be; if its buildings are completed upon the original plan, and it receives a reasonable support I have not the slightest doubt that it could be made the best Agricultural Institution in the world."[17]

By the fall of 1860, a year into his presidency, Pugh had won the confidence of the school's trustees. Writing to McAllister, Watts praised the new president. "Dr. Pugh writes frankly and generously and I must say the more

I know of him the better I like him." Watts noted that the task of hiring faculty should fall upon Pugh rather than the trustees, as was the original practice: "I have said to him . . . that the organization of faculty must be a work of time and that the duty of doing it well must devolve upon him ultimately—he has more interest and will have more zeal in doing the work well than even you or I. He is young . . . energetic and writes as if he had devoted himself to the object of building the institution up into fame."[18]

Increasingly, the completion of the College Building became a preoccupation. Little progress had been made since the late autumn of 1858, when the west wing was finally completed in the wake of the original contractor's bankruptcy. Meeting on December 5, 1860, the trustees heard Pugh stress the urgency of finishing the structure. Watts and his colleagues resolved to make that happen by applying for a $50,000 appropriation from the state legislature at its new session in January 1861.[19]

The new year, 1861, would prove fateful to the nation, as it split apart, eleven Southern states seceding, forming the Confederacy, and firing the opening salvos of the Civil War. Despite the hostilities, the efforts of Pugh, Watts, McAllister, the trustees, and their allies in the Pennsylvania legislature and the statewide agricultural community paid off. On April 18, a week after Fort Sumter had been fired upon, Pennsylvania Governor Andrew Curtin signed the legislature's appropriation of $49,900 for the building's completion—the second appropriation in the school's brief history. The groundswell of support was due in no small part to the perceptions of progress at the school since Pugh had come on board. Several county agricultural societies made their support known through letters and resolutions, and "friends of agriculture" across the state made visits to legislators and wrote letters as well. The agricultural press was vociferous in its support. And Pugh helped his case by taking a photograph of the incomplete building to the hearing before the House Ways and Means Committee. Nevertheless, there was opposition to the bill, which greatly frustrated Pugh. After the House's passage but before the Senate considered the bill, Pugh told his confidant Samuel Johnson that he was "a little blue about it." Pugh was even more distressed because his vacation time was "wasted with those legislative blockheads." But the Senate followed the House and passed the bill 18–12.[20]

The appropriation saved the school from failure, plain and simple. Pugh said the Keystone State "was saved the disgrace of allowing an Agricultural College it had attempted to found, to break up in the act of being founded. . . .

Our old Commonwealth has succeeded in bringing the first Agricultural School in the United States into successful operation."[21]

Watts was elated. He had never felt "more overjoyed than I do now at your success in Harrisburg," he told Pugh. The money not only would allow the institution to pursue its plans but also enable it to "build upon the confidence" that the legislature had expressed in the institution's management.[22]

The trustees moved quickly to get construction under way. Meeting in early May 1861, they appointed a special committee of Watts, Pugh, and McAllister to make any needed modifications to the original plan and hire a contractor to complete the building. They asked that it be finished in eighteen months, by November 1862. Watts and the trustees hired George Tate of nearby Bellefonte for $41,500 to complete the building. At their next meeting, nearly six months later, the trustees realized that the construction contract did not provide for the entire completion of the project, as it made no provisions for heating and furnishing the structure. Thus they authorized extending the contract with Tate to include these essential features at a cost not to exceed $20,000, for which another mortgage would need to be secured.[23]

Enrollments in 1861 dipped from 110 to 88, the war having siphoned off current and potential students. But in addition to the resumption of construction, progress was made in other key areas. Foremost among them, the school produced its first graduates. Of the fifty-five who entered with advanced standing as sophomores in 1859, eleven of them received their degrees in December 1861—the first bachelor of scientific agriculture degrees granted in America. The graduates were rank ordered on a scale of one to ten. In addition to finishing their coursework and passing examinations, they were required to complete a dissertation, teaming up in twos to accomplish the task. Topics ranged from an analysis of the iron ores of the Nittany Valley to an investigation of Indian corn as well as an analysis of artificial fertilizers and more besides. "This was also the first class that graduated at an Agricultural College in the United States," Pugh said, "and they graduated upon a higher scientific educational standard than is required at any other Agricultural College in the world."[24]

In addition to the rigorous "full course," which the first graduates pursued, Pugh expanded the curriculum in several directions. First came the Partial Scientific and Practical Course, designed for talented but mathematically challenged students whose interests were instead largely in the natural sciences. For students interested in gaining only a basic introduction to the agricultural arts and sciences in a briefer residency without the demands of more formal study, Pugh introduced the Practical Course. Pugh also established graduate work, offering the master of scientific and practical agriculture (M.S.A.) degree. The first M.S.A. graduate was C. Alfred Smith in January 1863; Smith had procured his B.S.A. degree in 1861 and stayed on at the school to assist Pugh in the chemistry laboratories. In addition, Pugh cast a wider net for students of more diverse backgrounds and interests. He reached out "to persons in cities who may wish their sons to become acquainted with the details of practical agriculture and science." He especially emphasized the school's proficiency in chemistry, which could lead to careers in pharmacy, manufacturing, mining, and engineering.[25]

The school's momentum carried into 1862, the year that can be considered the turning point in the institution's early history. Despite the fury of the Civil War little more than one hundred miles to the south, enrollments built back up from 88 to 110 and the school attracted "many . . . from other states, who could not be admitted," as the College Building still lacked the capacity to accommodate them.[26]

With the gains of the first three years, Pugh determined it was time to change the name of the school to better reflect its collegiate status and position it as the obvious beneficiary of the "agricultural college bill" recently introduced in Congress by Representative Justin S. Morrill of Vermont. The name change had been very much on Pugh's mind. Since the beginning of his presidency, he typically referred to it as the Agricultural College, not the Farmers' High School. At its charterings in 1854 and 1855, the institution was designed to be of collegiate grade conferring baccalaureate degrees. The founders' sense, however, was that the word "college" resounded negatively among the farming community, conjuring images of haughty "gentlemen" with idle habits and disdain for manual labor.

The name change did not occur without some discussion. Pugh wanted to take the matter to the Pennsylvania legislature for approval. He also wanted to include the word "State" somewhere in the new name, so as to ensure continuing financial support from the Commonwealth. Most likely, Pugh wanted to name it the Pennsylvania State Agricultural College or the State Agricultural College of Pennsylvania. Watts had other ideas, however. Though approving "entirely of your proposition to change our corporate name," Watts pointed out that it wasn't necessary to ask the legislature for approval. An act passed in 1843 empowered the Courts of Quarter Sessions in the Commonwealth, upon the petition of the parties in intent, to change the "name, style, and title of any corporation" within their respective counties. "From both education and experience I prefer a resort to a Court rather than the Legislature," Watts told Pugh. "As to the name: There is a 'Penna. Col.' at Gettysburg and I do not like the use of the word State—perhaps it is because I like brevity and I think with that omission in your proposition it will do and call it 'Penna. Agl. College.'"[27] McAllister presented the petition for change to the Court of Quarter Sessions for Centre County; after its approval there, the trustees ratified the name change at their meeting of May 6, 1862. Pugh had even designed a new seal for the college, which was also approved at the same meeting. Thus the Farmers' High School of Pennsylvania became the Agricultural College of Pennsylvania, a name it would retain until it became the Pennsylvania State College in 1874, which would be Watts's last year as president of its board of trustees.[28]

At that same May meeting, the trustees appointed a committee of three—Watts, Pugh, and McAllister—to prepare a report, a magnum opus, to be used for public relations purposes: to attract students, political support, and patronage. This became a sixty-three-page document, written entirely by Pugh and endorsed by Watts and McAllister, titled "The Agricultural College of Pennsylvania . . . September 1862." The work presented a detailed and lengthy history of agricultural science in Europe and America with an equally detailed history of the origins of the agricultural college in question. Also presented were "the aims, object and present conditions and prospects of the institution." The subtext was that the Agricultural College of Pennsylvania was the American culmination, at least as an educational institution, of the great scientific agriculture movement that had its roots in Europe two centuries previous. It presented the aforementioned "objects" or mission as an educational institution, a practical institution, and experimental/research institution, and a "servant of the state." It described the college's extensive scientific collections, equipment, laboratories, and other facilities, not to mention its grounds: a four-hundred-acre farm replete with vineyard, orchards, and small nursery, as well as experimental plots and various outbuildings, including the large barn of Watts's design. Circulated in mass quantities across the northern states, particularly to the agricultural press, and to Europe as well, the document characterized the Agricultural College of Pennsylvania as a hard-won success—the first successful agricultural college in the United States. Despite the war's continual drain of men and money, enrollment continued to grow. Equipment and amenities had been added and improved. The institution had adopted a new name to better reflect its purpose and stature. Most important, the college had graduated fifteen more students—the largest graduating class until 1890. After three and a half years of operation, the college seemingly had turned the corner.[29]

The Morrill Land-Grant College Act of 1862

Notwithstanding the college's progress, the most significant achievement for Pugh, Watts, and the trustees was their efforts to help gain passage of the Morrill Land-Grant College Act of 1862. This was deemed the proverbial manna from heaven that would provide perpetual funding for the college and allow it to build out to the grander dimensions they envisioned.

The Morrill Act—officially "An Act Donating Public Lands to the Several States and Territories Which May Provide Colleges for the Benefit of Agriculture and the Mechanic Arts"—marked the federal government's first policy involvement with higher education. The act appropriated federal acreage to qualified states—17.4 million acres in all—based on their population as represented by the size of their congressional delegation. The land was to be sold and the proceeds used to establish an inviolable endowment to support "at least one college where the leading object shall be, without excluding other scientific and classical studies, and including military tactics, to teach such branches of learning as are related to agriculture and the mechanic arts, in such manner as the legislatures of the States may respectively prescribe, in order to promote the liberal and practical education of the industrial classes in the several pursuits and professions of life."[30]

In nineteenth-century America, land was the coin of the realm, and the farsighted Thirty-Seventh Congress used it creatively to build up the country in the midst of the Civil War, looking to the conflict's successful conclusion and the resumption of Manifest Destiny. In addition to the Morrill Act and the establishment of the U.S. Department of Agriculture, the year 1862 produced other far-reaching legislation. The Homestead Act eventually distributed 234 million acres of federal land by allowing any qualified head of household to file a claim for up to 160 acres in exchange for five years of residence and the improvement of the property. The Pacific Railway Act began the practice of granting federal lands directly to corporations. The act chartered companies to build the transcontinental line from Omaha, Nebraska, to Sacramento, California, and the National Bank Act authorized the issuance of paper money to pay for the massive project.[31] By 1871, the federal government had granted 175 million acres to the railroads.

As the historian Ariel Ron has shown, the federal government's ownership of the vast public land domain constituted an unprecedented fiscal resource, a "reserve of wealth" that the government "spent" to support a wide range of policy goals, including immigration and settlement, transportation infrastructure, social welfare, debt financing, war and conquest, and public education, among other uses. Rather than resorting to increased taxation of the citizenry or borrowing from foreign governments, the government used the treasure trove of public lands—once the domain of Native American Indians—for the broad purposes of national development.[32]

The Morrill Act promised a bonanza for the more populous eastern states. New York, the largest state, received title to 980,000 acres. Pennsylvania, the second most populous, was awarded 780,000. Ultimately, the Agricultural College would realize $439,000, about 56 cents per acre, though the funds would not begin to materialize fully until 1867.[33]

The legislation had a significant impact on American higher education and the nation's socioeconomic development. Perhaps the best summation was provided by historian Roger Geiger, who observed that the act "conveyed far-reaching aims to institutionalize practical fields of study, meld them with liberal education, open them to a new class of students, and charge the states with finding the means to accomplish all of it. The act immediately affected the expansion and structure of higher education and, eventually, the productivity of the American economy."[34]

Pugh, Watts, the trustees, and the influential Pennsylvania agricultural community pushed hard for the act. Pugh, in particular, is credited with wielding considerable influence on the outcome. Penn State historian Margaret T. Riley says that Pugh went "to Washington in the line of duty, however, as did Penn State's trustees and leaders from other states, notably Illinois, Massachusetts, New York, Michigan, and Connecticut . . . to exert influence on the formulation and passage of the Morrill Act."[35] Robert Bruce, in his *Launching of Modern American Science, 1846–1876*, credits Pugh as being the only *scientist* actively engaged in the effort.[36] Earle D. Ross, the foundational land-grant college historian, said that Pugh was one of four college presidents who worked vigorously for the passage of the bill. Ross asserted that "Pugh led the Pennsylvania group with characteristic zeal and with effective if not determining influence on the final result."[37] Penn State historian Asa E. Martin, writing in 1942, was less specific. He said that "certainly the agricultural interests of Pennsylvania were extremely active in support of both the Morrill Act of 1857 [vetoed in 1859 by President Buchanan] . . . and that of 1862 . . .

and the Farmers' High School of Pennsylvania was expected to be the recipient of the financial benefits conferred by the act."[38] Nevertheless, there is no direct evidence of Pugh's personal advocacy efforts, or of any meeting or conversation with Morrill or other congressmen. Pugh was in Washington in late January and early February 1862, but his purpose was to confer with the director of the U.S. Bureau of Agriculture on how the anticipated U.S. Department of Agriculture might be structured, financed, and focused in terms of its research agenda. Pugh made no mention of any meeting during this time to discuss the Morrill bill.[39]

But given what was at stake, and given Pugh's intense drive to build the school, he was in no small way orchestrating the effort. He deflected credit especially to Centre County congressman and Agricultural College trustee James T. Hale as well as others in the state's agricultural community. In his 1864 plan for the organization of land-grant colleges, Pugh stated: "The friends of the Agricultural College of Pennsylvania secured the passage of the Land Grant bill by Congress. A member of their Board of Trustees (then as now a prominent member of Congress) devoted almost an entire session in Congress to its passage and other friends of the college visited Washington several times for the same purpose. Without their aid, the bill would not have passed."[40] The act passed Congress without appreciable opposition and was signed into law by President Abraham Lincoln on July 2, 1862.

The Morrill Act's Acceptance by the Commonwealth of Pennsylvania

It was one thing to work for Congress's passage of the Morrill Act; it was quite another to push the Pennsylvania legislature and governor to accept the terms of the act, as was required, and designate a specific institution to receive its benefits. The Morrill Act placed a number of requirements on the accepting states. A state was entitled to first claim its allotment of public land within its own borders. For the great majority of states, particularly in the Northeast, where no public land was available, they were to be issued land "scrip," a paper entitlement to the allocated amount of federal land. With land scrip, the states were forbidden from actually locating the land they wanted to sell within the borders of any other state; instead, they were free to sell the scrip to land speculators and private agents, who in turn could locate it in whatever state or territory they chose. To prevent a land grab in any one state, however, the act set a limit of one million acres per state that could be claimed by land agents and speculators.

Importantly, those states accepting the act had to do so before the deadline of July 2, 1864. Furthermore, the act required each state accepting its provisions to establish or designate within five years at least one college dedicated to the purposes of the act; thus, if a state accepted the provisions of the act on, say, July 1, 1864, it would have until July 1, 1869, to establish a land-grant college. The penalty for missing the five-year deadline would be a cancellation of the act and a reimbursement by the state to the federal government of all monies from its land sales. The act also required an annual report by the college to be sent to all other land-grant colleges and the U.S. secretary of the interior. Finally, the act required that monies realized by the land sales be invested in U.S. stocks not yielding less than 5 percent per annum in earnings used to establish an inviolable endowment for the support of the college. Nonetheless, the act mandated that the endowment's earnings could not be used for the "purchase, erection, preservation, or repair of any building or buildings." Thus the responsibility for the college's physical plant would rest with the state and the college proper, not the federal government.[41]

Watts and the trustees lost no time preparing for the state's acceptance. At their September 2, 1862, meeting—just two months after Lincoln had signed the law—the trustees formed a committee "whose duty it shall be to procure the action of the legislature on the subject." The committee consisted of Watts, Augustus O. Hiester, and McAllister. And so the race was on.[42]

The first snag they encountered was presented by the Pennsylvania governor, Andrew G. Curtin, a Centre County native and ex officio member of the college's board of trustees. Curtin wanted to divert the Morrill land-grant fund away from the college and toward homes for disabled Civil War veterans. Pugh asked trustee McAllister to intercede with the governor.[43] Meanwhile, believing that half a loaf was better than none, Watts drafted a bill providing that half the proceeds from land sales be dedicated to the college. Watts handed the draft to his local state representative, who referred the bill to the appropriate House committee. Then Watts realized his folly, a serious gaffe for a seasoned lawyer to make: The federal law would have prohibited the use of the land-grant fund toward soldiers' homes and other nonacademic uses. Watts rewrote the bill so as to give the college all of the money. As Pugh described it: "He [Watts] put the whole bill into better shape, talked to a number of members, found all friendly—put the Governor all right and thinks there will be no difficulty." Pugh copied Watts's rewrite and gave it to the chair of the Committee on Judiciary General. The bill was reported back to the full House on February 4, 1863.[44]

The House made a few minor amendments to the bill, but one change, passed unanimously, would prove ominous: that the annual income would go to the Agricultural College "until otherwise ordered by the Legislature of Pennsylvania." Thus the legislature essentially declared the Agricultural College as the placeholder as they looked at other uses of Morrill Act funds, as the governor had proposed earlier. One legislator wanted the funds to benefit additional colleges, and another wanted to benefit the common (elementary) schools. Nevertheless, a sense of urgency prevailed, fanned in no small part by the on-the-scene intervention of Congressman Hale with the Pennsylvania legislature. On February 26, 1863, the House overwhelmingly approved H.B. 119 by a vote of 82–9. In the upper chamber, the bill was championed by Senator Henry Johnson of Lycoming and Centre Counties. He outlined the Morrill Act's requirements—misunderstood by many—and boiled the issue down to one of two choices: either accept the act and apply it to the Agricultural College or accept it and build another such institution from scratch. "Those are the conditions under which we may accept this munificent grant . . . and we cannot accept it under any other conditions," Johnson declared. He went on to describe the Agricultural College not as a local school but a "State Institution, having been erected in part out of funds paid out of the Treasury of the Commonwealth, and in part by the contributions of citizens of this State—an institution which is in every particular just as such a one as is contemplated and described in this act of Congress."[45]

With Johnson's advocacy, the bill passed the Senate by a vote of 21–7 on March 23. But the bill's passage in both chambers was due largely to Congressman Hale's intervention and Pugh's behind-the-scenes work in Harrisburg. Hale visited the Pennsylvania legislature and "explained to members the necessity for a prompt acceptance on the part of the state." The outcome was an act directing that the fund "be temporarily devoted to the use of the Farmers' High School, we reserving to ourselves to say that it should remain there until otherwise ordered by the Legislature."[46]

From Harrisburg, Pugh reported the victory to McAllister: "Our bill passed (thanks to the industry and influence of Judge Hale) this evening. It is all right and ready for the Governor's signature, which Judge Hale will secure as soon as he comes home. . . . I trust it may never be so necessary to so wholly neglect my duties at the College for so long a time again, but I think the friends of the College will under the circumstances pardon the neglect."[47]

The act was signed into law—pledging "the faith of the State to carry the same [the Morrill Act] into effect"—by Governor Curtin on April 1, 1863.[48]

For Watts, Pugh, McAllister, Hale, and the rest of the trustees, it had been a banner twelve months, as their work had produced dramatic results: the passage of historic federal legislation, the Morrill Land-Grant Act of 1862, and the state's early acceptance of its terms that would, they hoped, provide the firm foundation to carry out the college's aspirations.

The Disruptions of 1863

The spring of 1863 marked an even higher tide than 1862 for the young institution. In addition to its successes in Washington and Harrisburg, the college increased its enrollment from 110 to 142; conferred its first master's degree in scientific agriculture; added new faculty, increasing from five when Pugh started to eight; and established a new preparatory department. The latter, which would enroll adolescents under sixteen years of age, was, in Pugh's view, vital for continued enrollment growth. Although many "literary" colleges had preparatory departments to feed their collegiate ranks, it was especially necessary for the Agricultural College to provide a *scientific* preparation that would ensure success in a scientific institution.

But the school's good fortune would soon turn and transmogrify into a year of disruptions, threatening the college's success. In June, in a bizarre twist of fate, Pugh and his fiancée, Rebecca Valentine, were injured in a buggy accident when it rolled into a Bellefonte creek. Pugh, whose left arm was badly broken by the fall, nonetheless extricated the unconscious Rebecca, pinned under the buggy. Though Pugh would manage to carry out his presidential duties for another month, in mid-July he left the college for advanced medical attention in Philadelphia. He would be gone from the college for more than ten weeks, returning in early October.

June brought an even bigger crisis to the school. The Army of Northern Virginia invaded Pennsylvania, battling the Army of the Potomac for three fateful early July days in Gettysburg. Lincoln had put out a call for one hundred thousand volunteers, and the college nearly emptied out of students bent on enlisting. But it did not close entirely. By early August, most of the students had returned to campus. Pugh did not, and his absence caused high anxiety among the more senior students, as their required chemistry courses were now in jeopardy. Pugh found a colleague to replace him temporarily, but he would not return to the classroom upon his return to campus because of the press of long-delayed administrative work. In the meantime, a certain "Dr. Thompson" plotted to have the trustees remove Pugh from the presidency, but the attempt soon fizzled. The trustees had vested high confidence in their young president, and they would not waver. By early November, things were nearly back to normal.

But another issue was weighing on Pugh, Watts, McAllister, and the trustees: completion of the College Building. Pugh was convinced that the contractor was not pushing hard enough to get the project finished; he wanted it completed so as to "leave a good feeling" among the students before they left in mid-December for their two-month winter break. December was also worrisome because Pugh's temporary chemistry professor was drafted by the U.S. Sanitary Commission and the college's vice president, David Wilson, resigned.[49]

The year was equally disruptive for Watts and the trustees. Having been consumed by their work to effect the state's acceptance of the Morrill Act, and then deterred by the Gettysburg campaign, they could not hold their first formal meeting of 1863 until September 2. Even then they could not muster a quorum; they nevertheless conducted their required annual election, unanimously putting Watts, James Miles, and Daniel Kaine into new three-year terms. The trustees tried to meet in December, but again could not muster a quorum, and so Watts put out another call for a meeting in Harrisburg on January 6, 1864.[50]

The largest threat, and the one that would dominate the winter and spring of 1864, was political. During Pugh's absence from campus, Watts and the trustees got wind of a growing interest among certain private colleges and state legislators to rescind or rework the state's acceptance act of April 1, 1863. Their intent was to remove the Agricultural College as the sole beneficiary and use the Morrill Act funds in other ways—mainly to benefit other Pennsylvania colleges.

To countermand the impending "land grant grab," Pugh produced a sweeping manifesto, his masterwork as a champion of industrial education, titled: *A Report Upon a Plan for the Organization of Colleges of Agriculture and the Mechanic Arts, with Special Reference to the Organization of the Agricultural College of Pennsylvania, in View of the Endowment of this Institution by the Land Scrip Fund, Donated by Congress to the State of Pennsylvania.* The thirty-five-page plan was "addressed to the Board of Trustees of the Agricultural College, Convened at Harrisburg, January 6, 1864." There was, of course, a much larger audience in mind, and the trustees immediately authorized the printing of three thousand copies, to be widely distributed.[51] The genius of the document was to position the institution as an *industrial* college (including both agriculture and engineering) rather than a purely agricultural institution, in compliance with the broader intent of the Morrill Act.

In building a detailed framework for industrial higher education, Pugh's organizational plan became the first and most farsighted document of his day. The land-grant historian Earle D. Ross called Pugh's plan an "elaborate report" constituting "the most complete and understanding contemporary statement of the financial and educational requirements of land-grant education. . . . The most thorough and understanding early analysis, both informing and interpretive."[52]

Essentially, Pugh called for industrial colleges to be organized on a large scale, larger even than Harvard, Yale, and Columbia, the leading American colleges. But Pugh's competitive set went far beyond American higher education. Even the best American colleges were inferior to those of Europe, he stated categorically. Using an almanac, Pugh benchmarked the top eighteen U.S. institutions on the basis of faculty, endowments, and annual expenses, and characterized all of them as deficient, not just in the resources they commanded but more so in the quality of education they offered. Pugh discerned "an absence of that *thoroughness* which characterizes the highest order of study. With very few exceptions, we will find Professors obliged to teach *too many* different things to teach *anything* very thoroughly, or to keep themselves posted on the progress of knowledge, in their own department, in the learned world." Pugh then picked a fight with Harvard. Although the richest and greatest American college, Harvard offered an "educational standard [that] is much below that of the best Universities of Europe."[53]

Industrial colleges, Pugh said, should be staffed by a faculty of at least twenty-nine professors and led by a scientist and should enroll between four hundred and eight hundred students—huge numbers by the standards of the day. They must emphasize research as much as instruction and be supplied with the facilities and equipment to facilitate the search for new knowledge. Pugh recommended the proper curricula for such schools, the need for large endowments and a large budget—minimally $47,000 per year in his estimation. He doubted that the proceeds from Morrill Act land sales would be sufficient to sustain industrial colleges and urged philanthropists to smile upon them. He then excoriated Pennsylvania's private "literary" colleges for grasping at the land-grant fund for which "they had not the *slightest legitimate claim*."[54]

Shortly after the document went to the printer, a bill was moved to give one-third of the land-grant endowment to Allegheny College in Meadville.

Pugh issued a protest, citing seven points: (1) the land-grant fund would hardly yield enough to support one college; (2) two or more colleges would not be able to provide industrial education efficiently and effectively; (3) the Agricultural College was a *state* institution, the state already having appropriated $100,000 for its support; (4) the Agricultural College could not use its property effectively without the land-grant endowment; (5) the friends of the Agricultural College secured the land-grant bill; (6) the Agricultural College had no other endowments and, if removed, would be more dependent on the state; and (7) Allegheny College was a " local denominational literary school," not a state institution, and it had no idea of how to provide an industrial education.[55]

The Battle Royal in the Pennsylvania Legislature

Pugh would have another opportunity to present the college's case to the legislature. On March 3, he testified before the House Judiciary Committee in Harrisburg. He emphasized the points presented in his organizational plan of January 6 but made new arguments as well. He sought to preempt other ideas rattling about the legislature for using the land-grant fund, including one proposal for establishing three separate colleges: one for agriculture, one for engineering, and one for military science. Pugh made a strong argument for the natural complementarity of agriculture and engineering and said they would be stronger yet when offered by a single institution. He cited the size and scale of German universities—Leipzig and Göttingen, each with 110 faculty members, and Berlin with 168—and made the case for a critical mass of faculty, students, and resources in proportions that far exceeded the average size of the two dozen private colleges in Pennsylvania. He said the "medium" ideal annual operating budget for an industrial college should be $87,800 per year—including $56,000 in faculty salaries and $31,800 for scientific research, museums, student aid, and building maintenance. Finally, he emphasized the demonstrably public character of the Agricultural College, as opposed to the private, sectarian nature of the state's literary colleges. It was, he said, the only college of its kind "belonging to the whole people of the State and controlled by them, as its property is held in trust by a Board of Trustees elected by delegates from all the county agricultural societies in the State, together with the Executive Committee of the State Agricultural Society." In addition, the Agricultural College had been in operation "longer and more successfully than any other Industrial College ever has in the United States. It has had a larger number of students, and hence enjoys a higher degree of confidence than any other." Its only other need was "an endowment to enable it to fulfill its entire mission of usefulness." The legislature was at a crossroads, he said. "You will either give to them [the state's citizens] one Grand Institution like Harvard University, or the world-renowned Educational Institutions of Europe . . . or you will transit to them a number of petty institutions, jealous of one another, who will come up to succeeding Legislatures to exhibit their poverty."[56]

Meanwhile, beginning in November 1863, Watts, Pugh, and the trustees had been considering yet another avenue for garnering legislative support: They would invite lawmakers to campus to see the institution's progress for themselves. The College Building was nearing completion, and some thought it was time to show it off. Trustee opinion was divided on the advisability of the open house, however, and Watts was particularly wary. Trustee Hiester told Pugh flatly that Watts "has no exalted opinion of them [legislators] and . . . all that we now require is to be let alone." The larger worry was that if they became more familiar with the college, "they may be disposed to tinker with it."[57] Trustee Daniel Kaine, a former legislator, opposed the idea as well: "Your report will be laid before them, and those who feel any interest in the

FIGURE 15 *The College Building, completed late 1863. Courtesy of The Pennsylvania State University Archives.*

institution will inform themselves, without going there. From my own experience in Legislative visits, I am not in favor of them."[58] Notwithstanding the dissension, they decided to hold the event, on March 18–19, 1864. "A goodly number" attended, with everything in operation and on display. "The members of the legislature and their wives and State officials inspected everything and then sat down and ate their fill," a student said. "Dr. Pugh told me he was afraid the dinner would cost more than the College would get out of it."[59]

None of these stratagems—the visionary organizational plan, Pugh's testimony before the Judiciary Committee, the legislative visit—would hinder the efforts to divide the land-grant fund. In fact, Pugh's examples of German universities and the "ideal" financial resources he recommended angered some legislators. Pugh was accused of wild extravagance. As one lawmaker said, Pugh told legislators that "eighty five thousand dollars annually . . . would be insufficient to sustain such an institution as he was ambitious to build up in Centre county. . . . When I heard that remark, I deliberately made up my mind that it was a most visionary affair, and that it would not be safe to leave the proceeds of this vast fund at the disposal of those who managed the institution."[60]

On April 14, the Senate Education Committee introduced S.B. 809. The legislation ordered the land-grant fund to be split among six institutions: Allegheny College in Meadville, the Polytechnic College at Philadelphia, the Agricultural College in Centre County, Pennsylvania College at Gettysburg, the University at Lewisburg in Union County, and the Western University of Pennsylvania at Pittsburgh. Furthermore, it required that the colleges advance the money for their share of land scrip at 80 cents per acre until the land had been sold and the fund was generating annual earnings.

A few days later, on April 19, the Senate Education Committee introduced another bill, just as ominous, to the full chamber for debate. S.B. 617 did not designate specific colleges to which it would direct the funds, but it repealed sections of the legislature's acceptance act of April 1, 1863, removed the Agricultural College as the sole beneficiary, and set the stage on which the Senate could designate the recipient institutions in a future session.[61]

Between April 14 and 21, the battle royal ensued in the Senate between proponents and opponents of the Agricultural College. Word of the Senate's debate got back to Pugh and turned him livid. On April 22, taking to his desk, he wrote a howling jeremiad against S.B. 809: "The effect of the bill is virtually to squander the entire proceeds for all time to come of the magnificent grant of public land from Congress to this state for the purposes of industrial education."[62] This would be Pugh's last public statement. As he wrote, he was seized by a violent chill but managed to rally and conduct what would be his last lecture, to his chemistry students. Then he was taken to his bed in the College Building.

Ironically, it was not S.B. 809, which purported to split the funds among six colleges, that would gain traction. Rather, it would be S.B. 617, which sought to remove the Agricultural College as the sole beneficiary. On April 28, S.B. 617, after some amendments, went to the House for consideration. Another intense debate occurred, with various amendments being offered.[63]

And then, on Friday, April 29, 1864, fate intervened. Evan Pugh died, the victim of the lingering effects of a broken arm, the stress from a crushing workload, and, finally, typhoid fever. He was just thirty-six years old. His death triggered a pause in the House debate, in deference to the Centre County representative Cyrus Alexander, who was excused to attend Pugh's funeral.

The House reconvened on May 4, when it voted by the slimmest of margins, 45–44, to resume its consideration of S.B. 617. Then procedural issues intervened. For any legislation to pass into a signable law at the end of a session, the rules required a two-thirds vote for both the House and Senate. Even if that might have been possible, another rule stipulated that no bill requiring the signature of the governor could be passed by either chamber on the day of final adjournment. And the day of final adjournment was Thursday, May 5. With these procedural hurdles looming larger by the minute, the House approved a motion, 47–44, to postpone "further consideration" of the bill indefinitely, and there the matter ended.[64] The issue would continue to haunt Watts and the trustees in subsequent legislative sessions, but for the time being, the Agricultural College retained its status as the sole beneficiary of the Morrill Act. It was, however, a Pyrrhic victory, the college having lost its brilliant young president in the battle.

CHAPTER 6

Watts and the College After Pugh

EVAN PUGH'S UNEXPECTED DEATH on April 29, 1864, shocked everyone associated with the Agricultural College of Pennsylvania and the American scientific community. The following day, the students drafted a resolution and sent it to newspapers across the Commonwealth. "To his wearied and cordial devotion to our interests, and his quick and clear perception of our needs, is largely due the success which has thus far attended us," they said, acknowledging that their future would be imprinted with "the stamp of his character and labor." En masse, they attended the funeral in Bellefonte on Tuesday, May 3.[1]

Testimonials came from far and wide. Alfred L. Elwyn, the trustee with whom Pugh had corresponded about a position nine years earlier, said Pugh "had to go through the almost desperate struggle . . . of attempting to place a new idea before indifferent and unprepared minds . . . we could never perceive that he had a selfish purpose, or any purpose but that of making the Agricultural College the first institution of its kind."[2]

The American Journal of Science and Arts called Pugh "one of the most able scientific men of the country. . . . The Agricultural College of Pa., the first institution of its kind established in this country, was attaining a high degree of success and usefulness, as a result of the rare combination of scientific and practical knowledge with administrative energy which characterized its lamented President. His death is a loss to Pennsylvania and the Nation."[3]

No one was more stunned by the sudden reversal of fortune than Watts. "I am greatly distressed at the death of Dr. Pugh and feel as if we were at Sea with regard to our College," he told McAllister. "But trust that Providence will take care of so good a project."[4] The board of trustees had not met since January 6 in Harrisburg, their attention having been focused on the battle royal in the Pennsylvania legislature and then on the matter of finding Pugh's successor. Finally meeting on June 15 at the college, some six weeks after Pugh's death, they resolved "that we now appreciate more highly than ever the value of his devoted attachment to the interests of Agriculture, his disinterested services to the Institution over which he so ably presided and the industry with which he prosecuted his noble purpose to elevate the public mind in its appreciation of the agricultural science."[5]

With Pugh's death, the momentum of the Agricultural College of Pennsylvania would begin to slow. Few if any American scientists/administrators had his background, energy, and vision to develop a new, experimental agricultural college into the national model in so short a time. Yale's Benjamin Silliman Jr., coeditor of *The American Journal of Science and Arts* (aka "Silliman's Journal"), is reported to have insisted that he "knew of but one man in the world who could bring the Agricultural College to the desired standard—and that man was Evan Pugh."[6]

Since his arrival in 1859, Pugh had built enrollments to a record 146 in 1864, thus becoming the largest agricultural college "in the world," as he put it. He created and sustained the highest scientific standard for his students in terms of a curriculum fitted to the aborning agricultural sciences, graduating students in 1861 with the first bachelor of scientific agriculture degrees in America. And he instituted graduate study with the master of scientific agriculture degree, also the first of its kind in America. Its reputation growing, the college attracted inquiries from prospective students and their families beyond Pennsylvania. In 1863–64, the college had enrolled eleven "resident graduates." One of the earliest "resident graduates" was Augustus King, son of Columbia College (later Columbia University) president Charles King.[7] Assessing Pugh's lost potential on the national level, the chief chemist of the U.S. Department of Agriculture in 1930 said: "Had his brilliant young life been spared we are confident that by the force of his leadership the great movement which began in the eighties [1880s] for the promotion of agricultural chemistry and scientific agriculture would have been advanced by at least a decade."[8]

Pugh's death signaled an inflection point for the college. However arduous the task of getting the institution founded and guided into successful operation, Watts and the trustees would find the years after Pugh to be even more daunting. They would be consumed with defending the institution against its enemies; attracting the needed finances and state support; fighting to retain the college's exclusive claim as Pennsylvania's Morrill Act designee; keeping the college on track educationally, consistent with the terms of the Morrill Act, yet entertaining wildly divergent curricular experiments; and struggling to regain the confidence of its increasingly disenchanted agricultural constituency. Through all of this, Watts and the trustees would be confronted with their greatest problem: a succession of problematic and troubled institutional presidencies—a problem, ultimately, of their own making.

The Search for Pugh's Successor

The indispensable man was now gone, but the trustees lost little time in searching for his successor. In the days immediately following Pugh's death, Watts and McAllister had the good sense to gauge the interest of Yale's Samuel Johnson, Pugh's fellow student at Leipzig and lifelong friend and confidant. Johnson would long outlive Pugh and win fame as the "doyen of American agricultural science," the most highly respected agricultural scientist of his day.[9]

Watts knew something of Johnson from Pugh. But he had some additional inside information, from "a young man employed in my office who graduated two years ago at Yale who says Prof. Johnson was very highly estimated as a practical chemist," as he told McAllister.[10] On May 10, Watts sent an inquiry to Johnson, simply to learn whether he "might be willing to give direction to its destinies . . . the scope of my information presents no name more likely to command the confidence of our friends than yours."[11] McAllister had sent a similar query to Johnson on May 6.[12]

Johnson certainly could have sustained Pugh's standards scientifically and educationally, but he turned the opportunity down. Although "honored" to be considered, he was aware of "the many difficulties" the college had endured before emerging as "a bright example of success and usefulness." Johnson added that he wished "my strength were equal to my will. But I am not strong enough for a situation of such responsibility. I am too easily tired out by brain-work and care to dare to attempt the work of carrying out the plans of your college."[13] Johnson surely knew from his friendship with Pugh how demanding

FIGURE 16
Samuel Johnson (1830–1909), Yale chemist and friend of Evan Pugh. Courtesy of The Pennsylvania State University Archives.

the job was. In any event, he was far more interested in scientific work than institutional leadership and administration, as his distinguished career at Yale, and later as founder of the first state-sponsored agricultural experiment station in America, would demonstrate.

With Johnson's dismissal of the presidency, the Agricultural College came to a major turning point, albeit unrecognized as such at the time. The question arises as to why Watts did not press Johnson for recommendations about potential candidates, trained in science, who could lead the institution in the direction Pugh had set. In 1864, Johnson was already nine years into his forty-year relationship with the Sheffield Scientific School at Yale. In 1855, he had returned from his European studies to take charge of the Yale Analytical Laboratory. A year later, Johnson also was appointed chemist to the Connecticut State Agricultural Society and shortly thereafter promoted to professor of analytical and agricultural chemistry at Yale.[14] A fast-rising star who would be elected to the National Academy of Sciences (f. 1863) in 1866, Johnson was widely traveled and well acquainted with the Who's Who of the developing agricultural sciences at the handful of other American scientific institutions. Despite Johnson's stature, Watts did not press him for advice or help to find a worthy successor to Pugh after he declined interest in the presidency; at least there is no evidence to that effect. Thus, it could be argued, the Agricultural College crossed the Rubicon—in the wrong direction.

Concurrent with the feelers sent to Johnson, Watts was considering another candidate: William Allen, the recently retired president of Girard College for Orphans in Philadelphia. "I write to Mr. Allen today," Watts told McAllister on May 4, the day after Pugh's funeral. "He is the only man I know who would be competent to the task."[15] The effort was successful. The fifty-six-year-old Allen was elected president on June 15, 1864, his appointment to "take effect from and after the commencement of the next session." In the meantime, Allen was empowered "to have such supervision of the Institution" wherever he was living until he and his wife could make their home on campus. Allen's salary was set at $2,500, well exceeding the $1,500 Pugh had been making.[16]

Watts had been personally acquainted with Allen in years past, as Allen had lived in Carlisle from 1836 to 1850. A graduate of Bowdoin College, Allen came to Dickinson College shortly after the school's reconstitution as a Methodist college. Allen first served as professor of chemistry and natural history, a post he held for ten years. He was then appointed to the chair of mental philosophy and English literature. In 1848, after the death of Dickinson's president, Allen was named to the presidency on an acting basis but was never considered a candidate for the post because he was not a clergyman.[17] In 1850, he was inaugurated as president of newly established Girard College for Orphans in Philadelphia, from which he retired in 1863.[18] Watts was certainly aware of Allen's sterling reputation as a Dickinson College professor. A contemporary faculty member said: "Allen . . . was a grand teacher. I have never seen his superior. . . . His lectures were the clearest and most philosophical I have ever listened to. They possessed . . . adhesiveness. That is, the student somehow could not forget them. And hence it was that the graduates of Dickinson knew more about these things than any of the other young men of the day."[19] Girard was a different proposition altogether. Established as a bequest by the richest man in America, the merchant Stephen Girard, the institution was a boarding school for "poor, orphaned, or fatherless" boys to be trained for the trades and professions of their era. Despite the name, it was not a collegiate institution.[20]

FIGURE 17
William Allen (1808–1882), president, Agricultural College of Pennsylvania, 1864–66. Courtesy of The Pennsylvania State University Archives.

At the Agricultural College of Pennsylvania, Allen would not be nearly as successful as he was at Dickinson and Girard. The central problem of Allen's administration was finances. The institution remained $50,000 in debt. The revenue from the $100 tuition was insufficient to cover operating costs, prompting Allen and the trustees to double it to $200 per year.

Meanwhile, the land-grant "fund," such as it was, was inactive and producing no revenue whatsoever. When the state accepted the terms of the Morrill Act in April 1863, it established a board of commissioners—composed of the governor, the secretary of the Commonwealth, and the auditor general—charged with selling the land; the same terms, however, prohibited any proceeds from being used to advertise the scrip and otherwise handle the sales. At the same June 15, 1864, meeting in which Allen was hired, the trustees approved a committee of Watts, McAllister, and Kaine to "procure the disposition to be made of the land scrip . . . to meet the necessities of the institution."[21] Shortly thereafter, the trustee committee met with the board of commissioners and reported that they had made "a satisfactory arrangement by which that business would be satisfactorily progressed in."[22] But it would be a long time coming. Scrip sales began haltingly in early 1865, but by the end of the year, only a small fraction of the 780,000 acres allotted the state had been sold.

Meanwhile, as the new legislative session opened in January 1865, the battle to wrest the land-grant designation from the Agricultural College resumed in full fury. Due to the confusion and misunderstanding about the Morrill Act that had been evident the year previous, the House printed five hundred copies of the Pennsylvania acceptance act of April 1, 1863, so that members could become better acquainted with its directives. To little effect, however: One new bill attempted to divide the fund among the six institutions as per the previous year. Nevertheless, it was the second bill, S.B. 120, that captured the lawmakers' attention. S.B. 120 removed the Agricultural College as the sole beneficiary. The bill also directed the board of commissioners to dispose of the land scrip at a price not less than 80 cents per acre, with the proceeds to remain in the treasury of the Commonwealth until further ordered. With this bill, opponents of the Agricultural College hoped to park the proceeds from land scrip sales in the state treasury, buying time until they could eventually figure out how to apportion the money.

The legislative debates over S.B. 120 became personal, vindictive, and fiercely ideological. The Agricultural College champions said the fund should be devoted in its entirety to an institution that focused primarily on agriculture and the mechanic arts, as Pugh had argued. Going further afield, Watts sent a memorial to the legislature attaching a statement from Ohio Governor John Brough describing the system of education propounded by the Morrill Act. Brough said the act inaugurated "a new and distinct species of education" whose purpose was to promote the agricultural and mechanical interests of the nation. Advocates for repeal argued otherwise. They maintained that the fund should be used "not to propagate a new system of education" but to dispense practical agricultural and mechanical knowledge to as many people as possible, diffusing such instruction among multiple institutions. The two sides also clashed over the value of manual labor. The Agricultural College deemed it necessary to elevate the legitimacy of industrial education and to sustain the students' tolerance for hard work—a bulwark against the idle habits and disdain for labor that they might obtain otherwise. The proponents of repeal argued for a less arduous student experience that would be "pleasant and agreeable."

To break the deadlock, Senator Hiester Clymer of Berks County offered a compromise. He proposed an amendment assigning one-third of land-grant proceeds to the Agricultural College in perpetuity and placing the other two-thirds in the state treasury, allowing additional colleges to apply for shares of the fund in the future. The bill passed the House and then the Senate on May 8, 1865. The one-third restriction for the Agricultural College would be codified into law the following year.[23]

Aside from issues surrounding the disposition of the Morrill Act, there were other pressing concerns, and they would metastasize into disenchantment with Allen's leadership. The same day that Allen was elected president, June 15, 1864, the trustees also appointed a professor of chemistry to fill Pugh's faculty position: George Caldwell, hired at $1,500 per year.[24] Caldwell had been a fellow student with Pugh in Germany, earning his Ph.D. from Göttingen. When Pugh absented himself from the college in July 1863 to seek medical attention in Philadelphia, he prevailed upon his old friend, then a professor at Antioch College, to take his place until he could return. Caldwell did so, staying until December 1863, when he was drafted into the U.S. Sanitary Commission in Washington, D.C. Soon after Pugh's death, the trustees prevailed upon him to return to the Agricultural College. Caldwell was somewhat reluctant, but "knowing that it would be so much in accordance with the wishes of my good friend that I should take his classes, at least till a better person can be found, and feeling much honored by your invitation as well as a deep interest in all such institutions as yours I have concluded to come to your aid for the present." Shortly after arriving, however, Caldwell protested Allen's appointment. "It seems to me a matter of the greatest importance that a *scientific* man should be placed at the head of the Institution—and if such a man cannot be found . . . then the one chosen should have a *just* and *hearty appreciation* of the importance of science in the management of the College—and you know as well as I how strong Dr. Pugh would have insisted upon this," he told McAllister.[25]

Caldwell would stay nearly four years at the Agricultural College, providing a standard of instruction that would have pleased Pugh. He left in 1868 at the invitation of Cornell University, opening for instruction that same year, to serve as founding chairman of its Department of Chemistry, where he would stay for the rest of his productive scientific career.[26] But his early protest of Allen's election as president in 1864 sowed the seeds of a faculty rebellion that would lead to Allen's departure.

A year after Caldwell's appointment, in July 1865, Allen hired a new professor of mathematics and astronomy and—in an effort to comply with the Morrill Act—lecturer in "military tactics": John Fraser, a Scottish immigrant and alumnus of the University of Aberdeen. Fraser had taught mathematics at Jefferson College in western Pennsylvania, then enlisted in the Union Army and was breveted as a brigadier general. Captured, he spent nearly a year in Richmond's Libby Prison. He emerged as a man of stern disposition, with strong ideas and the ambition to achieve them.[27] With Fraser's arrival, the college was able to offer its first formal program in "military tactics." But the mechanic arts—the remaining branch of land-grant education—were as yet to be formally introduced or even addressed. A collegiate curriculum in engineering was something in which the classically oriented Allen seemed to lack interest, and it would lead, in part, to his undoing.

In the meantime, soon after Fraser's arrival, a joint committee of Allen, trustees Watts and McAllister, and three faculty members (Fraser, Caldwell, and Jordan Whitman) was formed to develop a plan of reorganization. The plan was floated as a circular of the college on October 1, 1865.[28] Following up, the trustees at their next meeting, on February 8, 1866, requested the faculty to submit for consideration at the September 1866 meeting "such changes and improvements in the Literary and scientific departments," including changes to the manual labor requirement, as the plan of reorganization might recommend.[29]

The October 1865 "Plan of Reorganization" proposed that mandatory student labor be abolished, as military tactics and drill would provide a more suitable replacement; in fact, a four-year course in military science would be established. The college year would be altered radically, divided into two twenty-week semesters, starting in August and ending in June. Three curricula were proposed for adoption: General Science (which soon included several new engineering courses), leading to the bachelor of science; Agriculture, leading to the bachelor of scientific agriculture; and Literature, leading to the bachelor of arts.

Implementing the new plan would be another matter, assuming that trustees and delegates would grant their approval at the September 1866 meeting. With Fraser now the spark plug, firing up Caldwell's disenchantment with Allen, the faculty quickly mounted a rebellion of sorts, a de facto vote of no confidence in President Allen. At a faculty meeting of May 7, 1866, Fraser's resolution, supported by his colleagues, proclaimed: "The Agricultural College under the educational policy hitherto pursued, has failed, and in the judgement of the Faculty cannot but fail, to satisfy the expectations of the friends of enlightened practical education."[30]

The denouement of the Allen presidency came four months later, at the trustees' meeting on September 4–5, 1866. The board accepted Allen's resignation and elected Fraser to the presidency. Allen's problems with finances and curriculum were compounded by a cultural mismatch. He and his wife had long enjoyed the amenities of civilized life in Philadelphia. Although they now resided in the new house that Pugh had designed and partly financed, they became disenchanted with their rustic environs and social isolation. A professor remarked that Allen and his wife "seemed dissatisfied with their life at the college, apparently regretting that they had moved there." In any event, the classically educated and oriented William Allen had little conception of what land-grant education was to be and to do. After his resignation, Allen moved back to the Philadelphia area and was reelected president of Girard College in 1867, serving in that capacity until 1882.[31]

The rapid dissolution of the Allen presidency invites questions as to why he was selected in the first place. Watts's comment that Allen was "the only man I know who would be competent to the task" is telling. Evidently unwilling or unable to cast a wider net for a successor to Pugh, Watts considered only two candidates who were familiar to him—Samuel Johnson of Yale by reputation and William Allen of Girard by personal knowledge and reputation. After all, Allen had a record of success at both Dickinson as a professor and Girard as president. And Girard, not unlike the Agricultural College, was an experimental institution, albeit one that was preparatory rather than collegiate and heavily endowed. And, too, Allen was immediately available, having retired the year before as Girard's president. Allen also had a reputation as a man of unimpeachable character. And he had a connection to the Centre County elite: Allen's wife, the former Ellen Honora Curtin, was a daughter of Centre County ironmaster Roland Curtin and a sister of Andrew G. Curtin, a Dickinson College alumnus (1837) and sitting governor of Pennsylvania (1861–67) at the time of Allen's appointment.[32] Aside from these factors, expediency was certainly in play. Watts and McAllister felt an urgent need to get a successor to Pugh installed as soon as possible, so as to prevent the school from wobbling off its firm foundation. But Allen was so unlike Pugh. Despite his teaching of chemistry for a decade at Dickinson, he was not a practicing scientist nor did he have any sort of agricultural background or familiarity with the dictates of the Morrill Act. Unimpeded by any formal procedure for a presidential search-and-selection process, and having had their offer rejected by a candidate very much in the Pugh mold (Samuel Johnson), Watts and the trustees made a quick but unfortunate choice. The historian Wayland Dunaway pronounced a fitting epitaph to the Allen presidency: "Though a man of character and culture, he seems to have had no program of his own to promote and rose to no heights of leadership."[33] But in foisting such a poor choice upon the board of trustees, Watts, too, must share in the blame for this failed presidency.

The Memorial to the Legislature and the Bond Issue

Nonetheless, there were two notable achievements emanating from the Allen years. These resulted not from Allen but from Watts in order to shore up the college financially and politically. While there is no evidence to suggest that Watts was ever interested in assuming the Agricultural College presidency himself or from his colleagues suggesting as much, Watts would take command and control of the college as occasion demanded. Now was such a time.

The first action was a memorial to the legislature regarding the college's contested land-grant endowment and the establishment of experimental farms "in connection therewith." The second was a resolution to issue institutional bonds in the amount of $80,000, with "all the real estate of the Institution" offered as security. Both of these initiatives were approved at the trustees' February 8, 1866, meeting. Watts appointed a committee of three—which included McAllister—to draft a document "on the condition and wants of the college" that basically offered a quid pro quo: In return for the legislature's granting the entire land-grant endowment to the college, the institution would establish three experimental farms, in different regions of the state, to serve its agricultural constituents more effectively.[34]

The memorial Watts wanted was drafted quickly. It noted that, while the college was well adapted to agricultural instruction, the college farm was "not adapted for scientific experiments, sufficiently varied to benefit agriculture in parts of the State differing widely in soil and climate." Thus the legislature was asked to authorize "two additional experimental and model farms East and West in Pennsylvania. Upon lands of diversified quality, where the principles of agricultural knowledge may be tested by practical experiments." In return, the legislature would be asked to appropriate, "for the attainment of these objects, the fund arising from sale of the public lands granted to Pennsylvania."

The petition stated that the institution, since its founding, had spent $250,000—$100,000 of which was contributed by the state, $70,000 contributed by individuals and organizations, and $80,000 that would be generated through a bond issue, secured via a mortgage against the institution's property, to pay off the mounting debt load.

Watts and the committee construed the experimental farms as being essential to the success of the college and always a part of the trustees' original plan. Yet the farms could never be established "because there have *never been funds* at the command of the Trustees adequate to their establishment." Referencing the thousands of failed agricultural experiments across the state and nation, the memorial emphasized the need to conduct them under controlled circumstances and scientific method. The experimental results would be communicated to the public through a new "Agricultural Journal, to be edited by the Faculty, brought to the attention of every intelligent agriculturist in the State."

The memorial reiterated arguments that Pugh had made: that the endowment provided too little, not too much, for a single institution; that the Agricultural College was a state institution, controlled by delegates from all counties and an elected board of trustees; and that "it therefore needs and deserves more than other colleges, the fostering hand of legislation."

Attached to the memorial was a draft of the legislation that Watts wanted. It provided that the interest and income of "the entire residue" from the sale of lands be appropriated to the Agricultural College, on the condition that trustees establish and maintain three experimental farms under the immediate supervision of the professor of agriculture of the college. It also recommended that the state board of commissioners direct 10 percent of the total funds realized by the sale of scrip to purchase lands for the experimental farms.[35]

What the college received from the legislature on April 11, 1866, was a step in the right direction, but far short of what it sought. In passing its "supplement to the act to accept the grant of public lands by the United States . . . for the endowment of Agricultural Colleges," the legislature granted two provisions.

First, it authorized the board of commissioners to direct payment for the expenses of disposing the land grant scrip out of the general treasury of the state. The Morrill Act forbade expenditures for advertising, marketing, commissions to land agents, and other related expenses to be paid from the sale of land, so alternative sources needed to be found. In addition, the legislature provided that no more than one-third of the shares of land scrip be sold—in other words, no more than 260,000 of the 780,000 acres of land allotted the state could be offered for purchase. This provision was the formalization of the compromise legislation offered by Senator Hiester Clymer in May 1865: assigning one-third of land-grant proceeds to the Agricultural College in perpetuity and placing the other two-thirds in the state treasury so that other colleges might apply for these funds in the future.

Second, the act authorized the board of trustees to issue $80,000 in bonds, paying 7 percent per annum and maturing in ten years, secured by mortgaging the institution's property "to pay and consolidate all the debts of the institution."[36] The state's act of April 1866 moved things in the right direction, at least to some degree. But the action Watts and the trustees wanted above all else—the dedication of the entire land-grant fund to the Agricultural College and the authorization to establish experimental farms—was not forthcoming.

The Presidency of John Fraser and the Disposition of the Land-Grant Fund

The September 4–5, 1866, trustees' meeting was monumental in many respects. Allen's resignation was accepted and Fraser's appointment as the third president of the Agricultural College was approved. The trustees and delegates from agricultural societies approved the plan of reorganization, put forth nearly a year earlier. The board also approved Fraser's plan for reorganizing the faculty, as their contracts had to be terminated and new ones approved, given the recalibration of the academic calendar. Most ambitiously, the plan called for a large expansion of the faculty, from eight to twenty-three, but recommended that only so many be hired as could be sustained financially from the tuition of the student body; by that time, some 114 matriculants, 32 fewer than the enrollment of Pugh's final year, were attending. The plan also recommended that "resident graduates" be used to teach an hour a day in return for free room, board, and tuition—much in the manner of today's graduate teaching assistants.[37]

The Agricultural College was now Fraser's to lead. He would last only eighteen months, however. To his credit, he did demonstrate a much better understanding of the Morrill Act than did his predecessor, particularly in regard to the mechanic arts, or engineering. He quickly recommended new courses in mechanical and civil engineering, leading to a bachelor's degree in engineering, and in metallurgy, mineralogy, and mining, leading to a bachelor's

FIGURE 18
John Fraser (1823–1878), president, Agricultural College of Pennsylvania, 1866–68. Courtesy of The Pennsylvania State University Archives.

in mining engineering. He advertised far and wide for "resident graduates" to attend the college for two years, free of charge. And he introduced a practicum—a parallel course of laboratory and systematic field practice in concert with each science, engineering, and agriculture course. Fraser was betting that the addition of engineering and wider applied science studies would fulfill the industrial college curricula envisioned by the Morrill Act and generate an increase in enrollments. But sensing new pressures on institutional finances, the trustees limited expenditures such that they would be commensurate to the tuition revenue generated by a student body of only seventy.[38] The college was already $80,000 in debt, and though the legislature had approved a bond issue to cover that amount, Watts and the trustees were wary of sinking even further. Watts was exceedingly frugal, and the debt the college was carrying was a constant worry for him.

So at their December 20, 1866, meeting, Watts and the trustees gathered with one thing on their mind: money. At their previous meeting, they had expressed concern about the large amount of land scrip that had been issued to the southern states of the defeated Confederacy, depreciating the value of land and producing "a further glut in the market," which in turn threatened to depress the value of Pennsylvania's large allotment. With the trustees' support, Watts authored a new memorial to the legislature "exhibiting the financial condition of the college" and asking either that all the income from the sale of lands be appropriated to the Agricultural College or that the state take over the college, owning its property and assuming its debts.[39] It was, in modern football parlance, a Hail Mary pass.

And it worked. On February 19, 1867, the legislature finally threw its support to the Agricultural College by passing H.B. 215. The act appropriated the income and interest from the sale of the remaining scrip, in their entirety, to the Agricultural College. Evan Pugh had been dead nearly three years, but now his life's work was finally vindicated.

The act's passage came not without argument, however, most of it along the lines that had been deployed before. Opposition senators proposed measures to stall the bill, recommit the legislation to another committee, establish a minimum price per acre, and apportion one-third of the fund to Allegheny College. Similar debate took place in the House. But noting that other Pennsylvania colleges had not taken discernible steps to comply with the Morrill Act, Senator George Connell of Philadelphia maintained that the Agricultural College had firmly established itself as the obvious beneficiary, adding that "the feeling of the public has been gravitating toward the institution." On February 14, the House passed the bill overwhelmingly, 58–16, and on February 19, the Senate followed suit.[40]

The "act relating to the Agricultural College of Pennsylvania, and to the establishment of experimental farms in connection therewith," generally reflected the memorial Watts's committee had drafted the year previous. It repealed the first section of the act passed in April 1866, which limited the sale of land scrip to only one-third of the allotment and dedicated that share to the Agricultural College. It then directed that one-tenth of the proceeds from the sale of scrip be directed to the college to buy lands for experimental farms. Most important, it mandated that "the entire residue of the proceeds of the said lands . . . are hereby appropriated . . . to the Agricultural College of Pennsylvania for the endowment, support, and maintenance thereof, on condition that the trustees establish, conduct, and maintain, in connection with the College, three experimental farms; one near the College, under the immediate supervision of the Professor of Agriculture in the institution, another east, and the other west, upon lands of diversified quality, under the immediate supervision, respectively, of an assistant professor of agriculture."[41]

With the act's passage, the logjam of land-scrip sales broke apart. Up to that point, from late 1864 to early 1867, the board of commissioners charged with controlling the sales had generated little revenue. By February 8, 1866, for example, the commissioners had sold only 22,400 acres in all for a total of $18,258, or 81.5 cents an acre. After the legislature's act of April 1866, authorizing the use of state general funds to cover marketing and sales expenses, the board began to solicit large bids. After H.B. 215 passed, however, the commissioners moved much more vigorously. The sale of the remaining 520,000 acres of land was completed seven months later, by September 17, 1867. In toto, the sale of the 780,000 acres of land allocated to Pennsylvania generated $439,186.80, or 56 cents an acre on average.[42]

The land-grant "clock" was ticking in other ways as well. Section 3 of the Morrill Act required the states accepting its terms "to provide, within five years from the time of its acceptance, at least no less than one college . . . or the grant to the State shall cease." In Pennsylvania's case, that five-year term would have ended on April 1, 1868. The legislature resolved its ambivalence about the Agricultural College with little more than a year to spare.[43]

Meeting on March 13, 1867, the trustees accepted the conditions of H.B. 215 and appointed a committee to select the three farms and devise a plan for their development. The trustees decreed that that experimental farm to be located "at or near the College" should be on lands owned by the institution, and that it should comprise four hundred acres. As for the eastern and western farms, they should each contain about one hundred acres. Watts, as president of the board, chaired the committee that would figure out how to proceed with the farms.[44] Given Watts's long experience with innovative farm and barn design, he was the logical choice to lead the effort, as his expertise extended from grand plan to tiny detail. In early 1868, for example, Watts instructed George Tate, contractor for the new barn for the central farm, to build "racks . . . made of 4 inch Studs and faced in the upper and lower corners with light straps in the barn 12 apart rungs of 3/8 inch iron; the holes to receive them to be bored half through the beams, making each rung 16 inches long."[45]

Notwithstanding Watts's expertise, the process of establishing and managing the farms would become exceedingly complex, onerous, financially draining, and fraught with political peril. The experimental farms would require considerable time and attention that the trustees might otherwise have devoted to guiding the institution proper, but such was the price of their quid pro quo with the legislature.

Despite the promise of substantially more income from the sale of scrip—now entirely dedicated to the Agricultural College—the proceeds would be slow in coming. Only $6,300 was realized from the land-grant fund by early 1867. Furthermore, debt was accumulating at an even faster rate. Interest on the bond issue and early expenditures for the experimental farms cost more than $11,000 in 1867.

Worse, students stopped coming. Despite the new and much broader curricula—science, agriculture, mechanical and civil engineering, mining engineering, literary studies, and military science—enrollment plummeted, with only thirty undergraduates in residence at the start of the 1868–69 term. Penn State historian Michael Bezilla has offered that parents "must have balked at the prospect of sending their sons to a college whose curriculum embodied so many novel ideas. Perhaps students wishing to study agriculture doubted the commitment of the College to the subject, now that other courses of study were to be offered."[46]

Debt continued to accumulate: $17,000 more by the end of 1867. Fraser was severely constrained in his ability to finance the hiring of many more faculty, as he had envisioned. More ominous, the reduced emphasis on the once-solid agricultural science curriculum began to engender more criticism of the college, from eastern Pennsylvania in general and Chester County in particular. Fraser wanted to continue with his reforms and new programs but discerned that that would not be possible. Citing "the irreconcilable differences with the board of trustees as to scope and policies of this institution," Fraser submitted his resignation as president on March 14, 1868.[47] Watts brought Fraser's resignation to the board's May 27, 1868, meeting, and the trustees accepted it with regret.[48] Regardless of their official sentiments, there was concern that Fraser's emphasis on engineering might have compromised the college's focus on agricultural science and, in the process, further diminished the school's reputation in the eyes of its increasingly powerful agricultural constituency.[49] In any event, Fraser's last day of employment at the college was June 3, 1868.

Of the five presidents over the eighteen years from Pugh to Atherton, Fraser was the only internal candidate to succeed to the presidency. And he did so by fomenting a rebellion against his predecessor. Fraser's claim to distinction, however, is that he came closest to realizing what the Morrill Act meant and tried to expand the institution ambitiously along those lines. "He committed an error of judgment in attempting to carry out a program which was ideally desirable but practically impossible," said Wayland Dunaway. "Hence his administration was unsuccessful and expired in gloom."[50]

The College Retrenches, Buys Farms, and Searches for a New President

Meeting on May 27, 1868, Watts and the trustees opted for a severe retrenchment. They noted that the plan of reorganization adopted by the board upon the recommendation of the faculty two years previous "has failed to attract students as anticipated, and has proved too expensive to justify its longer continuance." Adding to their problems was the new burden of having to establish three experimental farms. The board slashed the faculty from eight to four, naming James Y. McKee as vice president and allowing him to move into the president's house until a permanent successor could be named. A professor of Greek and classical literature, McKee would lead the institution in each presidential transition henceforth, serving several times as acting president. Finally, the trustees retained two additional instructors at the parsimonious rate of $300 and $400 per semester.[51]

Critics of the college, who for more than a decade had derided its isolated location and lack of amenities, could now point to a looming existential crisis: The college that had been succeeding under Pugh was floundering in his absence. "I doubt very much the propriety of the policy of the Trustees in making the change in the general policy and management of the institution from that pursued by Dr. Pugh and imbodyed [*sic*] in the pamphlet," one critic wrote to McAllister. "In the death of the Dr. I fear the College, and Agricultural Education met with a loss that will be hard to replace. I am now satisfied that the selection of Mr. Frazer [*sic*] as President was a most unfortunate one for the College on account of his administrative abilities."[52] A Chester County agriculturalist said: "I have been pained to learn that the College is not prospering. Governor Geary told me when here a few weeks ago that there were not thirty students there this session which circumstance still further convinced me that the death of our worthy friend and the late talented Dr. Pugh was a public calamity."[53]

As the summer of 1868 got under way, the Agricultural College was teetering precariously. Watts and the trustees now had to find a new president, preferably one who could mollify the increasingly disgruntled farming community. And they needed to lose no time getting the experimental farms located, into operation, and producing results.

Pressure was mounting quickly. As soon as the legislature passed H.B. 215, Watts began receiving unsolicited offers to purchase farms from various parts of the state—from Westmoreland and Indiana Counties in the west to Bucks and Chester Counties in the east. Now, the trustees finally had the means to move ahead. As of late August 1868, they had $43,886.50 in hand for the purchase of three farms. The sum represented one-tenth of the $439,186.80 realized from the sale of land scrip, the proportion mandated by the legislative act of February 19, 1867, for those purchases. At a special meeting of the board on September 1, 1868, they allocated $8,000 for the construction of a house and barn on the experimental farm in the center of the state, a site adjacent to campus. They hired George Tate of Bellefonte, the contractor who had finished the main College Building in 1863–64, to do the work.[54] At their November 20, 1868, meeting, they authorized the purchase of a western farm located near Indiana (Pennsylvania) in Indiana County for $16,000. The deal required the county's citizens to raise $2,500—soon revised upward to $3,000—"towards stocking a suitable farm in their midst."[55]

The experimental farm in the eastern part of the state would be a different story, however. Located in Chester County, near West Grove (about eleven miles east of Pugh's hometown of Oxford), the farm would require more time and effort than the other two, the dynamics turning into a "political football" as the deeply agitated easterners exerted strong influence over the direction and management of the farm.

Concurrent with the business of the farms, Watts was searching vigorously for a new president. He immediately turned to a man with firsthand experience at the Agricultural College: David Wilson, who had served as vice president from 1859 to 1863, but whom Pugh had disliked and tried to remove from office. Wilson declined regretfully, "as I feel a deep interest in the success of that great enterprise, and I have unfaltering faith in its ultimate triumph over all prejudice and opposition."[56]

Also worth exploring is the curious question of whether Watts and the trustees ever considered the college's more recent vice president and professor of agricultural chemistry, George Caldwell, as a viable candidate for the presidency. Fraser certainly recognized Caldwell's administrative ability, appointing him as second-in-command. Although no documentary evidence can be found that even hints of Caldwell's potential for an eventual presidency, there is little question that he could have provided the kind of leadership the institution needed at this critical juncture. A graduate of Harvard (1855) and holder of a Göttingen Ph.D. in chemistry (1857) whom Pugh knew well and greatly

FIGURE 19
George Caldwell (1834–1907), professor of chemistry, 1864–68. Courtesy of The Pennsylvania State University Archives.

respected, Caldwell could have ensured a strong emphasis on agricultural science and continued Fraser's efforts to build the engineering disciplines.

The thirty-four-year-old Caldwell was highly respected in scientific circles, but, unfortunately for the Agricultural College, he was already out the door. He had been recruited to Cornell University by its president, Andrew White, as one of the first faculty members to be hired before the institution opened for instruction in the fall of 1868. Caldwell was one of four faculty members elected by the Cornell board of trustees on September 26, 1867, as professor of agricultural chemistry.[57] White later described his satisfaction with the appointment: "So, also, the steady work of Professor George C. Caldwell, whom I had called from the State College of Pennsylvania to take charge of the department of agricultural chemistry, won the respect of all leaders in agriculture throughout the State, and, indeed, throughout the country." White also recognized Caldwell's talent for administrative work, appointing him as secretary of the new university, a post in which he "discharged his duties admirably."[58]

Caldwell made the most of his opportunity. He spent the rest of his career at Cornell, building the department into a national leader. In 1869, a year after leaving the Agricultural College, he published the first English-language textbook on agricultural chemistry, *Agricultural Qualitative and Quantitative Analysis.* His reputation as an agricultural scientist, especially as a crop and soil scientist, increased by the year. He developed methods of analyzing foods and water for the U.S. Department of Agriculture and New York State's Department of Hygiene. His contributions to analytical chemistry transformed it from "mere technique" to the analysis of particle shape and size.[59] He was instrumental in founding the Society for the Promotion of Agricultural Science and served as president of the Official Agricultural Chemists. In 1892, he was elected president of the American Chemical Society.[60] Caldwell died in 1907 and Cornell memorialized him in 1913 with the naming of Caldwell Hall on the Ag Quad.

It is difficult to discern whether Watts and the Agricultural College trustees might ever have considered Caldwell as a viable internal candidate for the presidency. As soon as he arrived in June 1864 to take Pugh's professorial place, Caldwell voiced strong criticism to McAllister about Allen's appointment, believing his credentials unsuited for leadership of a scientific institution. Thus he may have alienated himself from Watts and McAllister at this early point in 1864. And as he was so closely associated with Fraser, who appointed him as vice president, he may have been viewed as a liability rather than an asset. At any rate, it is doubtful Caldwell would have considered the position, having seen firsthand the mounting problems of the Agricultural College. Like Samuel Johnson, Caldwell was dedicated to science, and so he committed to Cornell long before Fraser resigned on March 14, 1868. In fact, Caldwell's resignation was accepted by the trustees at their January 23, 1868, meeting.[61]

In any event, the man Watts eventually found for the presidency had impeccable educational credentials and a statewide reputation, but little in the way of scientific agricultural knowledge or practical farming experience. He was Thomas Burrowes, sixty-three years old, former state superintendent of the common schools, creator of the legislation that brought the state's normal schools (later teachers' colleges) into being, and the founding editor of the *Pennsylvania School Journal*, which he would continue to edit until his death.

But Burrowes was not without an appreciation for agriculture or practical education. He had, after all, attended the founding convention of the Pennsylvania State Agricultural Society in 1851. He addressed the Philadelphia

Society for Promoting Agriculture in 1853, pointing out the need for an institution like the one in Hofwyl, Switzerland, which emphasized industrial education. In talks before teachers' associations and institutes, he had displayed interest in the utilitarian aspects of education, and had spoken and written about industrial and agricultural education. Responding to a report issued by the Farmers' High School Board of Trustees in 1857, Burrowes noted that it was clearly distinguishable from an ordinary manual labor school. That same year, he wrote that "in the Farm School every lesson learned in the classroom or the laboratory, or the cabinet has reference to the active operation of the field and the bar, or the garden and the forest." Burrowes's biographer observed that Watts and the trustees were aware of his "known comprehension and sympathetic understanding of industrial and agricultural education in its relation to the public welfare."[62]

Notwithstanding his credentials, Burrowes's appointment, effective November 20, 1868, immediately stirred anger in Pennsylvania's agricultural community. "You have no idea of the almost universal prejudice against the college, among the farmers of eastern Penna. Our agricultural papers are constantly denouncing it; the political Press take up the cry and seem to vie with each other in the bitterness of their denunciations," J. Lacey Darlington, president of the Chester County Agricultural Society (and the son of Dr. William Darlington, Pugh's mentor) wrote to McAllister in December 1868. "The appointment of Mr. Burrowes has furnished them with another occasion for attack, and while they all acknowledge his eminent fitness for any educational post, they unite in predicting that his administration will be a failure—as the college is practically dead, past resurrection."[63]

Burrowes's appointment came about as a direct result of Watts's initiative, as had been the case with Allen. In the fall of 1868, Watts personally consulted "several prominent educators" to obtain their view on the best way to "fill the College with students." He invited the educator with whom he was most impressed—Burrowes—to address the board of trustees at a special meeting Watts called on October 29, 1868. Burrowes recommended that the "agricultural course *practice* must be made more prominent and *science* less so; that the President of the Faculty should have administrative ability as well as scientific and literary attainments; and that the expense of students must be diminished by making the tuition *free*, and the rates of boarding as low as possible."[64] A month later, after receiving a committee report on curricular changes and a new leader, the trustees elected Burrowes as president, at a salary of $2,000 per year plus the house that Pugh built.[65] Burrowes accepted the

FIGURE 20
Thomas Burrowes (1805–1871), president, Agricultural College of Pennsylvania, 1868–71. Courtesy of The Pennsylvania State University Archives.

trustees' offer at their December 10, 1868, meeting, but he negotiated for a better compensation package: a salary of $3,000 per year, the use of the president's house and grounds, plus "forage and feed for two horses and two cows."[66]

And so the year 1868 ended, not quite an annus horribilis but close to it. Now things were looking better. Two experimental farms had been purchased and were now in the formative state. A new president had been hired, and his new curriculum emphasizing practical agriculture had been approved. As the new year began, Watts and the trustees hoped for a reversal of fortune that would regain the confidence of the state's agricultural community and herald better days ahead for the struggling Agricultural College of Pennsylvania.

The Presidency of Thomas Burrowes

The advent of the Burrowes presidency signaled a nearly 180-degree swing in the college's orientation. Watts was in full support. In fact, Burrowes's educational philosophy of practical rather than scientific agriculture was close to Watts's own views of a college that existed chiefly for the education of farmers, although it was to be predicated on science. Burrowes's thinking was more in line with Watts's views than anything Allen or Fraser had proposed.

As Burrowes put it: "The chief hindrance encountered has been want of confidence naturally resulting from the failure of the institution by a departure from its proper work."[67] Abandoning Fraser's emphasis on introducing the engineering disciplines, Burrowes turned the school's emphasis to practical agriculture. The solution to the school's malaise, he noted in his reforms, was to devise a curriculum oriented to vocational agriculture, as opposed to the scientific agriculture Pugh had established. In a sense, it was the equivalent of a curriculum that would, in no small way, resemble a finishing school for farmers. In fact, Burrowes reduced the agricultural curriculum to three years, culminating in the degree bachelor of scientific agriculture. For those wishing more science, they could matriculate for a fourth year, taking additional science courses, and earn a second degree: the bachelor of science. And for those who wanted to round out their college education with literary and classical studies, they could opt for a fifth year and receive the bachelor of arts degree.[68]

Burrowes also reintroduced the old manual labor requirement, which had been replaced by military science in 1866. A fatherly figure, he actually worked in the fields alongside the students—his "lads," as he affectionately called them. And, as professor of civil government, practical agriculture, and French, he directed the agriculture experimental work himself, overseeing the college's central experimental farm adjacent to campus.

Seven months into his presidency, Burrowes instituted the first "Harvest Home" festival, in July 1869. He was convinced that the college was not well known among the state's citizens, and that publicity would prove a corrective. Harvest Home was his effort to showcase the college with its new emphasis on practical agriculture. The festival featured exhibits, demonstrations, and faculty presentations on agricultural topics, all in an effort to restore confidence in the school among the state's agricultural constituency. The event was repeated on a grander scale in 1870, attracting more than two thousand visitors. A highlight of the 1870 Harvest Home was a competition of thirteen mechanical reapers owned by farmers.[69] Harkening back to his introduction of the McCormick Reaper to skeptical Pennsylvania farmers on his Carlisle farm in 1840, Watts might have been pleased with the widespread acceptance of the machine thirty years later and with Burrowes's demonstration of their comparative features. Also of significance: the 1870 Harvest Home attracted a handful of alumni, the college now having graduated students for nine years, albeit in diminishing numbers with each passing year. The returning graduates took steps to organize an alumni association, electing a president and secretary-treasurer, although the organization would not formally charter itself until 1874.

The Experimental Farms

With a new president on board in late 1868, Watts and the trustees' preoccupying priority became the three experimental farms—which they knew had to succeed to satisfy the legislative act of February 1867 and recapture the faith of the state's agricultural community. Their meetings through 1869 and 1870 show inordinate concern with getting the farms into good working order. The farms were designed to be managed by a resident director: Thomas Harvey at the eastern farm in Chester County, William Huey at the central farm adjacent to the college, and T. P. Walker and, soon after, A. J. Hamilton at the western farm in Indiana County. The directors were to work closely with the local county agricultural societies and report annually to the president of the Agricultural College and the professor of agriculture as well. Despite the land-grant fund, finances were always precarious. "If we was only out of debt," Hamilton told McAllister in early 1871, "I would think that we could get along better, but by careful work this year, I expect to make the farm pay all expenses and the debt, with the assistance of a part of our appropriation. I see no other way."[70]

There was tension, as well, over the direction the farms were to take. One of the original intentions was to feature controlled experiments for comparative purposes across the three large regions of Pennsylvania—crops planted at the same time in plots of the same dimensions at all three farms to determine similarities and differences caused by local conditions. The results would generate new knowledge that would inform and improve agricultural practice in those locales. The competing philosophy was to use the farms as models rather than experimental farms—in other words, to *showcase* "best practices" up to that point rather than to use the farms for purely experimental purposes to *improve* agricultural practices.

The first annual report of the Eastern Pennsylvania Experimental Farm was submitted in January 1869, demonstrating its focus on experiments. In his remarks to the board of trustees, J. Lacey Darlington, president of the Chester County Agricultural Society, praised its superintendent, Thomas Harvey, whose experimental results showed "a zeal and industry over his charge." For his part, Harvey observed that "the [experimental] results may not be satisfactory to all, but we have to report them as they are," noting that the late start of the farm relative to the growing season, as well as the stringent finances and the absence of some skilled assistance, made it "difficult to get the work done at the right time, and in the proper manner." Harvey was particularly eager to show some of the results of lime application, however. "Our soil already contains a good supply of Phosphate of Lime, and the addition of more, in many cases, did not prove useful; thus showing the necessity for Farmer to know what their soils contain, and the composition of what they purchase to apply to them."[71]

Darlington, a champion of the college but increasingly worried about its fall from grace among eastern farmers, saw the experimental farms as the college's salvation. "I am confident that one of the surest ways to make friends for the College and regain lost confidence, is *through these Experimental Farms*." They needed to be run the right way, however. "Our Eastern Penna. Farm is . . . in the most intelligent and progressive agricultural district of the whole state, and unless everything about the Farm is up to the neighborhood, we are subject to ill-natured criticisms, and the blame is thrown upon you unfortunate Trustees 'who waste and spend the endowment fund at the College where nobody sees any results from it, instead of spending it on the Farm where everybody can appreciate,'" he added, asking for more money to be invested in the enterprise.[72]

Watts and Darlington had been appointed by the trustees as a two-person committee charged with overseeing the eastern farm. For Watts, it was difficult to visit or exercise his personal influence over the operation, so Darlington invited various farmers clubs and agricultural societies in his region to send a representative to form an advisory board of managers. The managers soon sought to take things over, "to run this farm in their own way—subject, of course, to the veto power if ever necessary of the 'Committee on the Farm' (you and myself)."

Darlington went further, however, testing whether Watts would rescind the resolution appointing the committee of two and then "give control of the practical operating of the Farm to the Agricultural Societies of Eastern Penna. It will relieve the College of that much responsibility and . . . it will go far toward allaying the prejudice so unfortunately existing against the College in Eastern Penna."[73]

Ultimately, Watts and the trustees would not relinquish control in the manner that Darlington had recommended. At their November 17, 1869, meeting, however, they expanded that control, slightly, resolving that management of the eastern farm be continued by Watts, Darlington, and a newcomer, Joseph C. Turner, a Chester County agriculturalist who had been elected to the board of trustees the previous September. These two prominent Chester Countians constituted something of a controlling interest in the three-man committee now managing the farm going forward, and the hope was that the Chester County constituency would be placated.[74] That did not happen, however, and the agitation drove Watts to distraction. Watts especially feared that, in the upcoming annual trustee election, agricultural society delegates from eastern Pennsylvania would vote in sufficient number to oust two trustees perceived as insufficiently sympathetic to their interests: A. Boyd Hamilton, the immediate past president of the state agricultural society who had served as an ex officio trustee since 1865 and was elected in 1869 to a three-year term, and Daniel Kaine, who served as an elected trustee from 1863 to 1879. "If these eastern men turn Hamilton and Kane [*sic*] out I am for letting them take the whole concern and manage it in their own way," Watts told McAllister in the summer of 1870. "If Hamilton is turned out I will not stay a minute."[75] Watts's frustration was clearly showing.

The college's experience with the eastern and western farms would prove increasingly problematic over the next eighteen years, by which time Watts was long gone from the board of trustees. For one thing, the farms were a drag on institutional finances. Having spent the $43,000 one-tenth share of the land-grant endowment for the farms, mainly in purchasing land and erecting buildings and facilities, the college could not spare more than $1,000 per year to sustain each farm. That was far too little to support scientific experiments and pay directors and staff. The college's perceived parsimony generated even more dissatisfaction among its agricultural constituency. In addition, coordination and direction from the college proved an issue, as farm supervisors and their local advisory committee often were at loggerheads with the professor of agriculture in charge of the farms, John Hamilton.

Neither did the criticism from Chester County abate; in fact, it intensified as the years rolled on. In 1880, a series of letters attacking the college and its failing experimental farms appeared in the West Chester *Register and Examiner* under the pseudonym "John Plowshare." The letters were reprinted in papers across the Commonwealth.[76] The next year, 1881, members of the Eastern Farm Club petitioned the legislature to rescind the college's land-grant status and give the endowment to another, or other, institutions. The bill that was generated passed the House but failed in the Senate, due to the intervention of

General James A. Beaver of Bellefonte, who had succeeded Watts as president of the college's board of trustees.[77]

The experimental farm saga would not come to an end until 1887. In the wake of the federal Hatch Act, establishing agricultural experiment stations at land-grant institutions, the college established its own such station in conformance with the legislation. The Pennsylvania legislature appropriated $12,000 for the erection of a station building and agreed to the sale of the eastern and western experimental farms.[78]

The End of the Burrowes Presidency

Meanwhile, the Burrowes presidency was heading for a tragic end. Leading his students on a mountain camping trip in the early winter of 1870, he and his entourage were overtaken by heavy snows. Burrowes, now sixty-five, suffered from cold and exposure, lingered for weeks, and died of pneumonia on February 26, 1871. His novel three-tier curriculum would die with him. Despite his efforts to revive the college with increased publicity and a curriculum centered on practical agriculture, enrollments did not climb sufficiently to generate the needed income. Student attendance ranged from 45 when he began his presidency in the winter of 1869 to 75 in 1871, with nearly one-third of that number—24 students—in the college's preparatory department or grammar school.[79] Put another way, the increased enrollment generated by Burrowes peaked at 75 in 1871—little more than half the enrollment of 146 (including 29 preparatory students) of Pugh's last year.

With the death of Burrowes, the college had reached yet another inflection point. In the seven years since Pugh's demise, the college had been through three troubled presidencies that had failed to move the enterprise into successful operation as a land-grant or industrial college. On the positive side of the ledger, however, the college was now, through legislative act, certified as the sole beneficiary of the land-grant fund, the initial balance of which stood at $439,000. But the several curricular experiments had failed. The experimental farms were struggling and incurring increased criticism. The college remained mired in debt and its finances were precarious at best. And the needed enrollments had not materialized, very bad news for an institution so heavily dependent on tuition revenue. The College Building, finished in Pugh's final months, contained 165 dormitory rooms, each accommodating 2 students, or 330 students when full. The occupancy rate by the end of

Burrowes's administration in 1871 was only 23 percent. The college had sunk into what Penn State historians have termed "an era of drift"—a period of "strange transmutations," as one alumnus called it—that would devolve into a severe existential crisis by the end of the 1870s.

One wonders what might have happened had Burrowes lived several years longer, say, until 1876. He was managing to increase enrollments somewhat and those increases might have persisted. But with his emphasis on practical agriculture and manual labor, the college was already well off-track as a developing land-grant institution and far removed from Pugh's vision as a scientific institution. For this turn of events, Watts must shoulder the major responsibility, for it was he who pushed hard for Burrowes's candidacy with the board of trustees and then supported the new curriculum based on practical rather than scientific agriculture.

By the summer of 1871, Watts was facing major changes in his life, personally and professionally. Now seventy years old, he was being pursued by President Ulysses S. Grant to serve as commissioner of agriculture for the United States. Watts was reluctant to consider the position, however. "You have doubtless seen the offer of Com. of Agriculture offered to me and the various versions of it," he told McAllister. "The truth is, the president offered me the appointment which I declined peremptorily because I could not think of breaking up my present home connections. The offer was repeated and pressed upon me by Mr. Scott and Mr. Cameron. My friends around me whom I consulted insisted upon my acceptance and I was prevailed upon to say that if the President still insisted upon it I would accept and added it is greatly against my inclination and if the President can suit himself with anybody else it will be exceeding acceptable to me, and thus the matter now rests."[80] A few weeks later, Watts accepted the post, although still reluctant. "The President persisted that I should take the Head of the Ag. Bureau at least for a time and he and my friends prevailed upon me to accept that appointment very much against my inclination," he told McAllister. "I will take Wm. Watts with me when I go. . . . I am really distressed that I can not be with you a few days but it is impossible. My son Fred (Agricultural College graduate, Class of 1862) goes up to attend the meeting of the Alumni and he knows how perplexed I am about not going with him."[81]

Watts would become the third commissioner of the U.S. Department of Agriculture, established by Congress with Lincoln's support in 1862. In addition to his law practice (from which he had largely retired), his presidency of the Cumberland Valley Railroad, his Carlisle farms, and his various civic and business interests, he would remain on the college's board of trustees, as president, for three more years, until the summer of 1874. His interest in the college would not abate immediately, but he would be hard-pressed to attend board meetings for the remainder of his term and devote his usual attention to the institution. Clearly, Watts was becoming overstretched.

More and more, McAllister would serve as the de facto president of the board. But McAllister, too, would soon pass from the scene, dying in Philadelphia on May 15, 1873. Before that, however, Watts would make his last presidential appointment, and this one would nearly doom the college.

CHAPTER 7

Final Years with the College and the Aftermath

WITH THE DEATH OF Thomas Burrowes on February 26, 1871, Watts began the search for the college's fourth president in seven years. Once again, he lost no time getting the process under way. At the trustees' meeting on March 10, 1871, they examined letters and statements recommending four men. One of them was the vice president of the Agricultural College, Professor James Y. McKee. Another was a college president in Michigan, albeit with Pennsylvania roots.[1]

The trustees quickly settled upon the latter. On March 21, 1871—less than a month after Burrowes's demise—they elected the Reverend James Calder, D.D., president of Hillsdale College, in Hillsdale, Michigan, as the fifth president of the Agricultural College of Pennsylvania. Calder's salary was set at $2,000 per year, one-third less than what Burrowes had been making, with payments beginning April 1, 1871.[2] On its face, it seemed an odd choice, and Pugh surely would have been apoplectic at the prospect of a minister now presiding over what just a few years prior was the nation's leading college of agricultural *science*. With the drumroll of criticism from the agricultural community over the college's drift from its land-grant mission, and the three troubled presidencies since Pugh, the hiring of Calder merits a closer look.

Calder was born in 1826 to a prominent Harrisburg family, making him forty-five years old when elected to the Agricultural College presidency. He graduated from Wesleyan College in 1849 and then entered into ministry with the Philadelphia Conference of the Methodist Episcopal Church. These were a denomination and conference with which Watts was familiar, as thirty-eight years earlier he had helped to engineer the transfer of Dickinson College to the same Philadelphia conference. A devout Methodist, Calder served as a missionary in China from 1851 to 1854; returned to the United States, where he continued his church work; and in 1869 was elected president of Hillsdale College.[3]

Originally a Baptist institution, Hillsdale was founded in 1844, providing a classical liberal arts curriculum. It was avant-garde in other ways, however, admitting women and blacks from the start, and, after the Civil War, enjoying robust enrollments. Calder was Hillsdale's third president, serving only three years before moving to the Agricultural College.[4]

Of the five presidents between the "founder," Evan Pugh (1859–64), and the "second founder," George Atherton (1882–1906), Calder would serve the longest, from April 1871 until January 1880. But his presidency featured an arc of antithetical dynamics, with some promising developments at the start but disaster at the end, resulting in the near closure of the college. The inflection point may well have been the summer of 1873, when McAllister and Watts, the two guiding lights on the board of trustees, were essentially out of the picture.

The new administration started auspiciously enough. "President Calder writes to me in good spirits," Watts told McAllister in the early summer of 1871.[5] The first early achievement was the introduction of a new baccalaureate program of study, which, upon the recommendation of Calder and the faculty, the trustees approved at their July 26, 1871, meeting. Gone was Burrowes's three-tier curriculum and in its place were three four-year curricula: Agriculture, Scientific, and Classical.[6] It was the classical curriculum, centered on Greek and Latin and literary studies, that would wax predominant over Calder's tenure, far eclipsing agriculture, the school's original curriculum, and science, its very foundation. The new classical curriculum would lead to "strange transmutations," in the words of C. Alfred Smith, Pugh's protégé, who had returned to the college in 1877 as professor of chemistry. "I realized how completely the Institution had become a 'mere literary College,'" Smith recalled upon his arrival. The scientific course was nominally in place but lacked "enthusiasm," with only one laboratory that could accommodate no more than twenty students. There were no specialized laboratories, and a portion of what once existed was now stored in the basement with the other

FIGURE 21
James Calder (1826–1893), president, Agricultural College of Pennsylvania and Pennsylvania State College, 1871–80. Courtesy of The Pennsylvania State University Archives.

part cut into kindling and burned. "In answer to my surprise, President Calder said, 'If Prof. Smith remains with us he will find that we are not devoting as much time to Chemistry as in the old years.'"[7]

Aside from the curricular changes—however dire they would prove to be—the second early accomplishment of the Calder administration was the admission of women. Ellen Cross of Omro, Wisconsin, and Rebecca Ewing of Angola, Indiana, had applied to the faculty for admission as day students.[8] Both had been students at Hillsdale and came to the Agricultural College at Calder's invitation.[9] The matter was approved quickly. At the September 5, 1871, meeting, the trustees authorized the president and faculty "to open the doors of the College to male and female students on the same conditions precisely, under such regulations as they may deem expedient."[10] The trustees explained their decision further in the 1871 college catalogue: "It was felt that the important trust committed to the Board would not be fully administered while one half of the youth of our State were denied its advantages; and the experience of other institutions, several of them Agricultural, justified the expectation of good results from the co-education of the sexes. Therefore, ladies are now admitted to the same courses of study as the gentlemen, are subject to the same general rules, and on the completion of their studies, will receive the same certificates and degrees."[11]

Rebecca Ewing would go on to complete the scientific course and graduate in 1873 with the bachelor of science degree, the first woman to graduate from the college.[12] Ellen Cross eventually transferred to the University of Pennsylvania, went on to earn a Ph.D., and was ordained into the ministry. Ewing and Cross residence halls on Penn State's University Park campus stand as their memorial.

As time rolled on, the enrollment of women increased from six in 1871 to forty-nine in 1879, a high-water mark that would stand for thirty years.[13] The number forty-nine is somewhat misleading, however, as only nine women were enrolled in the four collegiate classes (freshman through senior years) for 1878–79. Seventeen more were in the preparatory classes and twenty-six were categorized as music pupils (with a few women listed as both preparatory and music pupils).[14] As was the case at the Agricultural College, similar developments concerning the admission of women were taking place at land-grant colleges nationwide at roughly the same time, circa 1870, about five years after the Civil War. In fact, land-grant colleges broke the gender barrier a century before women were granted such privileges at elite private institutions in the northeastern United States and elsewhere.[15]

The third early achievement involved finances—an infusion of funds to increase the principal of the land-grant endowment, bringing it from $439,000 to an even $500,000. The state's surveyor general pushed a recommendation that, "as an act of tardy justice," the land-grant endowment be augmented by additional funds that would be consolidated into a single bond for $500,000. Trustees A. Boyd Hamilton, former president of the Pennsylvania State Agri cultural Society, and Frances Jordan, with Calder's assistance, took the lead in advocating for the measure with the legislature.[16] Their efforts paid dividends. Approved on April 3, 1872, the legislature's act authorized the surveyor general to sell all the current bonds constituting the land-grant fund, pay the proceeds to the state treasurer, and issue a new fifty-year bond for $500,000, payable to the Agricultural College at the rate of 6 percent annually.[17] The act's passage prompted a public celebration in the college chapel.

Given the undercurrent of criticism from the agricultural community, particularly in southeastern Pennsylvania, and the wobbly dynamics of presidential leadership since Pugh, it may seem counterintuitive that a measure to buttress the finances of the college could garner support in the legislature.

But, as the college's first historian suggested, the opposite sentiment may have prevailed: that the college was floundering precisely because the sale of land scrip generated far less than was originally anticipated.[18] Indeed, back in Pugh's day, the state Senate's unsuccessful bill to remove the college as the sole beneficiary also sought to set a minimum price for the land scrip at 80 cents per acre; theoretically, that would have brought in $624,000 for the state's allotment of 780,000 acres.[19] In any event, the $500,000 endowment would soon provide earned interest of $30,000 per year for the beleaguered institution.

The Great Unraveling Begins

The summer of 1873 marked the end of the old guard of leadership on the board of trustees. McAllister, the local trustee since the chartering of the school in 1855, died on May 5, 1873, at age sixty-three. McAllister had been the de facto president of the board since Watts left for Washington in August 1871. He and Watts had started the institution from scratch and guided it to its present state, through five presidencies. They were close colleagues and friends, irrevocably committed to the college. For Watts, Pugh's death was shocking enough, but now McAllister, too, was gone. "Many disappointments and difficulties have occurred in the management of the College in the last few years, but nothing so disasterous [*sic*], as the death of our friend H. McAllister," Watts wrote to Calder. "'Thy will be done, O Lord'! is the only consolation we have."[20]

Watts, at age seventy-two, was now consumed with running the U.S. Department of Agriculture, the college's board of trustees, and the Cumberland Valley Railroad. Though Watts would remain as the nominal trustee president for another year, the July 23, 1873, board meeting would be the last he would attend. He used the occasion to praise McAllister: "Whilst I highly appreciate the public eulogies which have been pronounced upon his public and private character, I desire that the Board shall make an enduring testimonial of the estimation in which we hold the invaluable services which he rendered in the establishing of this institution and in the conscientious and persevering energy in which he prosecuted its objects and purpose."[21] Watts's resignation as president of the board was accepted a year later, on July 29, 1874. General James A. Beaver, the law partner and son-in-law of McAllister, and also a resident of Bellefonte, was elected president in his place. Beaver would hold the board presidency until 1882.[22] Beaver would remain on the board, however, until his death in 1914. As governor of Pennsylvania from 1887 to 1891, he served as an ex officio member. In 1891, he was reelected to the board, serving as its president from 1898 to 1914, including a brief term as president pro tempore of the college (1906–7) after the death of Atherton.

But with Watts and McAllister absent after the summer of 1873, the college charted a new course. The prospect of greater munificence from the enlarged endowment prompted Calder to recommend, in 1874, the elimination of tuition altogether, except for a few minor fees. He also undertook a program of improvement to the college's physical plant, from the macadamizing of the college lane to the planting of trees and flora as well as improvements to the college building. Both of these measures created additional financial strains on the college, however.[23]

The new direction became fully evident when Calder recommended, and the trustees concurred, on July 29, 1874, the renaming of the college. Henceforth, the Agricultural College of Pennsylvania would be the Pennsylvania State College. As Calder explained: "The change of name was needful, because the old name not only failed to express the breadth of purpose contemplated by the laws under which the College received its endowment, but also misled many persons as to its real character. In many instances, students were prevented from entering, being under the impression that the College was designed for those alone who intended to be farmers. Under the change of name no change has been made in the courses of study or in the practical work of the institution."[24]

The name change may have been prompted, in part, by an insurgent effort in the legislature to establish a new, separate institution for engineering titled the Mechanics High School to "furnish skilled foremen for our Pennsylvania workshops." Calder and the trustees successfully parried the effort, maintaining that the college and state had accepted the terms of the Morrill Act, and that the mechanic arts rightfully belonged to the college rather than to a competing institution that would demand funding from the state.[25]

The funds spent on physical plant improvements and the money lost with the elimination of tuition put added financial pressure on the college. The institution was also staring at an $80,000 obligation coming due from the bonds issued by the Allen administration in 1866. In 1878, Calder and the trustees would persuade the legislature to make a special appropriation of $80,000 to the college to erase its debt. This was the first direct appropriation from the legislature since 1861, when Pugh had prevailed upon it to provide $49,900 for completion of the College Building. In return for the $80,000 appropriation, the legislature demanded that the faculty take a 10 percent pay cut.[26]

Under Calder's leadership, the Pennsylvania State College, or "Penn State" as it came to be called, did manage to increase and then sustain overall enrollments. But the growth came through rapid increases in its preparatory department or grammar school, which soon surpassed enrollments in the collegiate ranks. In Calder's first year, there were 75 students in all—51 in the collegiate ranks and 24 (or 32 percent) in the preparatory department. The following year, 1872, enrollment nearly doubled to 147, with 80 students in the collegiate ranks but 68 (or 46 percent) in the preparatory department.[27] Watts was buoyed by the news. "My great anxiety for the ultimate success of the College makes the information that you give me of the increase of numbers very acceptable," Watts wrote to Calder. "And I may add that I do feel that you must and will command success. The character of our State—the particular situation of our College and the object we all have in view must be successful at last."[28]

The celebratory spirit was short-lived, however, as enrollments in 1872 had reached their high-water mark for the decade of the 1870s. The following year, 1873, enrollments began to decline, but, more ominously, the pattern flipped: Preparatory students now outnumbered college students. That same year, enrollment topped out at 145, with 58 students in the collegiate ranks but the majority—87 students (or 60 percent)—in the preparatory department.[29]

This new enrollment dynamic—preparatory students outnumbering college students—held sway as the decade wore on. In 1875–76, 144 students matriculated: 54 college students and 90 (or 62.5 percent) preparatory students.[30] In the 1879–80 academic year, Calder's last, little had changed. The collegiate ranks held 58 students and the preparatory department held 66 (or 53 percent).[31] Contrary to expectations, the increased enrollments in the preparatory department during the 1870s failed to grow collegiate enrollments.

The nadir for enrollments occurred in 1882–83, after Calder and his successor had left office and during the first year of Atherton's presidency. That year, the collegiate ranks had only 23 students, not including 3 "resident graduates," and the preparatory ranks had 50 students (68 percent).[32]

For the collegiate ranks, Calder's administration increasingly emphasized the classical curriculum at the expense of the agriculture and science programs.

And despite the earlier nod to the mechanic arts, engineering was ignored altogether. Calder came out of the classical tradition and, as a minister, had no training in, or inclination toward, science and technology. Near the end of the 1870s, Penn State had devolved into a backwoods classical college, the very kind of institution Pugh had railed against in making his distinctive case for the Agricultural College as a scientific institution of the first rank. A dozen years after Pugh's death, the institution was not substantially different from the three dozen or so other classical or liberal arts colleges scattered across the state of Pennsylvania. Within half a decade, Calder had remade the Pennsylvania State College into something closely resembling Hillsdale College, whence he came. And in the process he had reduced the collegiate population to a permanent minority among the institution's matriculants.

The trustees were not oblivious to this new direction. In 1875, a year after Watts had officially retired, the college's charter was amended to increase the number of trustees from thirteen to twenty-three. This was an effort to make the institution more accountable to the state's agricultural interests as well as to state government and the Commonwealth's increasingly powerful industrial interests, particularly mining and manufacturing. Four new ex officio posts (the secretary of internal affairs, the adjutant general, the superintendent of public instruction, and the president of the Franklin Institute) were added to the extant four (the governor, the secretary of the Commonwealth, the president of the state agricultural society, and the college president), for a total of eight ex officio positions. Twelve more members were to be chosen by a combination of interests consisting of: the executive committee of the state agricultural society; the managers of the Franklin Institute; three representatives from each county agricultural society; and three representatives from each of the state's mining and manufacturing associations. In addition, the college's alumni were authorized to elect the remaining three members.[33]

The State's Agricultural Community and the Legislature Weigh In

Toward the end of the Calder administration, the state's politically active and agitational agricultural community, increasingly distraught with the college's direction, began to take matters into its own hands. In 1877, the Centre County Chapter of the Patrons of Husbandry, Pomona Grange No. 17, took a peek under the tent and gave the college passing marks: "After a careful and thoughtful examination, we have no hesitancy in commending this Institution to Patrons as first class in every particular."[34] A year later, the state Grange took its own peek and came to a quite different conclusion, essentially calling for a takeover of the institution. Although it "would recommend this institution to the patronage of all, and especially the farmers throughout the country, we deem it advisable that the State Grange should assume a supervisory control over the College, as far as is consistent with the chartered rights and privileges of others."[35]

The Pennsylvania State Agricultural Society also weighed in. At its 1878 annual meeting, the society passed resolutions demanding that the college strengthen its agricultural curriculum and reorganize its experimental farms into agricultural research stations. In the state legislature, criticism over the agricultural program and the failure to establish a mechanic arts curriculum culminated in the formation of a special joint committee in April 1879 to investigate the college. Led by Representative Albert Ackerly, the committee visited the college briefly and cursorily, concluding that "while evidence does not show actual fraud or disclose corrupt management, the institution has been very badly managed." A bill was then introduced to deny further funding to the college until things were straightened out. The measure passed the House but failed in the Senate.[36]

The death knell for the Calder presidency was tolling loud and clear. The trustees began pressuring him to resign. Faculty were distraught over the emphasis on classicism, not to mention their pay cut, and appeared to be on the verge of open revolt. Students were fed up with Calder's penchant for strict rules and regulations, and they, too, were at the point of rebellion. Seeing no solution, Calder announced his intention to resign in June 1880 but departed his office four months earlier, on January 22, 1880.[37]

The final president of this eighteen-year retrogression was an unmitigated disaster: Joseph Shortlidge, president of the Maplewood Institute, a "seminary for learning" chartered in 1870 and located in Concordville, Delaware County, in southeastern Pennsylvania. Shortlidge brought with him no higher education experience and even less political acumen. He lost no time in criticizing the legislature for its lack of funding and, with an authoritarian hand, alienated both the faculty and student body. The state's agricultural community remained up in arms over the school's lack of agricultural focus. A faculty committee took matters into its own hands and recommended substantial changes to the curriculum, especially to include engineering. They also argued for Shortlidge's removal. He quickly resigned and was gone by April 8, 1881, his tenure lasting little more than ten months.[38]

In early 1881, as the Shortlidge presidency was falling apart, the trustees launched their own investigation of the college, an inquest that was welcomed by the faculty. As one frustrated faculty member wrote to Trustee President Beaver: "After 22 years of experimenting, we are today the laughing stock of the state. . . . As an industrial College we are a failure. . . . When the complaint is made that we do so little for agriculture, the reply is that we are no longer exclusively agricultural. Unfortunately we are not anything *in particular*."[39]

It was as near to extinction as the college would ever come. As Penn State historian Wayland Dunaway summed it up: "In his mistaken policy, President Calder had sown the wind and the institution was now about to reap the whirlwind. Had his successor in office [Shortlidge] measured up to his high station, the situation might have been saved, but he served only to bring the school into further disfavor and to add fuel to the fire of criticism burning fiercely on every side."[40]

A faculty committee appointed to revise the curricula did so quickly, with its chairman, Professor I. Thornton Osmond, issuing a report clearly delineating two distinct eras: one closing in 1880–81 and a new one, with substantial curricular changes, opening in 1881–82.

In 1880–81, the college had "nothing whatever in mechanic arts or engineering"; the principal focus was the classical course and also a scientific course—"just the usual courses common in small colleges at the time"; and an agricultural course differing from the scientific by only three hours per week in studies and some practicums, a mere shadow of its former self.

With the opening of the 1881–82 academic year came a new era with a marked change in the college's academic character: two general courses, scientific and classical, and four technical courses: agriculture, natural history, chemistry and physics, and civil engineering. Also added were new engineering practicums and more agriculture practicums. "The College has been distinctly differentiated from the other Colleges of the State, and correlated with the Land Grant Act of Congress of 1862," the faculty report concluded.[41]

The turnaround did not end there, however. A new joint committee of the Pennsylvania legislature was appointed to "investigate the affairs" of the college, reporting its findings in February 1883. In nearly four hundred pages, the report issued a glowing conclusion: "The State College is in good faith fulfilling the trusts committed to it by the State . . . much of the misconception respecting it arises from a lack of easily obtainable information. We believe it has passed its worst days. Its courses of study, in the opinion of experts, are well organized; its facilities good, and in some particulars unusually complete; its faculty is composed of competent, and many of them highly experienced professors . . . and the entire spirit and work of the institutions . . . are directed to the promotion of industrial education." The legislative committee was convinced "that the time has come when the State should give it much fostering care as will make it not only an object of just pride, but a source of immeasurable benefit to our sons and daughters."[42]

At the time the report was issued, the president who would in time become known as the college's "second founder" had been in office for just six months. In his twenty-four years in the presidency, George Atherton would further reconcile the institution to its land-grant mission, strengthening both engineering and agriculture substantially, as well as the liberal arts and sciences. He would build up the faculty and student body to nearly eight hundred at the end of his tenure and add new buildings and facilities. By the year of his death, 1906, Atherton had set the college firmly on course for success in the twentieth century.

But the nine years between 1873 and 1882 had resulted in a near-death experience for the Pennsylvania State College. After Watts and McAllister were gone from the scene in 1873, the college wobbled terribly as it abandoned its industrial college and Morrill Act mandate. The institution lost students in its collegiate ranks, incurred the wrath of the state's agricultural constituency, attracted criticism from the press, alienated its faculty and students, and endured sharp scrutiny from the legislature. At the eleventh hour, the faculty and trustees managed to right the institution and save it from being closed for good.

Confrontation and Investigation at the National Level in the 1870s

Daunting as they were, the travails of the Agricultural College of Pennsylvania / Pennsylvania State College on the state level were not unique among land-grant institutions. On the national level, the tribulations were even more severe. The 1870s, in fact, were a time of intense scrutiny and confrontation for the new land-grant institutions, which, after the end of the Civil War in 1865, were being established quickly in state after state, especially as the states of the former Confederacy were brought into the fold. The champion who would lead the colleges out of the political wilderness, as it were, was the man who later became Penn State's so-called second founder, the aforesaid George Atherton.

The first challenge in 1873 was a confrontation from the presidents of leading eastern colleges, particularly Princeton and Harvard. The second challenge in 1874 was an investigation of the colleges by the U.S. Congress. The third challenge in 1875 was another investigation, this time by the national Grange. Atherton, then the Vorhees Professor of Constitutional Law, History, and Political Economy at Rutgers College, would lead the colleges' collective efforts to defend themselves during these years.

The first battle lines were drawn at the August 1873 convention of the National Education Association, in Elmira, New York. President James McCosh of Princeton criticized a bill introduced a few months previous by Senator Justin Morrill to further support the land-grant colleges. McCosh called for an investigation of the schools and voiced opposition to the "principle of partiality," which the federal government demonstrated in supporting the land-grant colleges. If such grants were to be made, he argued, they should go to the strongest colleges (such as Princeton), not the weakest. He also said federal dollars should go to support secondary schools, not colleges. President Charles Eliot of Harvard called the land grants "a demoralizing use of public money." He voiced visceral opposition to all federal grants to education at any level, claiming they were injurious to the nation's democratic values of independence and self-reliance.

The response was a carefully prepared paper by Atherton, titled "The Relation of the General Government to Education." Atherton had prepared a statistical analysis of the land-grant colleges proving that they had more than justified the federal government's cost in establishing them. "The nation as a nation must educate," he thundered, arguing for a strong federal role in education. "There is no argument to prove the duty of the state governments in this respect which does not apply with at least equal force to the national government." Atherton's address was well received among his peers and positioned him as a leading spokesman for the colleges.[43]

Nevertheless, Atherton's defense of the land-grant colleges at Elmira was not sufficient to prevent the investigation McCosh had demanded. In February 1874, the U.S. House committee on Education and Labor launched its inquest. Senator Morrill asked Atherton and his colleague at Rutgers to advise the colleges as to how they should respond. Atherton prepared a circular with instructions for responding, and the result was a positive finding by the House committee: "There is no reason to believe . . . that there has been any serious mismanagement of the fund received from the United States. . . . There is nothing in the results thus far attained that can be called discouraging . . . a

FIGURE 22
George Atherton (1837–1906) in 1875, as a professor at Rutgers College; later president, The Pennsylvania State College, 1882–1906. Courtesy of The Pennsylvania State University Archives.

few of those earliest organized have already found time to take high rank among the institutions of the land."[44]

The most challenging confrontation was issued, ironically, from a new national farmers' organization, and it came on the heels of the congressional investigation. The Patrons of Husbandry, better known as the Grange, was galvanized as a potent political force by the Panic of 1873, sparked by the financial misadventures of financier Jay Cooke and his brother Henry; their bankruptcy quickly led to a nationwide depression.[45] The economic malaise was especially hard on American farmers. Although agricultural productivity increased during this time, prices for farm products declined and land values fell sharply. The result was financial ruin for many farmers, especially those on the margin. The "Great Depression," as the Panic of 1873 was called until the 1930s, cut a much wider swath through the American economy. Half of the country's railroads defaulted on their loans and thousands of workers lost their jobs. By 1878, more than ten thousand businesses had collapsed, including banks, small factories, iron furnaces, and mines. At the same time, the crisis provided golden opportunities for wealthy industrialists—John D.

Rockefeller, Andrew Carnegie, Jay Gould, and others—to consolidate their industries into huge monopolies.[46]

The Grange was founded in 1867 as a fraternal and advocacy organization to promote political power and economic benefits for farmers. By 1873, the Grange had 200,000 members. As the panic spread, Grange membership swelled to 850,000 by 1875. Its strongest support was in the eastern states, where after 1880 state Granges increased their membership by 5 percent annually over the rest of the century.[47] As historian Nathan Sorber has shown, the Grange was particularly powerful in New England. In fact, the Grange and its allies eventually muscled the Morrill Act funds away from their original institutional designees in three states: from Dartmouth to the New Hampshire College of Agriculture and the Mechanical Arts in Durham (now the University of New Hampshire) in 1891, from Yale to the Storrs Agricultural School (now the University of Connecticut at Storrs) in 1893, and from Brown to the Rhode Island College of Agriculture and Mechanical Arts at Kingston (now the University of Rhode Island) in 1894. And had it not been for the personal intervention of Senator Justin Morrill in his home state, the University of Vermont would have lost its land-grant status to a new institution.[48]

Nationally, the Grange became a militant antagonist of the land-grant colleges. It maintained that the colleges had failed farmers, particularly by producing insufficient numbers of agricultural graduates. It also argued that agricultural research should be conducted by agricultural organizations or the state, not the colleges. In fact, the Grange investigation of 1875 resulted in a report a year later with two recommendations: (1) a permanent Grange committee to monitor and report annually on the state of the land-grant colleges and (2) a demand that "the agricultural colleges ought to be under the exclusive control of the farmers of the country."[49] Accordingly, the Grange opposed the colleges' efforts at enacting the federal legislation that resulted in the Hatch Act of 1887 and the Morrill Act of 1890.[50]

Through all of this turmoil, Atherton formed a strong working relationship with Senator Morrill. The two cooperated throughout the 1870s and 1880s in drafting bill after bill to generate additional federal support for the land-grant colleges. Not until 1890 would such a bill finally succeed. Before that, however, Atherton took the lead in drafting the Hatch Act of 1887 and finding a legislative sponsor, Representative William H. Hatch of Missouri. The act established federally funded agricultural experiment stations in every state, most of them attached to land-grant colleges, but the affiliation with the colleges was not a requirement of the act, courtesy of an amendment sponsored by the Grange, which continued to oppose the colleges at every turn. The states were thus free to establish independent experiment stations, although in nearly every case circumstance dictated their affiliation with a land-grant college, where the scientific expertise and research facilities were located.[51]

The era of confrontation at the national level produced something of an unanticipated consequence: Forced to defend themselves and their purpose time after time, the land-grant colleges organized themselves into the nation's first association of peer higher education institutions. After a preliminary convention in 1885, called by the new commissioner of agriculture, Norman J. Colman, Atherton as head of the executive committee called for an organizational convention in 1887. This second conclave in Washington, D.C., formally established the Association of American Agricultural Colleges and Experiment Stations, which wielded consummate skill in negotiating a strong relationship with the federal government. In recognition of his leadership, Atherton was elected founding president of the association, serving two consecutive terms, from 1887 to 1889.[52]

After years of confrontation and challenge, the land-grant colleges turned the corner from struggle to stability around 1890. They did so largely as a result of the permanent financial underpinning provided by the federal government through the Hatch Act and Second Morrill Act.

So where was Frederick Watts in all of this? As is shown in the final chapter, Watts, as commissioner of agriculture from 1871 to 1877, strove to guide the collective development of land-grant colleges during that contentious decade, with mixed results at best. As a matter of policy, he would not directly involve the U.S. Department of Agriculture in any partisan fashion with respect to the political challenges initiated by Congress and the Grange, whose sharply critical report was issued toward the end of his tenure. While he promoted the colleges generally, his vision continued to be limited to their role as primarily agricultural schools rather than the broader industrial institutions the Morrill Act envisioned. And early on in his administration, he encountered stiff resistance when he sought to consolidate the Department of Agriculture's control over the colleges in the realm of agricultural research.

In the latter half of his departmental administration, Watts also would be challenged by the fast-deteriorating fortunes of the American farmer. In the 1850s, Watts had characterized the Pennsylvania farming community as "lethargic," lacking the class consciousness and energy to organize and agitate for political, social, and economic parity with the rest of American society. He quickly whipped the Pennsylvania State Agricultural Society into a powerful organization designed to remedy the situation. Now, ironically, the "lethargic" agricultural constituency he had worked so hard to motivate in his native state had joined forces with the national agrarian reform movement—a movement growing exponentially, as the Panic of 1873 devastated farmers nationwide. (Even as the depression bottomed out, commodity prices continued to fall. Profit from a bushel of corn fell from 45 cents in 1870 to 10 cents in 1889.)[53] Agrarian discontent was quickly organizing itself through the Grange, the National Farmers' Alliance, and other kindred bodies. Their anger fueled the populist movement, with bitter grievances over the federal government's perceived support of business interests over labor, and with long-lasting implications for American political life. Watts as commissioner of agriculture would have to overcome the agrarian community's initial negative perceptions of him as an exemplar of their despised business interests. He was, after all, both a lawyer and a railroad president, and now he was the head of a federal agency presumably designed to solve their problems and champion their cause.

CHAPTER 8

U.S. Commissioner of Agriculture

Frederick Watts's final contributions to American agriculture were made as chief executive officer of the U.S. Department of Agriculture, from August 1871 to March 1877. He did not seek the appointment but accepted it reluctantly, acquiescing only after being pressed hard by President Ulysses S. Grant as well as colleagues and friends to assume the office.

His reluctance stemmed from several factors. In 1871, he was in his sixteenth year as president of the Board of Trustees of the Agricultural College of Pennsylvania, an institution roiling from a succession of three troubled presidencies in the span of seven years and requiring his continual attention. He was in his thirtieth year as president of the Cumberland Valley Railroad, an enterprise still close to his heart. He had essentially retired from his law practice in the early 1860s, but as one of the Commonwealth's eminent lawyers and jurists, "Judge Watts" was occasionally consulted on legal matters. His civic interests, including his lay leadership in the Episcopal Church, created additional responsibilities. And though he had sold his third farm west of town in 1867, he still had two farms on the Conodoguinet Creek and a townhome and office in Carlisle to manage.

And now he was seventy years old, having attained his biblical "three score and ten" when life expectancy for white males who survived childhood was fifty-eight years.[1] The prospect of taking on new and vastly increased responsibilities at the federal level was surely daunting. Additionally, he would have to move his wife, Henrietta, to Washington, D.C., for the duration and live penuriously. In fact, among the reasons for his refusal of the initial offer was "the insufficiency of salary for that position."[2] The enabling legislation for the department had set the commissioner's salary at $3,000 annually.[3]

Nonetheless, despite his many responsibilities in Pennsylvania, Watts's lifelong interest—the improvement of American agriculture—held sway. Since the 1840s, he had worked to transform isolated, tradition-bound farmers into a potent political, social, and economic force while championing a new form of higher education that would infuse science and its benefits into their enterprise. Here was an opportunity to do even more. Resultantly, Watts was in Washington working as commissioner on August 1, 1871, his appointment being confirmed by the U.S. Senate on December 11, 1871. True to form, he was living frugally. Watts and his family, for a while at least, "occupied several rooms on the upper floors in the west end of the Department building, as living apartments."[4]

After nearly twenty years, Watts had come full circle. In 1852, the newly organized Pennsylvania State Agricultural Society, with Watts as founding

FIGURE 23
Frederick Watts, U.S. commissioner of agriculture, 1871–77. Courtesy of The Pennsylvania State University Archives.

president, appointed a committee to press Congress to establish an independent federal agricultural department. The federal government's role in agricultural improvement had begun in 1836, when the U.S. Patent Office initiated surveys designed to improve agricultural productivity. In 1837, the patent office began distributing seeds and plants, prompting Congress in 1839 to establish the Division of Agriculture, with a small appropriation, within the Patent Office. Congress continued to fund the division, focusing on increased crop production and marketability, but its efforts were deemed insufficient by the increasingly powerful agricultural societies.[5]

The pressure from Pennsylvania to establish an independent federal department was considerable. The Philadelphia Society for Promoting Agriculture added its endorsement to the initiative of Watts's state society. The resulting National Agricultural Convention, held in Washington, D.C., in July 1852, appointed Watts as a vice president. The convention became the motive force behind the establishment of the United States Agricultural Society, which in turn advocated for the establishment of a federal department of agriculture. The constitution of the U.S. Agricultural Society called for a national board of agriculture, the membership of which would be appointed by the various state agricultural societies. The Pennsylvania State Agricultural Society appointed three members: Watts, McAllister, and John Ewing.[6] Thus Watts and his Pennsylvania colleagues played a role in the seminal events that led to the eventual establishment of the U.S. Department of Agriculture in 1862.

Watts was the third commissioner of the department. He succeeded Horace Capron, who had resigned to oversee the development of agriculture for the Japanese Empire, shortly after that nation's government had been reconstituted under the Meiji Restoration of 1868. Like Watts, Capron was a champion of industrial colleges. "I am confident that these institutions are destined to become a vital power in the land and to wield an influence which colleges weighted with a 'curriculum' of studies of classical ages can never exert," Capron said in his final annual report. He called for a congressionally authorized commission, under the direction of the Department of Agriculture, to conduct a detailed study of the existing colleges to benefit those institutions still in the formative stage.[7] The idea for the commission died with Capron's departure, however. Watts did not revive the idea, as he had a different agenda for the land-grant colleges.

The national agricultural community greeted Watts's appointment with something less than unabated glee. He was not Grant's first choice; it was rumored he angled for the appointment by his obsequiousness with Grant on a fishing trip, though his reluctance in taking the post would seem to belie such a story. And despite his prominence in Pennsylvania, Watts lacked national stature. Additionally, his professions as both lawyer and railroad company president were anathema to farmers and the agricultural press beyond Pennsylvania's borders.[8] Further, his leadership as board president of the troubled Agricultural College of Pennsylvania and its struggling experimental farms did not sit well with farmers, particularly in southeastern Pennsylvania.

Criticism also came from later writers. A historian writing in the 1940s summarily dismissed Watts's six years of leadership. "His primary interest was railroading, and he permitted Department work rather to slide along as best it might under the supervision of his son, who in turn delegated his responsibility to the chief clerk," the historian wrote, adding that "Watts practiced picayune economy but had little interest in farm buildings."[9] It should be noted, however, that within two years of his commissionership Watts quit his presidency of the Cumberland Valley Railroad, in October 1873. The charge that he had little interest in farm buildings seems particularly strange. Farm buildings, per se, were a matter beyond the purview of the national commissioner, and, in any event, Watts had devoted considerable thought and creativity to improved designs for farms and barns throughout his life.

The most unflattering critique, however, was turned in by a former employee of the department, writing at the beginning of the twentieth century:

> Commissioner Frederick W. Watts . . . was well advanced in years at the time of his appointment in the Commissionership. Partly for this reason, and partly because he failed to grasp the fundamental purpose for which the Department was really created, he failed to comprehend the possibilities of the work of the Department, believing that the seed distribution to be the main feature of its usefulness. He inaugurated no new work, and spent but little time in his office at the Department, leaving the conduct of the official work to the Chief Clerk, his son, who, in turn, because of chronic inebriety, shifted the burden of responsibility to a favorite clerk in his own office who practically ran the Department. This statement is absolutely true. The redeeming characteristic of Judge Watts' official life was economy in the service. He believed that the people's money should not be wasted in useless expenditures and he practiced this

> gospel at all times, when in personal supervision of departmental affairs, which unfortunately was comparatively seldom. As an illustration, he would occasionally go into the large packing room in the basement of the main building and quietly observe the employees tie up bundles of seed and when he saw a man, in cutting his string, have a long end, he would call him down good and hard, also the room superintendent who permitted the wastefulness. He lived up to this same idea in other small things entering into the daily affairs of the Department, like furniture, stationery, etc., demanding that all purchases be made as economically as possible, both as to price and quantity.[10]

It is difficult to discern the motives behind such a negative characterization. The employee, Frank P. Evans, was hired in 1875, rather late in Watts's tenure, to work in the mailing room of the seed division. Within a few months, Watts promoted him to the statistical division. In 1890, Evans was appointed cashier and in 1893 was named chief, division of accounts, a post he held until his resignation in 1906. In any case, the complaint is in certain ways suspect. Consider the charge that Watts "failed to grasp the fundamental purpose for which the Department was really created . . . believing that the seed distribution to be the main feature of its usefulness." In point of fact, seed distribution *was* a major goal of the department. Its enabling legislation in 1862 posited a twofold mission: "to acquire and to diffuse among the people of the United States useful information on subjects connected with agriculture in the most general and comprehensive sense of that word, and to procure, propagate, and distribute among the people new and valuable seeds and plants."[11] Watts took the seed distribution mandate seriously and expanded the program liberally—an imperative he viewed as especially important to the recovering South and the developing West.

The complaint against Watts's son—Frederick Watts Jr., an 1862 alumnus of the Agricultural College, having earned the bachelor of scientific agriculture degree—also bears scrutiny. In 1873, Watts appointed his thirty-year-old son as chief clerk, a position not created by Watts gratuitously but mandated by the enabling legislation. This was long before federal civil service reform was written into law. Nonetheless, one newspaper complained that the department's offices were now "all in the family."[12] Another newspaper painted a different picture entirely. It observed that Watts the younger gave "great satisfaction to all with whom he is brought in contact in the discharge of his official duties. How onerous these are, may be inferred from the fact that the

Department is in receipt of from one to three thousand letters daily, many of which require the personal attention of the chief clerk, on whom also chiefly devolves the duty of receiving the calls and attending to the applications of persons having business with the Department, toward whom he exhibits a uniform courtesy and affability which makes him deservedly popular."[13]

Finally, Evans's charge that Watts "inaugurated no new work" is demonstrably suspect, as is shown later.

One of the more intriguing aspects of Watts's tenure as commissioner, however, was his agenda for the nearly three dozen agricultural or industrial colleges (eventually called land-grant colleges) then coming into existence—an agenda entirely overlooked by his several biographical profilers.

The enabling legislation for the colleges, the Morrill Act of 1862, had been passed only nine years before Watts took office as commissioner. Aside from the three state-sponsored agricultural colleges that had been brought into some stage of actual operation by the eve of the Civil War, the development of additional state-sponsored schools had been stopped cold by the conflict. Several other agricultural colleges in the Midwest and Northeast had been chartered in the late 1850s. But they were unable to open for instruction before the outbreak of hostilities and would not get into operation until the war's end. Additionally, the Morrill Act barred those states in "rebellion or insurrection against . . . the United States" from qualifying for the act's benefits.[14]

By the late 1860s and early 1870s, the rush was on to establish new colleges. At the outset of his tenure, Watts felt it imperative to bring the fledgling institutions into what he termed a "cooperative" working relationship with the equally new Department of Agriculture. In addition, he presented brief commentary and extensive data on the year-to-year progress of the colleges in each of his annual reports, though he continued to construe them as essentially agricultural colleges rather than the broader institutions the Morrill Act envisioned. The Morrill Act required the colleges to make annual reports of their progress, including statistical information, to be sent to all sister colleges and the U.S. secretary of the interior. The U.S. commissioner of agriculture also was required to make an annual report to both the president of the United States and the Congress. The first commissioner, Isaac Newton, incorporated a section on agricultural colleges in his annual reports, a practice that continued with his successors, Horace Capron and Frederick Watts.

After making summary comments about the colleges in his annual reports, Watts published each college's report in a lengthy section titled "Progress of Industrial Education." As a whole, these reports detailed the growth and development of the new land-grant colleges at a time when they were coming under increasing scrutiny and criticism from the private college presidents, Congress, and the Grange. Watts would not embroil the Department of Agriculture in political fights with the latter two organizations, but he did take umbrage at the first volley of criticism leveled against the colleges at the National Education Association Convention of 1873.

"This Department has never been unmindful of the expression which Congress gave to its purpose to improve the condition of the agriculturist by the act of 1862, which made provision for the establishment of a college in every State of the Union, whereby he may obtain scientific knowledge, and thereby elevate his calling to that standard which will give him a place in the race of competition in which all the world is engaged," Watts wrote in his 1874 report.

> I have taken much pains . . . to promote this great object, because it cannot and should not be concealed that the purely literary institutions of the country are hostile to the success of what they please to call a "new education." Indeed, the president of one of the most distinguished of these institutions . . . at an educational convention at Elmira, N.Y., took occasion to condemn the entire policy of the national and State governments regarding scientific and industrial education. There is perhaps no employment on earth which so constantly brings into requisition the principles of science as that of agriculture, and the Representatives of the people can render no better service to the cause of humanity and universal prosperity than to educate the farmer.[15]

The Chicago Convention of 1871

Coincident with the beginning of Watts's appointment as commissioner was the first national gathering of the "friends of agricultural education." Assuming office on August 1, 1871, Watts had no role in planning the conclave, nor did he attend. Held August 24–25, 1871, in Chicago, the meeting had the earmarks of a newly self-conscious movement of American industrial colleges bearing a distinctive identity as federally sponsored institutions with a shared mission and constituency. Representatives of twelve agricultural colleges and a kindred institution in Ontario invited the presidents of agricultural colleges, professors of agriculture, and other interested persons "for the purpose of organizing, consulting and cooperating in the great work of advancing the cause of agricultural knowledge and education, especially by experimentation with similar crops under similar conditions at all the agricultural colleges."[16]

Twenty-nine delegates showed up, including a number of college presidents. John M. Gregory, the chief executive of the Illinois Industrial University (later the University of Illinois at Urbana-Champaign), was elected president of the convention. The president of the Agricultural College of Pennsylvania, James Calder, who had assumed office a few months earlier, did not attend, but John Hamilton, a recent graduate of the Agricultural College and newly appointed professor of agriculture at the same school, did participate. In fact, Hamilton and a professor of botany at Cornell were elected as the two secretaries of the convention.

Most of the discussion centered on agricultural research and experimentation. How could the colleges, as a collective force, cooperate in planning and executing research on a national scale? A committee submitted a plan that called for experiments testing "the variation of soil on adjacent plats, the planting of corn in hills and drills, and the uniform application of manures on adjacent plats."[17]

The delegates then veered into the murky arena of agricultural education: What to teach and how best to teach it? Writing years later, Hamilton recalled: "Agricultural education at that time was new in this country. There were no suitable textbooks to be had and few courses of study to use as a guide. What we adopted [at the Agricultural College of Pennsylvania] was wholly of my devising." He recalled the Chicago Convention of 1871 and said, "I put the question as to the duties of a professor of agriculture and could get no satisfactory definition."[18]

The delegates also discussed the desirability of forming a permanent organization, meeting at least annually to discuss experimental work and even becoming "an organization of agricultural colleges and technological schools." But a motion to that effect was laid on the table, and there the matter ended.

The topic of agricultural research stations then took center stage. A resolution came forth praising the examples of European agricultural research stations and called for "not less than one such station in each of the several states." The convention called for a committee to petition Congress and the states "for the speedy establishment of such stations throughout the country."[19]

Watts's 1872 Convention of Industrial Colleges

On December 20, 1871, nine days after his Senate confirmation as commissioner, Watts issued a call for a national convention of agricultural policymakers related to the industrial colleges. He asked for a wider swath of representation than had been in attendance at Chicago: two delegates from each agricultural college, state agricultural society, and state board of agriculture to convene in Washington, D.C., on February 15, 1872. The response was robust: Delegates, including many college presidents and agricultural scientists, came from thirty-two states, three territories, and the District of Columbia. The sponsor of the land-grant college act, Senator Justin Morrill of Vermont, and the patron of New York's land-grant college, Ezra Cornell, were among the luminaries in attendance. Delegates from the Keystone State included President James Calder of the Agricultural College of Pennsylvania, who was elected secretary of the convention; trustee McAllister; and professor of agriculture John Hamilton. George Loring was elected president of the convention. Loring was a bit miffed because, as president of a *regional* society—the New England Agricultural Society—rather than a state society, he had not been among one of the three groups explicitly invited to attend. The resulting ambivalence and even anger about which delegates would be credentialed added a sour note to the convention's first day.

Watts gave the convention's introductory address. He explained that the meeting's central purpose was to bring about the cooperation of the colleges, state agricultural societies, and boards of agriculture with the U.S. Department of Agriculture, which he construed as "a head separated from a body." He said that the people "in their aggregate capacity, in the shape of agricultural societies and colleges and horticultural societies, were the great body of agriculture, and this Department a separate head." He lamented that "there is no co-operation between us at all." Then he announced his agenda, telling the delegates "you have been brought together here mainly for the purpose, almost exclusively, for creating this system of co-operation between this head of agriculture and your body."[20] This directive caused immediate dissension among the delegates, as the call Watts had issued in December characterized the convention more generally as a "consultation between friends of these interests . . . for the purpose of conferring upon subjects of mutual interests."[21] Delegates inferred that Watts wanted the Department of Agriculture to control colleges and agricultural societies as subordinate institutions.

At that early point, Watts lost control of his agenda as the delegates took matters in a different direction. In particular, the agricultural college representatives and their allies controlled the discussion and focused on the issues they deemed of greatest importance. As a result, the convention's business committee created a new agenda with four items: (1) the need to petition Congress for additional land grants to support the colleges, (2) the importance of establishing experimental farms and research stations, (3) the modification of mandated military instruction in the colleges, and (4) in a concession to Watts, the issue of cooperation between the various agricultural organizations and the federal department.[22]

In another concession to Watts, the business committee asked him to read to the full convention a paper that he had submitted to the same committee. The paper not only reflected his sense of what the convention should consider but also revealed his philosophy of what land-grant education should be and should do. In sum, Watts viewed the colleges as mainly agricultural institutions, guided by scientific principles, devoted to the business of "educating farmers." He called for agricultural colleges to embrace several principles: (1) That the institutions should be "instinctively agricultural in their government and teachings." While not excluding other fields of learning articulated by the Morrill Act, the "main design" should be a knowledge of natural science and practical skill that contribute to "a finished agricultural education." (2) That manual labor should be "practiced and taught." (3) That females "be admitted as pupils."

In his push for cooperation, Watts also advised that horticultural and agricultural societies and agricultural colleges "should unite on any plan of education." Finally, he recommended that the department of agriculture establish a relationship with such organizations to facilitate "a continuous exchange of information, seeds, roots, plants, and publications as shall be mutually advantageous."[23]

Watts's presentation was largely ignored. The convention instead turned its attention to the matter of additional land grants to the colleges. In fact, discussion of that topic alone consumed half of the convention's time. Delegates discussed a variety of ideas, ranging from grants of five hundred thousand to two million acres per state, or perhaps splitting the proceeds among common schools, normal schools (teacher education), and land-grant colleges, as John Gregory of the Illinois Industrial University recommended. A resolution was introduced asking Congress to donate to each land-grant institution an additional one million acres of land. Nothing passed until Senator Morrill generalized the intent with a resolution that finally met with approval: "that, as a sense of this convention, we deem it of paramount importance to ask of Congress . . . for an additional donation of land, or proceeds of land, sufficient to found a professorship of some of the branches of practical science in each of the colleges now . . . sustained by the previous land grant of Congress." The same resolution petitioned the War Department to assign an officer to teach military instruction at each land-grant college.[24]

Morrill's resolution for additional land grants drew strong opposition from other quarters, however. Representatives of state agricultural societies, whose attendance at the convention far outnumbered the college delegations, showed little regard for the new institutions. Skeptical of the colleges' management and commitment to agricultural education, they called for a committee of "intelligent practical farmers" at each land-grant college "to assist in the examination of the agricultural classes . . . and that no graduate . . . shall receive a diploma till he shall pass a satisfactory examination before such committee."[25] The resolution did not pass, but it foreshadowed the attempts by the Grange a few years later to exert similar control over the colleges.

Watts did not speak to the resolution for farmers to examine prospective graduates. Neither did he voice support for the resolution petitioning Congress for additional land grants. In fact, it was said that Watts in private conversations at the convention "washed his hands" of the proposal for additional land grants.[26]

The matter of agricultural experiment stations generated further momentum with the report of a committee (in cooperation with the Chicago committee) that included the noted chemist Samuel Johnson—Pugh's lifelong friend and confidant who was rapidly building his reputation as the "doyen of American agricultural science."[27] John Hamilton of the Agricultural College of Pennsylvania was part of this five-man committee as well. The report emphasized the importance of quickly establishing experiment stations across the nation, through the efforts of not only the colleges but also individuals, agricultural societies, the states, and, of course, the federal government. It cited the contributions of European research stations in advancing agricultural productivity and noted that American stations cannot be self-supporting. "Experiments cost money," the report said. "Stations must be procured, equipped, set in operation, and kept in operation permanently. They require continual outlay of labor and money, and return nothing but information and ideas."[28] In general, however, the report was devoid of specific requirements for the stations. Johnson was asked to prepare a further report on the value of such stations, to be published by Watts's department.

Nevertheless, in the span of six months, the seeds had been planted for the harvest of American agricultural experiment stations to come, though it would take years of unrelenting effort. The first state-sponsored agricultural experiment station would be established by Johnson in 1875, in Middletown, Connecticut. Desultory efforts were made by agricultural colleges in various states to follow suit, including an unsuccessful attempt by the Pennsylvania State College. Not until the federal Hatch Act of 1887, drafted and promoted most vigorously by George Atherton of Penn State, would the agricultural experiment station movement be chartered nationally and sustained with annual federal appropriations.[29]

In addition to the major agenda items, other matters were brought up and discussed briefly at the Washington convention. The topics included the destruction of timber resources, the importance of entomological research, the elevation of the department's commissionership to full cabinet status, and more. For the delegates, the convention ended on a positive note, but not for Watts. For him, the convention had been hijacked and his central issue of "cooperation" largely ignored. To many of the delegates, including the colleges, Watts's priorities smacked of intrusive control. In particular, Watts's plan would have made the department of agriculture the collector, adjudicator, and broker of the land-grant colleges' research agendas. The colleges balked mightily and Watts's effort failed ignominiously, impairing his credibility and relationship with the land-grant colleges at the outset of his commissionership. The convention resolved to meet again in a year, but Watts refused "either to unite with the [convention's] Committee in the call . . . or to allow the Convention to assemble within the walls of the Agricultural Department." Ironically, without the support of Watts, the de facto association of colleges and societies fell apart.[30]

Despite his rebuff by the Washington convention, Watts continued his quest for coordination and control, although realizing he had to do it with the proverbial carrot rather than the stick. In May 1872, he sent a circular to representatives in every county in every state, appointing them as a "competent reporter" to respond to inquiries from the department about "the amount and quality of crops, numbers, conditions, etc., of farm stock, and any other subjects connected with local general agriculture." Watts intended to send frequent questionnaires to the reporters to gain such information. Nevertheless, he knew he could not compel any responses. Thus he appealed to the "public spirit of intelligent and progressive farmers" as his "only resource" for the information. In return, he offered to reward the reporters by "a generous remembrance in the distribution of seeds, monthly and annual reports, and by all other practical courtesies."[31]

As for the land-grant colleges, Watts in the autumn of 1872 sought to elicit detailed information by sending "interrogatories"—the responses to which he would publish "in order to aid these Institutions, to keep the country advised of their progress, and induce Congress to appreciate their importance." In addition to some general questions (number of faculty and students, status of the library, value of the land-grant fund), the vast majority of the sixteen questions were related to the agricultural mission of the college (e.g., "What system of plowing, manuring, and general cultivation has been practiced with the most marked success?" "What experiments have been conducted on the farm the present year?" "What number of students have been graduated in the agricultural course of study since the opening of the College, and how many have engaged in agricultural pursuits?" etc.).[32] The questionnaires further illustrate his conception of the colleges as predominantly agricultural institutions and little else.

After the Washington Convention, there would be no other such gathering of land-grant college leaders until Watts was out of office. The next conclave took place December 27–28, 1877, in Columbus, Ohio. The delegates discussed courses of study, military training, the aim and scope of land-grant education, and an increased congressional appropriation.[33] No further national conventions of agricultural college presidents and scientists were held in Washington, however, until 1883. Two years later, the new commissioner of agriculture, Norman J. Colman, issued a call for a new convention to convene on July 8–10, 1885. This would come to be known as the "preliminary convention" of what two years later would become the formally established Association of American Agricultural Colleges and Experiment Stations—the first formal organization of peer higher education institutions in the United States. Atherton of Penn State was elected as its founding president, serving two years, 1887–89.[34] And the additional federal aid for land-grant colleges, after several bills failed during the 1870s and 1880s, would finally arrive in 1890—the Second Morrill Act, providing annual federal appropriations (rather than land grants) to each college for the full range of academic programs.[35]

Illustrating the Progress of Industrial Colleges

During his tenure as commissioner, Watts continued to focus attention on the development of agricultural or industrial colleges. In his first annual report for the year 1871 (dated November 15, 1871, but published in 1872), industrial education was the first topic he addressed. His conception of "industrial colleges," however, would remain unchanged. He would maintain that their primary orientation should be agricultural, focused on the provision of education for farmers and scientific research designed to elevate their enterprise.

"These institutions are about to perform a most important part in the destinies of their country," Watts said. "They are yet in their infancy; professors and teachers are themselves untaught; agricultural education in this land is a new idea which has but now struck the public mind and is yet to be matured." Presaging his priorities for the Washington convention he would soon organize, he observed that

> if these institutions will but confer together, and adopt such principles of action as shall be common to them all; establish subjects of study and rules of discipline and graduation . . . and recognize and act upon the fact that this Department and they are engaged in the prosecution of a common cause, and the Department may be made the nucleus around which may be collected the knowledge of inventions, statistics, and rare facts, new and improved seeds and plants, to be disseminated, distributed, and experimented upon by the instrumentality of the agricultural colleges, the farmer will be benefitted to a degree which will be felt throughout every vein and artery of our common country.

Ominous as it would soon prove for the convention, Watts called for the colleges' experimental results to be conveyed systematically to the Department of Agriculture to be further analyzed and published for the benefit of the farming class. "An intimate relation between this department and the agricultural colleges of the country would produce the most profitable information," he declared.[36]

Watts also would hold fast to the idea that industrial colleges retain their distinctiveness from traditional colleges by mandating student labor. Even though the manual labor requirement was soon to be eliminated (for the second time) at his own college, Watts believed that every student should be required to perform compulsory labor for at least twelve hours a week, "thus training their tastes and habits, and inuring them to the daily occupations of a farmer's life, and thus, also answering the objections often made to agricultural colleges, that their graduates at last choose business or professional life."[37]

In his section on the progress of industrial education, Watts reported that the United States could now boast thirty-two industrial colleges and universities, twenty-six of which were in operation, with the rest expected to follow suit in 1872. As a whole, they employed 310 professors educating more than 2,000 students. Of particular interest was the urgency of the former Confederate states in establishing their institutions: Arkansas on March 27, 1871; Texas on April 17, 1871; Alabama on February 26, 1872; Virginia on March 19, 1872, establishing two racially segregated institutions; and Georgia on March 30, 1872.[38]

Watts also included a section devoted to the progress of women in industrial colleges—the first and only time the topic would be addressed formally by the department under his leadership: "We are inaugurating a new era in industrial education. . . . Is not here an open door for a radical reformation of female education?" He praised the "free and progressive" western states for being wide open to the admission of women but complained that in the eastern states "the sex is knocking persistently for permission to enter." But that knock was beginning to be heard, he added. Vermont's agricultural college had decided to admit women beginning in 1872. In Pennsylvania, he noted, "women were not received . . . for twelve years of its existence. After careful consideration of the question, the trustees decided that they could not take the responsibility of denying its advantages to half the youth of the State, and voted, in 1871, to admit both sexes upon equal conditions."[39]

Watts then ventured beyond his philosophical musings on the admission of women. After describing the heavy workload of farm women, he made suggestions as to how an agricultural college could offer a curriculum of applied science that would profit them greatly:

> There are industrial arts which have been, and probably will continue to be, measurably controlled by women. The care of the farm dairy, the preservation of fruits, the preparation of fruits for markets, the keeping of bees and poultry, the care of the flower-garden, and sometimes the management of the vegetable garden, will continue to furnish congenial and profitable occupation to women; and in all these avocations, applied

> science will enhance skill and more certainly insure success. A practical education, if supplemented with a knowledge of what is essential in literary and polite accomplishments, will deepen and intensify female charms of mind and person in all healthful and rightly constituted society.[40]

But here, once again, Watts revealed his conception of industrial colleges as being primarily agricultural institutions, for women as well as men. He seems not to have grasped the broader purposes of the Morrill Act. Alternatively, it could be argued that Watts was commissioner of agriculture, not higher education, and thus his deepest interest would of necessity be centered on the agricultural character of the colleges.

In his report for 1872, Watts observed that twenty-three of the thirty-seven states in the Union had sold all of their land scrip, totaling 6,120,000 acres for a total of $4,126,000. That amounted to about 67 cents per acre, far lower than what had been hoped for and far less than the standard U.S. government benchmark of $1.25 per acre.

But now thirty-eight industrial colleges were established in thirty-five states, including two each in Massachusetts, Mississippi, and Virginia. All were in operation save those of five states—Florida, Indiana, North Carolina, Ohio, and Texas. Faculty had grown by 13 percent, to 350, and student enrollment had swelled by 50 percent to 3,000.

The academic credentials of the presidents of these industrial colleges, as listed in the statistical table for 1872, are particularly intriguing. Of the thirty-five colleges reporting, fifteen of them—nearly 43 percent—were led by *ministers* with the Doctor of Divinity (D.D.) degree.[41] Evan Pugh might have rolled over in his grave at this happenstance. Pugh had fiercely maintained that the president of an industrial college must be "a scientific man . . . because the expenditures for *material, as auxiliaries to study* in a Scientific College must always be great, and they are such as can only be properly *regulated, encouraged* and *controlled* by a scientific man."[42] At the time of Watts's 1872 report, the presidency of the Agricultural College of Pennsylvania had been recently assumed by a minister, the Reverend James Calder, D.D. (an appointment in which Watts had played the leading role), and the Calder presidency eventually drove the institution to the brink of extinction. One can only speculate as to how the appointment of so many other Protestant divines might have retarded the development of their nascent land-grant colleges as well—particularly during a decade when they came under heavy criticism and needed presidents conversant with industrial education and the science and engineering that underlay it.

A year later, Watts's report for 1873 showed appreciable gains in the sale of land scrip—to 7,868,473 acres totaling $10,560,263 in revenue for the collective endowment principal, a 156 percent gain in value in a year's time. Watts also provided a snapshot of the overall economic value of the colleges: "All the states . . . have added something to the congressional land-scrip grant . . . in buildings, lands, and apparatus, yet several States have contributed largely in money. . . . The amount these colleges have received as donations from the States, counties, towns, and individuals is $7,292,841 . . . for every $100 given to these colleges by the Government the people have contributed $69, or more than two-thirds as much. The entire property of all colleges is valued at $17,535,475."[43]

Total faculty had increased 9 percent, to 389, while enrollments had climbed 30 percent, to 3,917. In the span of two years, enrollments had fairly doubled, from 2,000 to nearly 4,000, while gains in faculty had been much smaller by comparison.

Among the college reports, that of the Agricultural College of Pennsylvania noted the drag on the college's finances presented by the experimental farms. Though the endowment was said to produce about $30,000 per year, "so large are the drafts on this for carrying on the three experimental farms that the faculty, consisting of seven professors, including the president, and three assistants, receive only $11,300 for their services during the year."[44]

Watts's 1874 report showed that thirty-six of the thirty-seven states (Nevada the lone exception) had established thirty-nine industrial colleges. The number of professors grew to 435, a gain of 12 percent, but student enrollments declined by 6 percent, dropping to 3,669.[45] The decrease likely reflected the effects of the Panic of 1873, which was especially harmful to agriculture. It is possible, too, that the rising tide of criticism of the colleges—from the National Education Association Convention of 1873 and the impending congressional investigation, news of which was carried by the nation's newspapers and magazines, and the vociferously angry Grange—affected enrollments as well.

Watts's 1875 report reflected a slight growth in faculty and students (a gain of only thirty-four) to 3,703. He reported that the total number of graduates of land-grant colleges since 1862 was 1,524. He rationalized the slowdown in growth as due to the older colleges having "settled down upon a fixed policy of requiring of their students a thorough scientific and practical education in the principles of agriculture and the mechanic arts. The prevalent idea seems to be, that it is better to educate a few thoroughly than many superficially, with the belief that those thus educated will diffuse agricultural intelligence among the farmers around them."[46]

In this same document, Watts incorporated a report on agricultural experiment stations in Europe, with an eye to reviving interest on the part of the federal government in establishing similar facilities across America. The report was drafted by Wilbur O. Atwater, who had received his Ph.D. at Yale under Samuel Johnson and had earlier delivered a preliminary report at the Washington Convention of 1872. In 1875, Atwater was appointed to conduct a two-year program of agricultural experimentation, funded by the Connecticut state legislature, at Wesleyan University in Middletown. Two years later, this fledgling experimental station would become, with the legislature's support, the Connecticut Agricultural Experiment Station, under Johnson's direction, and moved to Yale.[47]

Atwater's report traced the growth of experiment stations across the whole of Europe, from the first in 1852 at Moeckern, near Leipzig, to sixty-two by 1872 and seventy-nine by 1876. Most were in Germany, with fifty stations, followed by Italy with thirteen. In addition to the seventy-nine, there were twenty-nine "other agricultural laboratories" in Europe, including three in England. "Their success has been most remarkable and the fruits of their work have already reached a value beyond calculation," Atwater said, in hopes that America would soon follow suit.[48]

It would take America twelve more years to do so, however, courtesy of the federal Hatch Act of 1887. Nonetheless, Watts as commissioner and advocate of scientific agriculture did what he could to provide visibility for the movement. He is credited by the historian of Pennsylvania agriculture for being "influential in developing public sentiment for the establishment of Agricultural Experiment Stations."[49]

By 1876, the year of Watts's last report, the nation's industrial colleges had recovered somewhat from the dip in enrollments two years prior. Faculty now stood at 473 and students at 4,211—a gain of nearly 15 percent. Watts was still sensitive to the constant criticism that land-grant colleges were not graduating many agricultural (and engineering) students, however. He addressed the situation by pointing to current impediments but offering, perhaps too optimistically, that the problem would correct itself over time:

> The number of students pursuing agricultural or mechanical studies is much smaller in proportion to the number in attendance than in others. This may be owing to several causes. In some cases the colleges have been recently established, and have not yet been brought into practical working order; in others the students were poorly prepared when they entered, in consequence of the low standard of education in the surrounding country; and in others inducements were greater to enter upon other courses of study which seemed to promise more immediate profit; but these embarrassments are gradually becoming less, and when agriculture and the mechanic arts require higher qualifications for their practice and become more remunerative, they will, no doubt, disappear entirely. Some of the colleges have already attained a high standard of excellence, considering the time they have been in operation and the fact that they have largely to educate their own educators.[50]

The case of the Pennsylvania State College bears this out. In the 1878–79 catalogue, the institution published a list of all alumni who had graduated with baccalaureate degrees, from 1861 through 1878. Of the ninety-five alumni, a plurality—forty-four—had earned the bachelor of agriculture degree, although most of them had graduated in the earlier years of the 1860s. And of the forty-four agriculture alumni, only twelve were listed occupationally as farmers. Most agriculture graduates had gone into other professions, as lawyers, druggists, coal dealers, physicians, chemists, iron manufacturers, and so on.[51]

The final verdict on Commissioner Watts's relationship with the colleges is mixed. Historian Alan I. Marcus says that Watts's vision of a unified, or at least coordinated, national system of agricultural policy organizations "stressed the elevation of colleges to the first rank." Agricultural college presidents and faculties supported his position that the colleges (and, eventually, their experiment stations) should be the primary research organizations within the states as opposed to state agricultural societies. But they opposed Watts's efforts to make the colleges and their research agendas subordinate to the department of agriculture, under his control. Among practical farmers, however, Watts came to be regarded as "an object of derision and scorn." This animus emanated from his "blatant disregard for farmer-dominated institutions such as state agricultural societies."[52] This purported loss of esteem with the farming community presented yet another major irony for Watts, given his earlier work as founding president of the Pennsylvania State Agricultural Society. In that role, and long after, he strove to inculcate class consciousness and political activism among practical farmers so as to elevate their standing in society. With respect to the various actors on the stage of agricultural higher education and research in the 1870s, Watts was battered and buffeted by competing interests. Nevertheless, he continued to champion the colleges—albeit with a limited vision of what the Morrill Act intended them to be—as well as the experiment station movement.

Major Priorities as Commissioner

Watts's work with the agricultural or industrial colleges was only one facet of his tenure as commissioner. His other priorities included: (1) a vastly expanded seed distribution program across the American agricultural community, (2) an initiative to help rebuild the agriculturally devastated South, (3) the establishment of a new microscopy division within the department, with a focus on studying parasitic fungi that advanced the systematic study of plant diseases, (4) the drawing of attention to the rapid deforestation of the United States and the inauguration of the program that grew into the U.S. Forest Service, (5) a comprehensive response to the grasshopper plagues destroying crops in the western states, and (6) the design of extensive exhibits showcasing the progress of American agriculture for the U.S. Centennial Exhibition in Philadelphia in 1876. Throughout his tenure, he managed an underfunded federal agency frugally, without a hint of scandal, during a presidential administration characterized by graft and corruption. And through new monthly reports (in addition to annual reports), he provided information to American farmers on a timelier basis.

Expansion of the Seed Distribution Program

Watts saw the seed distribution program as a central purpose of the Department of Agriculture—one of two major missions set forth in the enabling legislation of 1862: "to procure, propagate and distribute among the people new and valuable seeds and plants."[53] Watts interpreted that mandate liberally and expanded the program significantly. Although he was constantly searching for new seeds and plants, that search did not preclude the dissemination of those that were merely "valuable," in and of themselves, and not necessarily "new"—an improved variety, perhaps. Familiar as he was with federal and state legislation benefiting industrial and mercantile interests, he sought over his lifetime to create similar support for the agrarian interest, and an expanded seed distribution program fit this purpose perfectly well, he determined. "There is, perhaps, no occupation in life which so greatly needs the fostering care of the Government as that of farming," he wrote in his first annual report.[54] And taking office only six years after the Civil War, Watts was greatly concerned with rejuvenating the agriculture of the South and facilitating the settlement of the West, as the Homestead Act of 1862 was intended to do. An expanded seed distribution program was an essential means to those ends.

Seed distribution increased sharply under Watts's leadership. About thirty varieties were sent out annually. In his first year, for example, 26,000 quarts of wheat seed were mailed. In 1876, near the end of his tenure, 67,000 quarts were disseminated, an increase of 158 percent. But Watts sought to do more than merely distribute seeds and plants. He wanted the recipients to send back reports of what worked and what did not so that the results could be recorded and checked.[55] Watts also put an emphasis on quality as well as quantity. "It has been a special employment of this Department to seek to obtain seeds of a superior quality, appropriate them to the climate best adapted to their profitable use, and place them in the hands of the careful cultivator, upon the sole condition that he will correctly advise the Department of their success or failure."[56] Had things gone as Watts intended, this reciprocal program might have amounted to a continuous national quality improvement program on a grand scale, but the program failed, as few reports of success or failure were returned to the department.

Despite the expansion of the program, Watts was constantly haunted by the methods of distribution. The system he favored, and the system in place when he took office, was to have packages of seeds mailed by congressmen through their franking privilege to farmers in their districts, thus keeping the U.S. government "visible" to its constituents while saving the department the large expense of distribution. This was a time-consuming, onerous process for the congressional staffs, however, and their compliance was uneven at best. Watts also believed the amounts distributed were insufficient. "I am satisfied that the mode [of distribution] heretofore pursued is erroneous," he said in his first report. "The quantity sent is entirely too small even for an experiment. A pint or a quart of wheat or oats, or other cereal, cannot be successfully grown, and such experiments almost uniformly fail because the quantity is too small."[57]

In 1872, for instance, Watts chastised John Hamilton, professor of agriculture at the Agricultural College of Pennsylvania, for planning "small plot" experiments for seeds rather than a larger scale. "When the Department obtains a seed which it has reason to believe is an improved one, and desires to propagate it, it can not do so by putting two or three quarts of it into the hands of an individual," Watts said. "My conviction is that so small a quantity of grain will not grow successfully any where, and hence my fears of the satisfactory result of your small plot experiments . . . my idea was to put a larger quantity, say 20 bushels of seed into the hands of some one in whom I had confidence that it would be carefully cultivated and the proceeds returned to the Department, upon terms that would fully compensate the grower."[58]

In his last report, Watts recommended a cheaper, more efficient method of sending seeds. Rather than quart bags, which cost $24.70 per thousand, he wanted a "paper box" that would be more convenient and safer, costing $8.20 per box. He proposed to buy a machine for $5,000 to make the boxes, which over time would save the government "from $5,000 to $7,000 per year."[59]

During his tenure, the franking privilege allowing congressmen to send seeds and information free of charge was in danger of being revoked. Watts was infuriated on two grounds, philosophical and financial. "It takes from him [the farmer] the impression that he has a representative here who cares for his wants and necessities." Further, if Congress were to make its usual appropriation to the department for seeds and documents without a subvention to Congress for distribution, "then the present clerical force of this Department must be increased by at least six clerks" to handle the workload.[60]

Notwithstanding the several challenges to increased seed distribution, Watts deemed the program a success. "A correspondence with all parts of the country gives me the assurance of the wonderfully beneficial results which have been attained by this distribution of superior seeds," Watts proclaimed in 1875. "I do not hesitate to say that the crops of wheat and oats in this country have been increased many millions of bushels by reason of the qualities of seeds distributed by this Department."[61]

The department's finances reflect Watts's priority on seed distribution. In 1872, Watts's department spent $179,339. The highest amount, $68,814, went for salaries. The second-highest amount, $45,000, was spent on seeds.[62] Even as the department's budget increased incrementally, this spending pattern—salaries first, seeds second—held constant over his tenure.

When Watts left office, his successor, William G. LeDuc, immediately undid his extensive seed distribution program. "The distribution embraced very many common vegetable and flower seeds, and finding no authority in the provisions of the organic law of the department for the distribution of these, or indeed any other description of seeds than those which were 'new and valuable,' I deemed it my duty to limit the distribution to such seeds as were clearly within the meaning of the law."[63] LeDuc pointed to a section of the law that defined "new and valuable" as meaning "rare and uncommon." He also took what was left of the program out of Congress's hands for distribution and returned that process to the department where it could be systematically regulated.[64] Notwithstanding the department's reversal of policy after his departure, Watts felt justified by—and, indeed, proud of—his expanded seed program with what he deemed were its extensive benefits for American farmers and a rapidly developing nation.

Rehabilitating the South

Watts felt a responsibility to help bring Southern agriculture, devastated by the war, back to sustainable life. This would require some dramatic changes: "The course of agriculture in the Southern States has not been conducted with the care, skill, and regard for ultimate results which have characterized the operations of farmers in other States. While their lands are continuously devoted to cotton and tobacco until they arrived at a state of exhaustion, those of the North are continually improving by rotation of crops. . . . These impressions have induced me to turn my attention to these States to seek some mode by which the influence of this Department may be directed to benefit them." Watts's remedy was to encourage the planting of grasses, which would diversify and increase the region's agricultural products and make crop rotation necessary. "It will be an effort of this Department to introduce this idea, as well as the seeds by which it may be carried out."[65]

Going further, Watts introduced and promoted new plants, specifically ramie and jute, to the South, "the climate of which is alone adapted to their successful production."[66] Ramie is an Asian shrub, in the nettles family, that yields a fiber useful in making textiles. Jute, which the Department of Agriculture imported from East India, is a strong, coarse fiber used for making burlap, gunny, cordage, and the like, though it is difficult to separate the fiber from the plant's resin. Watts continued to emphasize the adoption of these plants in the southern states to replace, at least in part, their traditional emphasis on soil-depleting cotton and tobacco. "I have taken great pains to impress upon the southern planters the importance of turning their attention to the cultivation of jute," Watts said in 1873. "Its cultivation will probably become one of the established industries of the Southern States."[67] Two years later, Watts grew even more determined. "There is no one subject . . . in which I have taken more interest than . . . fibrous plants, especially ramie and jute. These have been brought into notice within the last four years through the influence of this Department." The problem of separating the fiber from the gummy principal and green covering of the plants had been solved "by the invention of machinery which . . . separates the fiber perfectly and economically."[68] After Watts's departure, ramie and jute never caught on to the extent he had hoped for and failed to emerge, as he had also hoped, as the salvation of the South. Cotton continued to be the fiber of choice; only after the boll weevil threatened to destroy the crop around the turn of the nineteenth century did peanuts move more to the fore (courtesy of George Washington Carver), keeping southern agriculture viable. Watts also looked to New Zealand flax, a crop that appeared to thrive in swampy areas not suited to cotton or corn, but this, too, was met with little enthusiasm in the southern latitudes, a region resistant to change and innovation.[69] In sum, his efforts to revive southern agriculture were largely unsuccessful.

Inaugurating the New Microscopy Division

When Watts took office in 1871, the U.S. Department of Agriculture had six divisions: Botany, Chemistry, Entomology, Horticulture, Seeds, and Statistics, with the department's library supporting all of them. After a year's time, he reported that the divisions are "judiciously associated and admirably adapted to the promotion and care of the agricultural interests of the country."[70] This was not a complacent endorsement of the department's services, however. Watts's lifelong interest was on the practical application of science to agriculture, so he was always pushing forward, never content with the status quo. Accordingly, he would discontinue certain lines of work and begin new ones. In 1872, for example, he suspended the department's publication of meteorological data, recommending that the work be turned over to the U.S. Army Signal Service. Congress adopted the recommendation.[71]

That same year, he initiated his most significant scientific contribution as commissioner, the new Division of Microscopy, charged with investigating "all subjects relating to agriculture which require more minute observations than can be made with the naked eye." With this addition, the department could begin the systematic study of plant diseases, under the direction of the newly appointed scientist Thomas Taylor. Educated in his native Scotland and in medicine at Georgetown University, Taylor was highly skilled with the instrument in medical investigations and now championed its use in agricultural research. Watts gave the Division of Microscopy the responsibility for *all* work with microscopes in the department; not until 1895, when the division was abolished, would the other divisions be permitted to use their own microscopes.[72]

Taylor's impact was immediate, and he went on to make significant contributions related to plant diseases. Taylor made some initial analyses of the organic structure and modes of growth of various plants, "but his attention has been chiefly directed to their diseases, and especially to those which are supposed to originate from a class of very minute organisms called parasitic fungi. . . . Potato-rot, peach-yellows, onion-rust, pear-blight, orange-blight and other diseases have been thoroughly studied," Watts reported in 1873. "These investigations will be continued in the future with increased energy."[73] By 1874, Watts reported, Taylor's research program had expanded to study parasitic fungi in relation to "black-knot fungus . . . which is the scourge of the plum and cherry trees . . . apple speck or rot of winter-apples in Eastern Arkansas; potato-rot; pear-tree blight; and cranberry rot."[74]

Pear-tree blight was an extensive problem across the United States, destroying trees in a matter of hours. The National Pomological Society requested that Watts and Taylor study the problem and find a remedy. Watts also sent Taylor, at the request of the Cranberry Growers Association of New Jersey, to investigate the subject, which he did, with "successful results . . . a saving to the cranberry-growers amounting to hundreds of thousands of dollars."[75] These and other findings of the division of microscopy were published, with intricate drawings, in the various monthly reports the department of agriculture made available to farmers.[76]

As the nation's Centennial Exhibition in Philadelphia approached, the division of microscopy found itself immersed in a wider public education mission. The division was now "principally engaged" in preparing for display an extensive collection of "finely executed water-color drawings" of microscopic fungi on some six hundred plant specimens, including edible and poisonous mushrooms and textile fibers. Watts was particularly interested in exploring the nutritive value of mushrooms and promoting their consumption. "The importance of the mushroom as an article of diet has never been properly understood in the United States, nor is it generally known how abundant our supply of edible mushrooms is," Watts said. "Many of those popularly supposed to be poisonous are not merely innocuous but highly nutritious, containing as they do many of the elements of animal food."[77]

Stirring the Government's Interest in Forestry

Watts set in motion the series of events that, after his departure, led to the creation of the U.S. Forestry Service within the Department of Agriculture. Presciently, he rang the alarm in his first annual report: "The season has been marked by local droughts, high winds, and floods. . . . It is to be feared that the destruction of forests by devastating fires and for supplies of timber will render drought, winds, and floods more frequent and severe."[78]

The American Association for the Advancement of Science (AAAS) was turning its attention to the matter as well. At its 1873 annual meeting, scientist Franklin B. Hough of New York presented a paper on the need for cultivating timber and preserving forests. The AAAS presented a memorial on the issue to Congress.[79] That same year, Watts asked his division of botany, directed by the remarkable scientist George Vasey, to create "a full collection of sections . . . of all the forest trees of our country." Watts foresaw the collection of tree specimens as having value in presenting to scientists and students "instruction in this department of knowledge." Looking ahead to the Centennial Exhibition, he requested a special appropriation from Congress of $2,000 to fund the project and present it as part of the Department of Agriculture's exhibitions.[80]

In 1875, out of the sum appropriated for the purchase of seeds, Watts was directed by Congress to instead spend $2,000 to hire a scientist who could "prosecute investigations and inquiries with a view of ascertaining the annual amount of consumption, importation, and exportation of timber and other forest products, the probable supply for future wants, the means best adapted to their preservation and renewal, the influence of forests upon climate, and the measures that have been successfully applied in foreign countries . . . for the preservation and restoration or planting of forests."[81]

Watts complained that the appropriation was far too little, given the charge. But he managed to hire Hough, whose report to the AAAS three years prior "On the Duty of Governments in the Preservation of Forests" made him the obvious choice. On August 30, 1876, Hough's appointment was confirmed as special forestry agent—the first federal expert on forestry with the charge of investigating the forest and lumbering situation and making reports. After

Watts's retirement in 1877, Hough's work laid the foundation for discussions of declining forest conditions at the height of the Industrial Revolution. In 1881, Hough became the first chief of the U.S. Forestry Division, as it was formally established within the Department of Agriculture, remaining in the post until 1883.[82]

Responding to Insect Pestilence

Watts developed measures to advance agricultural science and its applications for the American farmer as well as the emerging agribusiness sector of the national economy. He was adept, as well, at responding to crises.

The worst emergency imaginable descended on the Great Plains in the summer of 1874—a massive plague of locusts, or grasshoppers, darkening the skies and devouring everything in sight. This pestilence occurred in the widening wake of the Panic of 1873, the unusually hard winter of 1873–74, and an early summer drought. The plague of Rocky Mountain locusts invaded the territories of Dakota, Montana, Wyoming, and Colorado, Indian Territory in present-day Oklahoma, and the states of Iowa, Minnesota, Missouri, Nebraska, and Texas. The crop damage exceeded $200 million that summer and disrupted the settlement of the Great Plains, causing many homesteaders to head back east or move farther west. The nation responded in multiple ways, through the actions of state and territorial governments, the railroads' shipment of goods and supplies free of charge, and the U.S. Army's distribution of rations and raiment to beleaguered families. But beyond emergency relief, the larger concern was for obtaining seeds to plant in the spring of 1875 and for means of preventing the plague's recurrence.[83]

"There has been no period in the history of this country when farmers' crops have been so extensively depredated upon as in the past year," Watts wrote in October 1874, "and this has brought into active exercise the knowledge and industry of the Entomological Division of the Department. There is increasing demand for information with regard to insects injurious to vegetation, and much pains have been taken to investigate the character of insects sent here, to point out their modes of infliction and the means by which their depredations may be avoided."[84]

In addition to researching the problem, Watts's department undertook the supplying of seeds to all who requested it. He procured an emergency appropriation for that purpose from Congress. A year later, when the plague had subsided, he reported that "Congress wisely interposed . . . and through this department made provision for a supply of seed for the coming year by an appropriation of $30,000." One farmer wrote: "The seed is most acceptable, for it relieves me from a state of hopelessness; but it cannot do me half as much good as it does to know that we have a Government that cares for her distressed people."[85]

Showcasing American Agriculture at the Centennial Exhibition of 1876

The Centennial Exhibition of 1876 in Philadelphia—the nation's first official World's Fair—offered an unprecedented opportunity for Watts to showcase the progress being made in all realms agricultural, progress in which he took great pride. "Farmers and planters now realize that there is something else in this important work beyond the mere drudgery of sowing, reaping, and curing," he said in preparation for the exhibition. "Men of science and learning have turned their attention to the subject, and have so plainly and interestingly illustrated the nature of plants, the purposes to which they may be applied, their cultivation and products, as well as the injurious insects which depredate upon them, as to make the subject intelligible to the plainest comprehension."[86]

The Centennial Exhibition—officially the International Exhibition of Arts, Manufactures and Products of the Soil and Mine—included thirty-seven countries beyond the United States and attracted nearly ten million visitors over its six-month duration. The Centennial Exhibition was considered to be the sixth major international exhibition of its type after the Crystal Palace Exhibition in London in 1851, Paris in 1855, London again in 1862, Paris again in 1867, and Vienna in 1873, although many other world-class exhibitions of lesser scale were held both before and between these events. For the United States, however, it was the first in a long line of world's fairs and represented a "coming out" party for the nation as an industrial power. It was an exhibition of national pride and, not incidentally, provided an opportunity for the nation to come together and "forgive and forget" the Civil War.[87]

Sited at Philadelphia's Fairmount Park, with thirty-four structures on fifty acres overlooking the Schuylkill River, the exhibition paid due obeisance to the still largely agricultural nation. The third-largest structure was Agriculture Hall, a massive building designed to look like various barn structures pieced together. Agriculture Hall featured the latest in farm machinery and equipment, and its acres of farm and livestock exhibits drew large crowds. Not far away stood Horticultural Hall, designed to feature the work of professional and amateur gardeners.[88]

Watts had been anticipating the exhibition for several years, and had directed his six divisions to create extensive displays of their work. His department also conducted twenty-one "special display" days over the course of the exhibition, on such topics as pomological products and vegetables; early grass butter and cheese; early summer vegetables; trials of reaping machines; exhibition of horses, mules, and asses; autumn vegetables, and so forth.[89]

"This Department has contributed largely to that exposition in the exhibits it has made," Watts said. "Statistics, chemistry, botany, microscopy, and the seed division, are all there to represent the prodigious progress which has been made in this country in the last one hundred years; and I am extremely gratified to be enabled to say that their display has made a lasting impression of the wonderful achievements which have been accomplished in the agriculture of the United States."[90]

Leaving Office

The Centennial Exhibition provided a triumphant note for Watts as his tenure was winding down. President Grant, who had appointed Watts in the summer of 1871, had declined to run for a third term in 1876, opening the gates to one of the most controversial and contested elections in U.S. history. Republican nominee Rutherford B. Hayes beat Democratic nominee Samuel Tilden, who had won the popular vote by more than two hundred thousand ballots. A compromise solution between Republicans and Democrats awarded twenty contested electoral votes to Hayes in return for an agreement to withdraw federal troops from the South, thus ending Reconstruction.[91]

With Grant stepping down in March 1877 and his seventy-sixth birthday in view, Watts was preparing to retire as commissioner and return to his home in Carlisle. His leadership of the U.S. Department of Agriculture had provided mixed results. He did initiate advances in agricultural science through the introduction of new programs in microscopy and forestry. His department's response to the locust devastation in the West was fast, comprehensive, and effective. His contributions to the Centennial Exhibition were widely judged as successful. His ambitious national seed distribution program provided benefits to American farmers and the settlement of the West but was summarily dismissed by his successor. His efforts to reform agricultural practices in the

South produced no lasting impact. And his efforts to create a national system under departmental control to coordinate the work of agricultural colleges, state agricultural societies, state boards, and other agricultural policy organizations collapsed ignominiously at the Washington Convention of 1872. In that last respect, Watts met his Waterloo at the beginning of his administration rather than at the end. Nevertheless, he left office with his integrity intact. As a contemporary newspaper observed: "Amid all the criticism to which some of the Departments of Government have been exposed during the last administration, the Department of Agriculture, under the admirable direction on Hon. Frederick Watts, has never been touched by the breath of scandal."[92]

He was both criticized and praised for his extreme frugality. In his last full year, ending June 30, 1877, he returned a balance to the U.S. Treasury of $52,497 out of a total appropriation of $264,120. Watts wanted to move some money around between his divisions, but the secretary of the treasury disallowed his requests.[93] Over his term, he had requested larger appropriations for various purposes, but the year-to-year increases were incrementally small. In 1870, the year before he took office, the department's budget was only $130,000; it slightly more than doubled during his tenure to $264,000. It was hardly enough to allow the department to do everything that was asked of it nor was it enough to allow Watts to accomplish everything he had hoped. The Department of Agriculture was an independent and autonomous federal agency, but not a cabinet-level department, with no senior officer above the commissioner; thus his requests for more funds could be easily overlooked or ignored by Congress.

But Watts was adept at achieving much with meager resources. From his experience with Dickinson College, the Cumberland Valley Railroad, the Pennsylvania State Agricultural Society, the Farmers' High School, and the Agricultural College of Pennsylvania, he knew how to move new or distressed organizations into viable operation with little of their own money while proving adept at garnering additional support from their governmental sponsors—the Pennsylvania legislature in these cases, but, in his last tour of duty, not so much from Congress. As one writer concluded: "Perhaps one important accomplishment not so easily seen was his ability to do so much with so few funds."[94] In any event, it was time to go home.

EPILOGUE

Frederick Watts, soon to turn seventy-six years old, left office as U.S. commissioner of agriculture in March 1877. He returned to his beloved Creekside farm, where he would reside for the remaining twelve years of his life. There is little record in the *Carlisle Daily Herald* and other local newspapers of Watts's activities during his retirement. The presumption of one biographer is that his work as commissioner "no doubt caused a slowing down of the pace at Creekside." He occasionally sold off excess animals and farm equipment. Whether he actively managed the farm or hired a manager is not known.[1] Also unknown is the extent to which he engaged in the practice of law, from which he retired in the early 1860s. With his extensive knowledge, experience, and reputation, he likely was consulted on legal issues from time to time.

In any case, Frederick Watts was revered as the grand old man of Carlisle and Cumberland County, its most eminent citizen of the nineteenth century. He died on August 17, 1889, at age eighty-eight. His youngest daughter, Mrs. Samuel B. Johnson, recalled that "his mind was clear, his faculties good. He was simply worn out and went quietly to sleep without an illness."[2]

The *Carlisle Daily Herald* lauded him generously: "Certainly no man ever held a position in Cumberland County at all comparable with that Mr. Watts filled. Of all the noted men of the valley he was foremost in power, ability, and his hold upon the people." Calling him "facile princeps"—easily the first or best—the *Herald* cited "his innate nobility of character . . . preeminent ability . . . hatred of wrong . . . and sense of justice." His fellow citizens "had unlimited confidence in him and he never abused it. His simple word had the sanctity of an oath with them, and the accusation of enemies and of the envious only emphasized the towering probity of his character."[3]

In its resolution of August 20, 1889, the Cumberland County Bar praised Watts for his accomplishments and influence as a practicing lawyer for more than half a century: "Of great integrity, clear perception, unusual mental power, high moral courage, and of strong convictions, he was the unrivalled

FIGURE 24 *Watts with grandson John M. Mahon Jr., ca. 1886. Courtesy of the Cumberland County Historical Society, Carlisle, Pa.*

leader of the bar, and of the people of his native valley, and his influence and example elevated the oral tone of lawyers and laymen, and left an impression upon them the effect of which will be apparent for years to come."[4]

Another contemporary writer defined Watts's most prominent characteristics as "force of character and abiding self-confidence," calling him a man of "large intellect, sterling integrity and unblemished honour."[5]

But praise can be overblown at times, as occurred in a 1930 address to the Cumberland County Historical Society. The speaker, I. Thornton Osmond, appointed in 1879 as professor of physics at Penn State but long since retired, waxed hyperbolic: "Though I have not sufficient evidence to warrant asserting it as fact, I believe from what evidence I have, that the Land Grant Act of 1862, and also that of 1859, originated with the trustees of the Pennsylvania College; and that Hon. Frederick Watts was the author of its essential idea, the kind of colleges to be established, and that so he is the Father of all the State Colleges."[6] There is no question that Watts and his colleagues in the Pennsylvania State Agricultural Society played the indispensable role in getting an early state-sponsored agricultural college up and running, and they lobbied hard for Morrill's agricultural college bills. But other actors in other states—Michigan, Maryland, Iowa, Minnesota, New York, Illinois, and elsewhere—were working along the same lines, not to mention Morrill himself, whose 1862 bill federalized the land-grant college movement.

Today, Frederick Watts is little known. As the writer Saul Bellow declared: "The rule for the dead is that they should be forgotten. After burial there is a universal gradual progress toward oblivion."[7] Watts is not quite to that point, however. Some physical reminders remain, such as a state historical marker at the site of his experimental farm outside Carlisle and an eponymous residence

FIGURE 25
Graveside monument of Frederick Watts and wife Henrietta (Ege) Watts, Old Carlisle Cemetery. Courtesy of the Cumberland County Historical Society, Carlisle, Pa.

hall, built in 1923, on Penn State's University Park campus. Watts Hall was the first to be built in the West Halls complex, where six dormitories are named for various Penn State founders. And, of course, the Watts gravesite reposes prominently in the old Carlisle cemetery, not too many paces from the monument of Revolutionary War heroine Molly Pitcher.

But upon deeper analysis, the Watts legacy is extensive. His life is an important reminder of the oft-overlooked nineteenth-century "men of affairs," "men of progress," and "gentleman farmers" who contributed greatly to the development of American society at a time *before* the federal government emerged as the triumphant bureaucratic state of the twentieth century and *before* the age of the great industrial fortunes that quickly transformed the nation's economy (and, in response, the reforms of the Progressive Era).

The historian David Hackett Fischer characterized the United States as "an open society which is organized on the principle of voluntary action."[8] Nowhere is Fischer's thesis more vigorously demonstrated in antebellum America than in the growth of the voluntary associations known as agricultural societies. As more recent historians have shown, these societies forged a vast agricultural "lobby" that pushed state and federal governments to develop complex organizational structures able to respond to the needs of their agricultural constituencies. Originally, these societies were organized by elites, men of affairs and gentleman farmers such as Frederick Watts—an exemplary polymath with interests in law, jurisprudence, higher education reform, railroading, business, and civic leadership but above all else agricultural improvement. Watts's early contributions prior to 1840 in terms of innovative barn design, Mediterranean wheat, and the McCormick Reaper illuminate the altruistic motives of such men in improving conditions for the farming class—motives that would lead to organizing that same agrarian community to advocate for their interests through the political process.

Pragmatic and politically astute as he was, Watts also held a spiritual view of farming. "With regard to our occupation we should rather look upon this lovely earth as the beautiful landscape of God's creation, imbued with the powers of life, to breathe and feed, yielding its elements and products to the delicate and nursing operations of our hands," he told a group of Cumberland County farmers in 1870.[9] Of course he wanted them to do more than regard their livelihood beatifically. Thus he labored to forge farmers into a self-conscious community organized to work—and advocate, when necessary—for social, economic, and political parity with the rest of America. To his formula for the advancement of the farming class he added a new model of higher education. His model was designed to incorporate and develop scientific agriculture and to produce graduates able to put such knowledge to use in improved farming practices.

These were his lasting contributions to bettering the lot of the agrarian community, which he viewed as being isolated physically, culturally, and intellectually; wedded to traditional farming practices; unorganized politically with no collective voice to protect or advance their interest; and generally floundering as the "left behind" and disrespected denizens of a rapidly developing nation. (And on various speaking occasions, he would characterize his agrarian audiences in those same pejorative terms, directly and bluntly, in hopes of awakening them to new possibilities.)

Watts's career also exemplifies the values of the Whig Party. Formed in opposition to Jacksonian policies in the 1830s, the Whigs transformed themselves into a potent force advocating progressive policies to unify and develop the nation economically. The Whigs favored a strong central bank as the foundation of an efficient national fiscal system; tariffs to protect emerging industries from foreign competition; infrastructure projects such as canals, railroads, roads, and other internal improvements; education reform benefiting newer classes of people; science and technology as engines of progress; and, in the North, opposition to the extension of slavery in new states and territories. Lasting twenty years until the mid-1850s, the Whig Party was succeeded by the new Republican Party, which elected its first president in 1860. Described as an "ardent Whig," Watts personified those same principles, particularly in the arena of "internal improvements" involving railroading and educational and agricultural reform predicated on science and innovation.

Watts's lever for elevating the agrarian community was the Pennsylvania State Agriculture Society, which he led as founding president in 1851. The society organized large state fairs, awarding premiums for livestock, produce, and other farm products, and holding demonstrations of new machinery and improved farm practices. These agricultural exhibitions—in Harrisburg, Lancaster, Pittsburgh, and Philadelphia—attracted hundreds of thousands of visitors during Watts's four-year tenure. In addition, the exhibitions were instrumental in pulling together, for the first time, the state's vast agricultural community as a strong, self-conscious community. Watts's leadership ability manifested itself in moving the Pennsylvania society into a position of national leadership and influence in relatively quick order, catching up to if not surpassing the older agricultural societies in neighboring states.

Watts's state fairs of the early 1850s have since morphed into today's Pennsylvania Farm Show, held every January at the state Farm Show Complex in Harrisburg. Marking its 104th year in 2020, the state Farm Show bills itself as the largest indoor exposition in the nation, with ten thousand competitive exhibits, six thousand animals, and three hundred commercial exhibits.[10] The Pennsylvania Department of Agriculture, another eventual "state-building" result (1895) of Watts's earlier movement, oversees Pennsylvania's large agribusiness industry. This economic sector encompasses production agriculture, food products, and related businesses—a multibillion dollar enterprise that has kept the state competitive in agricultural, food, and lumber production.[11] In 2018, among the northeastern states, Pennsylvania ranked first in "top ten" placements in thirty-two U.S. Department of Agriculture categories, compared with twenty-nine for New York and thirteen for New Jersey.[12]

Watts's most important legacy, however, is the land-grant institution that became the Pennsylvania State *University*—tardily renamed as such exactly one hundred years after his 1853 resolution calling for an agricultural convention to establish the Farmers' High School. In its present-day College of Agricultural Sciences, the university carries out the mission originating with the Farmers' High School.

This new school was a top priority of the Pennsylvania State Agricultural Society, whose quick successes earned respect as a powerful sponsoring agency for the enterprise. Watts wrote the first business plan and the drafts of bills that provided the basis of the state legislature's charters of 1854 and 1855. Despite this quick ratification and gubernatorial support, Watts was frustrated because the charters did not provide for state funding.

Notwithstanding that deficiency, Watts assumed the critical role of prime mover in getting the institution sited, built, into operation, and on track to early success. And he resigned his presidency of the state agricultural society to devote his energies to the new college. To review his additional contributions:

On the trustees' site selection committee, he advocated for the school's location in Centre County, his recommendation ultimately being approved.

He was elected by the trustees as president of the board in September 1855, a leadership post he would hold for nineteen years.

He designed the first building for the institution, a large barn completed in 1856; hired a superintendent to get farming operations under way;

hired a Carlisle-based construction firm to erect the main building; and secured the first state appropriation of $25,000 in 1857 to fund it.

He guided the school through the Panic of 1857, hired a new contractor to complete the west wing of the main building, wrote the first two annual reports (1858, 1859) of the institution, and opened the school for instruction in 1859.

He hired a brilliant young president, Evan Pugh, Ph.D., who quickly built the new school into the nation's first successful agricultural college, as Watts expected, until Pugh's untimely death in 1864.

From 1864 to 1867, Watts successfully led efforts to defend the Agricultural College against legislative attempts to wrest the land-grant fund away and distribute it to other institutions.

He engineered the memorials to the legislature that resulted in authorization to issue $80,000 in bonds to arrest institutional debts, in 1866, as well as the quid pro quo proposal that finally induced the legislature, in 1867, to dedicate the entire land-grant fund to the college in return for the establishment of three experimental farms across the state.

Notwithstanding Watts's manifold contributions as prime mover in the founding of the institution, the blot on his legacy is the succession of failed presidencies during the Pugh aftermath. Watts rushed to fill four presidential vacancies with men unsuited to lead a new scientific institution and assented to the presidents' various curricular experiments. The eventual result was disastrous. The college slipped into a downward spiral, antagonized its core constituency, abandoned its land-grant mission entirely, and narrowly escaped being closed for good. Here Watts holds major culpability. Without painstakingly searching for a scientist/administrator capable of building on Pugh's accomplishments, Watts led the effort to hire successors, hurriedly and seemingly haphazardly, who had little knowledge or inclination (save perhaps Fraser) about how to build out the land-grant or "industrial college" model. Even more damning, he acquiesced in these presidents' plans to alter the direction the school would take—a direction that moved further and further away from the land-grant vision of a school of rigorous scientific agriculture and engineering, as Pugh had outlined in his visionary 1864 plan. The dynamics of these presidencies have been analyzed in some depth in this narrative, and some critics might be tempted to place the blame for the college's failings entirely on these presidents themselves. But the process starts at the top, with search and selection, and the responsibility for that lies with the governing board and especially its president, Frederick Watts. Accordingly, this episode serves as an early case study of the importance in adhering to the institutional mission and finding the right leader—no matter how long it takes—capable of advancing that mission.

The deleterious inflection point came in the days following Pugh's death, when Watts and McAllister had the great good sense to turn to the brilliant Yale agricultural chemist and Pugh confidant Samuel Johnson. But Johnson summarily turned them down. One wonders how the college's trajectory might have been sustained and strengthened had they prevailed upon Johnston to help find a worthy candidate. That was the proverbial road not taken.

Subsequently, Watts turned to personal acquaintances to fill the post: William Allen, the retired Girard College president, who lacked vision, energy, and interest in land-grant education, and Thomas Burrowes, who abandoned scientific agriculture in favor of practical agriculture, turning the institution into something resembling a finishing school for farmers. The worst decision was to hire the Methodist minister James Calder, who after some early successes turned the institution entirely away from the land-grant model until it resembled a backwoods classical college—in the image of Hillsdale College, whence he came. Although Watts had effectively left the board of trustees in 1873, his decision in hiring Calder in 1871 lingered on, to the institution's great detriment. By the end of Calder's administration, the core agricultural constituency was fighting mad, the legislature greatly disturbed, the trustees distraught, the faculty and students angry to the point of mutiny. The institution was on the verge of shutting down for good.

Thus questions arise as to the degree of Watts's own commitment to the land-grant model, which became institutionalized with the Morrill Act of 1862. For his part, Pugh made a seamless commitment, arguing for the complementarity of engineering and scientific agriculture within the industrial education model. Indeed, Pugh saw agricultural and land-grant colleges as primarily *scientific* institutions. Although a proponent of science and innovation, Watts's vision of the schools was somewhat more limited, as primarily agricultural colleges charged with educating the sons and (later) daughters of farmers—and not necessarily the scientifically advanced institutions Pugh envisioned. In accepting Burrowes's and Calder's wildly divergent curricular models, Watts acquiesced with their plans to pretty much sweep the college's once strong scientific core out of the equation. For Watts, then, the primary consideration in his selection of presidents seems to have been expediency over educational philosophy. His overriding concern was to keep the wobbling college operating above all else, without inviting an appreciable gap in presidential leadership that could lead to even more problems and criticism.

And yet there is some ambivalence in that assessment. As commissioner of agriculture, a position that was for three years (1871–73) concurrent with his presidency of the college's board of trustees, Watts strove for a stronger, centrally coordinated agricultural research program across the expanding universe of land-grant colleges. His plan met stiff resistance from the colleges, resulting in an early defeat for the new commissioner at the Washington Convention he organized in early 1872. Nonetheless, he continued to champion the colleges—although he viewed them as primarily agricultural institutions and little else. But he actively supported their nascent effort to establish agricultural experiment stations across the county. And as U.S. commissioner of agriculture, he made at least two significant contributions to building up the scientific capabilities of that department. He established the Division of Microscopy, an important step that enabled the systematic investigation of parasitic fungi and other plant diseases and led to the development of effective treatments. And he advocated for systematic forestry research, the beginnings of which were established under his leadership and which resulted in the formal establishment of the U.S. Forestry Division within the Department of Agriculture in 1881.

Over his nine decades, the man of affairs and gentleman farmer that was Frederick Watts engendered success in nearly every endeavor he took on, though he had his share of setbacks and disappointments. Aside from the many accomplishments of his first fifty years, it was the second act of his life that proved more significant. As "by far the most outstanding figure in Pennsylvania agriculture" between 1850 and 1880, Watts brought the new Pennsylvania State Agricultural Society into prominence as a powerful agricultural lobby, generated strong statewide support for an agricultural college, got the Farmers' High School chartered, sited, and into successful operation as the nation's first successful agricultural college, and eventually moved to the national stage, making significant contributions to American agriculture as commissioner of the new federal agency.

Notwithstanding the unraveling of the Pennsylvania State College in the 1870s, Watts deserves credit for his work in establishing the institution and hiring a president who, for one brief shining moment, made it the national model, the first successful agricultural college in America.

In any event, the college did survive its "era of drift," its great unraveling, its near-death experience. As the faculty revamped the curriculum at the eleventh hour, and as the presidency of George Atherton (1882–1906) got under way, the college began to recover and grow, greatly strengthening its basic mission as a land-grant college, expanding its arts and sciences capabilities, stabilizing itself financially, and positioning itself for success in the twentieth century. After World War II, the university began to flourish. In 1958, it was elected as the thirty-fourth member of the Association of American Universities, the elective consortium of the sixty-five best research universities in North America. By 2019, Penn State had secured recognition as a preeminent global research university, ranking forty-third among the one thousand institutions evaluated by the Center for World University Rankings.[13] The year previous, according to the National Science Foundation's 2018 rankings of research expenditures, Penn State placed first with eighteen "top ten" finishes in the thirty-two academic fields and subfields measured, followed by Johns Hopkins with sixteen, Michigan with fifteen, and MIT with thirteen.[14] With twenty-four campuses, thirty-one thousand faculty and staff, nearly one hundred thousand students, a research program surpassing $1 billion annually, an endowment of $3.2 billion, and an annual budget of $6.5 billion, Penn State had grown to proportions unimaginable in the 1850s.[15]

Watts's legacy also extends to the development of the U.S. Department of Agriculture. Despite some programmatic setbacks, he made key contributions to its development as a scientific agency. And through his aggressive seed distribution program and relief efforts during the great locust plague, he provided widescale support to the American farmer. Held at arm's length by Congress during the early administrations of Watts and his two predecessors, the U.S. Department of Agriculture became a secretary-level cabinet agency reporting directly to the president of the United States in 1889. From that point, it quickly grew into the world's outstanding scientific research organization. Under Secretary "Tama Jim" Wilson (1897–1913), the department made major advances in the identification and study of viruses, in plant genetics, and in reforestation studies, as well as introducing consumer protection legislation. By 1912, the Department of Agriculture had grown to a staff of more than eleven thousand and a budget of $21.2 million[16]—a far cry from Watts's last budget of $264,000 only thirty-five years earlier.

In sum, the work Frederick Watts so determinedly began in the 1850s—to organize and advance the interests of the Pennsylvania farming community through an influential statewide association, to create a new agricultural college predicated on science and guide it to rapid success as the national model, and to serve the nation as its chief agricultural executive while improving the effectiveness of the U.S. Department of Agriculture—constituted important contributions in helping to bring the American agricultural enterprise to a massive scope, scale, and global impact in the twentieth century.

APPENDIX

Report of a Plan for Organizing the Farmers' High School of Pennsylvania, by Frederick Watts, January 20, 1854.

To His Excellency, Wm. Bigler, *Governor of Pennsylvania*:

In the month of January, 1851, a few individuals, whose enterprising spirit of benevolence for their fellow-men, and care for the honor of their own State, assembled at the Capitol to organize a State Agricultural Society. Of the number of intelligent men who are found in every enlightened community, there are comparatively few who are so unselfish as to devote themselves, and expend their time and money to promote that which is but a great public good, and promises to them individually no particular benefit. And when spirits like these do step out to lead the way, the cynic criticizes them, the indifferent frown coldly upon them, the jealous impugn their motives, and under this influence, the power of the State itself withholds the cheerful light of its countenance and aid of its laws from them. The founders of our Society have not this to complain of. Their first meeting had but adjourned, when the Representatives of the State, seconded by the sincere and ardent support of the Executive, took up the subject, organized the society by a charter, and made, in aid of its funds, a liberal annual appropriation. The combined efforts of energetic men, and the earnest support of the representatives of the people, must accomplish the object in view.

The constitutional organization of our Society, regarding the choice of its officers, wisely embraces every portion of the State; each congressional district having an official representative, and all these representatives manage the affairs of the Society. Thus are the duties and labors divided, and interests and knowledge, as various as the climate and soil of our State, associated.

The officers of the Society, forming its Executive Committee, repeatedly met during the first year of existence, and under its auspices the first "Annual Exhibition" was held in the vicinity of Harrisburg. With the little experience we have now had; with the fruit which has already been so manifestly gathered from our short existence, we look back upon it as a most strange truth, that the year 1851 should have found the State of Pennsylvania without the organization of a State Agricultural Society. There are few States in the Union so purely agricultural as our own; and none which offered so many inducements and facilities, or whose wants in a greater degree demanded the establishments of a State Society. It was not surprising, therefore, that the farmers of the State took hold of the subject with avidity, and gave to its first exhibition a show of numbers and contributions which promised for the future their hearty support. On the third Tuesday of January, 1852, the Society met at Harrisburg, in the Capitol, when a report of the transactions of the past year was submitted and considered, some amendments of the constitution made, and the officers for the ensuing year elected.

At this period the question was mooted as to the expediency of giving to the Society, with regard to its annual exhibitions, a permanent locality. The subject was discussed and decided by the executive committee, composed of the officers of the Society, exclusively upon the consideration of what course would produce the greatest amount of benefit to the State at large. The conclusion was to change the place every year. In pursuance of this arrangement, it was determined to hold the next "Annual Exhibition" of the society at Lancaster. It is only necessary here to remark that in this exhibition the highest anticipations of the Society were realized, as to numbers in attendance; the only limit was the capacity of railroads and other conveniences to carry the people; and the contributions greatly increased with a single year's experience.

At the period appointed by the constitution, January 18, 1853, the Society held their second annual meeting at the Capitol. The transactions of the Society for the past year were reported, and, with various subjects of interest, were discussed; and the officers elected for the ensuing year. At this meeting a committee was appointed to enquire into the expediency of establishing a "State Agricultural School," which resulted in a report favorable to the project, and recommending "a general convention of delegates from all parts of the State to meet at the Capitol; when a full expression of public sentiment could be had." This report was adopted and the eighth of the following March was fixed for its meeting. The convention met; and with an unparalleled unanimity recommended the establishment of a school for the education of Farmers, and gave the subject in charge to a committee to have it enacted into a law, and carried into effect. The late period, in reference to the session of our Legislature, at which this business commenced, rendered it impracticable to procure the charter of such an institution at that session, and it yet remains to be done.

There are circumstances connected with the consideration of the subject of a school for the education of Farmers which command the attention of every enlightened citizen of the State. That farmers require education to place them in that rank of society where they are entitled to stand, as well as to give effect to the important business of their life, is a point which needs no discussion. But *how* they shall be educated is a subject not so well understood. It must be conceded, that our institutions of learning, as at present constituted, are not adapted to the education of young men for the business of agriculture. The expense is too great, and the character of the education they acquire, unfits them for the occupation of a Farmer. The body, by an uninterrupted application to books at a period of life when the habits of a man are formed, is rendered, in a measure, incapable of labor; and the mind is trained to an inclination and course of thought ill adapted to the practical operations of the farm. But a school for the education of Farmers may be so organized as to avoid these objections. It is not proposed so thoroughly to educate young men, as to fit them for the professional pursuit of scientific subjects; but to teach them that which is valuable for a farmer to know. They should be taught the English language, mathematics, geography, chemistry, botany, astronomy and such other kindred subjects as are practically useful; and with these, the art of farming. Certain hours of every day should be devoted to the manual labor of the farm, and to the construction and use of implements. This labor, well directed, would be productive, and thus the institution would be in a measure self-sustaining. Such an institution is loudly called for.—Many farmers throughout the State would be glad to educate a son, if it were not at the risk of destroying his usefulness for active life. A few figures will best illustrate how this project can be achieved. Adopting the spirit of caution and economy which characterizes the habit of thought and action of the farmer, it is deemed most expedient that such an institution should grow from a small beginning, that its value may be tested, and its growth strengthened by confidence in its practical usefulness.

A farm of 300 acres, having a variety of soil and ordinary house and barn, can be purchased at $60 an acre	$18,000.00
Additional buildings for the accommodation of boys	10,000.00
Stock, implements, &c	3,000.00

Furniture, books, instruments, &c	5,000.00
Contingencies of organization	2,000.00
	$38,000.00

Let the State appropriate	$20,000.00
The State Agricultural Society	10,000.00
Mortgage the property for	8,000.00
	$38,000.00

This puts the institution upon its feet; then how is it to be supported? It will require for the support of the professors and pupils, annually	$10,000.00
Salary of principal professor	2,000.00
Do..of two other professors	3,000.00
Do..of one other professor	1,000.00
	$16,000.00

To this object the State Agricultural Society would appropriate annually	$5,000.00
200 pupils at $75 each, to include all expenses at the institution	15,000.00
The produce of the farm under such culture may be estimated at	2,000.00
	$22,000.00

Leaving an excess of	$6,000.00

to be appropriated to extend the capacity of the institution for the accommodation of a greater number

Graduates of other colleges, competent to teach the several branches of Natural Science, would seek an opportunity to become tutors, that they might learn and fit themselves for professors of such an institution, of whom, it must be admitted, there are now so few.

When it shall be understood that a farmer may educate his son in that business of life in which he most confides, at an entire expense of seventy-five dollars a year, the only question will be who shall be admitted and who excluded for the time; for it may be most confidently expected, that the applicants will be far greater in number then can be at first accommodated. It may be safely estimated, however, that when the institution shall have been built and properly established, the contribution which the State Society may annually make, the product of the labor of the pupils, and the sum of seventy-five dollars paid by each of them, will be amply sufficient for its maintenance.

It may, with some degree of plausibility, be said, this project is too limited and parsimonious for the great State of Pennsylvania. Perhaps it is; but it is not proposed that the beginning shall be the end; but that a great, extensive and useful institution shall grow out of a beginning that shall be felt and tried, and have the confidence which experience always begets. This view accords with the genius and habits of that class of our people which is intended to be benefitted.

If the influence of such an institution were added to that of the State Agricultural Society, and the various county societies throughout the Commonwealth, the benefit to be derived from it could not be estimated. In view of the political economy of the project, we should not hesitate a moment.

By the fifth section of the act of incorporation of the State Agricultural Society, the Legislature contemplates, that, through the medium of the county societies, the agricultural knowledge and experience of their individuals members, shall be preserved and transmitted to the State Society, manifestly that the agricultural transactions of our State shall not be lost, but published, and placed in the hands of every farmer, that he may examine, judge and improve himself. The advantage of such a publication can not be questioned. Some pains have been taken to collect this information, and with some degree of success, as much so, indeed, as the newness of the project would permit us to anticipate. But as soon as the value of such information shall be universally known, and the system by which it may be collected and diffused shall be understood, we will not be without a volume of annual transactions such as will redound to the credit of the State and its agricultural history.

We propose to include within this, our first volume, a brief of all the transactions of the society, from its origin to this time, so that no part of its history shall be lost.

FRED'K. WATTS,
President of the Pennsylvania State Agricultural Society.
January 20, 1854.

An Act of Incorporation of the Farmers' High School of Pennsylvania, Approved February 22, 1855

SECTION 1. *Be it enacted by the Senate and House of Representatives of the Commonwealth of Pennsylvania in General Assembly met, and it is hereby enacted by the authority of same.* That there be and is hereby erected and established, at the place which shall be designated by the authority, and as hereinafter provided, an institution for the education of youth in the various branches of science, learning, and practical agriculture, as they are connected with each other, by the name, style, and title of the Farmers' High School of Pennsylvania.

SECTION 2. That the said institution shall be under the management and government of a board of trustees, of whom there shall be thirteen, and seven of whom shall be a quorum, competent to perform the duties hereinafter authorized and required.

SECTION 3. That the Governor, Secretary of the Commonwealth, the president of the Pennsylvania State Agricultural Society, and the principal of the institution, shall be each *ex-officio* a member of the board of trustees, and they, with Dr. Alfred L. Elwyn and Algernon S. Roberts, of the city of Philadelphia; H. N. McAllister of the county of Centre; R. C. Walker, of the county of Allegheny; James Miles, of the county of Erie; John Strohm, of the county of Lancaster; A. O. Hiester of the county of Dauphin; William Jessup of the county of Susquehanna, and Frederick Watts, of the county of Cumberland, shall constitute the first board of trustees; which said trustees and their successors in office, are hereby enacted and declared to be a body politic and corporate in law, with perpetual succession, by the name, style, and title of the Farmers' High School of Pennsylvania, by which name and title the said trustees, and their successors, shall be able and capable in law to take by gift, grant, sale, or conveyance, by bequest, devise, or otherwise, any estate in any lands, tenements, and hereditaments, goods, chattels, or effects, and at pleasure to alien or otherwise dispose of the same to and for the use and purpose of the said institution: *Provided, however,* That the annual income of the said estate so held, shall at no time exceed twenty-five thousand dollars; and the said corporation shall, by the same name have power to sue and be sued, and generally to do and transact all and every business touching or concerning the premises, or which shall be necessarily incidental thereto, and to hold, enjoy, and exercise all such powers, authorities, and jurisdiction as are customary within the colleges within this Commonwealth.

SECTION 4. That the same trustees shall cause to be made a seal, with such device as they may think proper, and by and with which all the deeds, diplomas, certificates, and acts of the institution shall be authenticated, and they may at their pleasure alter the same.

SECTION 5. That at the first meeting of the board of trustees, the nine named, who are not *ex-officio* members, shall, by themselves and by lot, be divided into three classes of three each, numbered one, two, and three; the appointment hereby made of class number one, shall terminate on the first Monday of October, one thousand eight hundred and fifty-six; number two on the first Monday of October, one thousand eight hundred and fifty-seven, and number three on the first Monday of October, one thousand eight hundred and fifty-eight; and upon the termination of such office of such directors, to wit; on the first Monday of October in every year an election shall be held at the institution to supply their place, and such election shall be determined by the votes of the members of the executive committee of the Pennsylvania State Agricultural Society, and the votes of three representatives duly chosen by each county agricultural society in this Commonwealth which shall have been organized at three months preceding the time of election, and it shall be the duty of said board of trustees to appoint two of their number as judges to hold such election, to receive and count the votes, and return the same to the board of trustees with their certificate of the number of votes cast, and for whom, whereupon the said board shall determine who have receive the highest number of votes, and who are thereby elected.

SECTION 6. That on the second Thursday of June after the passage of this act, the board of trustees, who are hereby appointed, shall meet at Harrisburg, and proceed to the organization of an institution and selection of the most eligible site within the Commonwealth of Pennsylvania for its location, where they shall purchase or obtain by gift, grant, or otherwise, a tract of land containing at least two hundred acres, and not exceeding two thousand acres, upon which they shall procure such improvements and alterations to be made, as will make it an institution properly adapted to the instructions of youth in the art of farming according to the meaning and design of this act. They shall select and choose a principal for said institution who with such scientific attainments and capacity to teach as the Board shall deem necessary, shall be a good practical farmer; he with such other persons as shall, from time to time, be employed as teachers, shall comprise the faculty, under whose control the immediate management of the institution, and the instruction of all the youth committed to its care, shall be subject, however, to the revision and all the orders of the board of trustees; there shall be a quarterly meeting of the board of trustees at the institution, and as much oftener as shall be necessary, and they shall determine; the board shall have power to pass all such by-laws, ordinances, and rules as the good government of the institution shall require, and therein to prescribe what shall be taught to and what labor performed by the pupils, and generally to do and perform all such administrative acts as are usually performed by and within the appropriate duty of a board of trustees, and shall, by a secretary of their appointment, keep a minute of the proceedings and action of the board.

SECTION 7. That it shall be the duty of the board of trustees as soon and as often as the exigencies of the case may require, in addition to the principal, to employ such other professors, teachers, or tutors as shall be qualified to impart to pupils under their charge a knowledge of the English language, grammar, geography, history, mathematics, chemistry, and such other branches of natural and exact sciences as will conduce to the proper education of a farmer; the pupils shall, themselves, at such proper times and seasons as shall be prescribed by the board of trustees, perform all the labor necessary in the cultivation of the farm, and shall thus be instructed and taught all things necessary to be known by a farmer.

SECTION 8. That the board of trustees shall annually elect a treasurer, who shall receive and disburse the funds of the institution, and perform such other duties as shall be required of him, and from whom they shall take such security for the faithful performance of his duty as necessity shall require; and it shall be the duty of said board of trustees annually on or before the first of December, to make out a full and detailed account of the operations of the institution for the preceding year, and an account of all its receipts and disbursements, and report the same to the Pennsylvania State Agricultural Society, who shall embody said report in the annual report which, by existing laws, the said society is bound to make, and transmit to the Legislature on or before the first Monday of January each and every year.

SECTION 9. That it shall be lawful for the Pennsylvania State Agricultural Society, to appropriate out of their funds to the object of this act, a sum not exceeding ten thousand dollars, whenever the same shall be required, and to make such further appropriations annually, out of their funds, as will aid in the prosecution of this object, and it shall be the duty and privilege of said society at such time as they shall deem expedient by their committees, officers or otherwise, to visit the said institution and examine into the details of its management.

SECTION 10. That the act to incorporate the "Farmers' High School of Pennsylvania," approved the thirteenth day of April, Anno-Domini one thousand eight hundred and fifty-four, be and the same is hereby repealed.

APPROVED—The 22d day of February, A.D. 1855.
James Pollock, Governor

Law of Congress

An Act Donating Public Lands to the Several States and Territories Which May Provide Colleges for the Benefit of Agriculture and the Mechanic Arts.

Be it enacted by the Senate and House of Representatives of the United States of America in Congress assembled, That there be granted to the several states, for the purposes hereinafter mentioned, an amount of public land, to be appropriated to each State a quantity equal to thirty thousand acres for each senator and representative in Congress to which the States are respectively entitled by the apportionment under the census of eighteen hundred and sixty; *Provided,* That no mineral lands shall be selected or purchased under the provision of this act.

SECTION 2. *And be it further enacted,* That the land aforesaid, after being surveyed shall be apportioned to the several States in sections or subdivisions of sections, not less than one quarter of a section; and whenever there are public lands in a State subject to sale at private entry at one dollar and twenty-five cents per acre, the quantity to which said State shall be entitled shall be selected from such lands within the limits of such State, and the Secretary of the Interior is hereby directed to issue to each of the States in which there is not the quantity of public lands subject to sale at private entry at one dollar and twenty-five cents per acre, to which said State may be entitled under the provisions of this act land scrip to the amount in acres for the deficiency of its distributive share; said scrip to be sold by said States and the proceeds thereof applied to the uses and purposes prescribed in this act, and for no other use or purpose whatsoever: *Provided,* That in no case shall any State to which land scrip may thus be issued be allowed to locate the same within the limits of any other State, or of any Territory of the United States, but their assignees may thus locate said and scrip upon any of the unappropriated lands of the United States subject to sale at private entry at one dollar and twenty-five cents, or less, per acre; *And provided further,* That not more than one million acres shall be located by such assignees in any one of the States: *And provided further,* That no such location shall be made before one year from the passage of this act.

SECTION 3. *And be it further enacted,* That all the expenses of management, superintendence, and taxes from date of selection of lands, previous to their sales, and all expenses incurred in the management and disbursement of the moneys which may be received therefrom, shall be paid by the States to which they may belong, out of the treasury of said States, so that the entire proceeds of the sale of said lands shall be applied without any diminution whatever to the purposes hereinafter mentioned.

SECTION 4. *And be it further enacted,* That all moneys derived from the sale of the lands aforesaid by the States to which the lands are apportioned, and from the sales of land scrip hereinbefore provided for, shall be invested in stocks of the United States, or of the States, or some other safe stocks, yielding not less than five per centum upon the par value of said stocks; and that the moneys so invested shall constitute a perpetual fund, the capital of which shall remain forever undiminished, (except so far as may be provided in section fifth of this act.) and the interest of which shall be inviolably appropriated, by each State which may take and claim the benefit of this act, to the endowment, support, and maintenance of at least one college where the leading object shall be, without excluding other scientific and classical studies, and including military tactics, to teach such branches of learning as are related to agriculture and the mechanic arts, in such manner as the Legislatures of the States may respectively prescribe, in order to promote the liberal and practical education of the industrial classes in the several pursuits and professions of life.

SECTION 5. *And be it further enacted,* That the grant of land and land scrip hereby authorized shall be made on the following conditions, to which, as well as to the provisions hereinbefore contained, the previous assent of the several States shall be signified by legislative acts:

First: If any portion of the fund invested, as provided by the foregoing section, or any portion of the interest thereon, shall, by any action of contingency, be diminished or lost, it shall be replaced by the State to which it belongs, so that the capital of the fund shall remain forever undiminished; and the annual interest shall be regularly applied without diminution to the purposes mentioned in the fourth section of this act, except that a sum, not exceeding ten per centum upon the amount received by any State under the provisions of this act, may be expended for the purchase of lands for sites or experimental farms, whenever authorized by the respective Legislatures of said States.

Second: No portion of said fund, nor the interest thereon, shall be applied, directly or indirectly, under any pretense whatever, to the purchase, erection, preservation, or repair of any building or buildings.

Third: Any State which may take and claim the benefit of the provisions of this act shall provide, within five years, at least not less than one college, as described in the fourth section of this act, or the grant to such State shall cease; and said State shall be bound to pay the United States the amount received of any lands previously sold, and that the title to purchasers under the State shall be valid.

Fourth: An annual report shall be made regarding the progress of each college, recording any improvements and experiments made, with their cost and results, and such other matters, including State industrial and economical statistics, as may be supposed useful; one copy of which shall be transmitted by mail free, by each, to all the other colleges which may be endowed under the provisions of this act, and also one copy to the Secretary of the Interior.

Sixth: No State while in a condition of rebellion or insurrection against the Government of the United States shall be entitled to the benefit of this act.

Seventh: No state shall be entitled to the benefits of this act unless it shall express its acceptance thereof by its Legislature within two years from the date of its approval by the President.

SECTION 6. *And be it further enacted,* That land scrip issued under the provision of this act shall not be subject to location until after the first day of January, one thousand eight hundred and sixty-three.

SECTION 7. *And be it further enacted,* That the land officers shall receive the same fees for locating land scrip issued under the provisions of this act as is now allowed for the location of military bounty land warrants under existing laws: *Provided,* Their maximum compensation shall not be thereby increased.

SECTION 8. *And be it further enacted,* That the Governors of the several States to which scrip shall be issued under this act shall be required to report annually to Congress all sales made of such scrip until the whole shall be disposed of, the amount received for same, and what appropriation has been made of the proceeds.

APPROVED, July 2, 1862.
A. Lincoln.

An Act to Accept the Grant of Public Lands by the United States to the Several States, for the Endowment of Agricultural Colleges

WHEREAS, By an act of Congress, passed the second day of July, one thousand eight hundred and sixty-two, a grant of land was made to the several States and Territories, which may provide colleges for the benefit of agriculture and the mechanic arts, equal to thirty thousand acres for each Senator and Representative in Congress to which the States are respectively entitled, by the apportionment under the census of one thousand eight hundred and sixty, which act of Congress requires that the Several States, in order to entitle them to the benefit of said grant, should within two years from the dates of this act, express their acceptance of same:

And whereas, the Legislature of Pennsylvania has already shown its high regard for the agricultural interests of the State, by the establishment of the Agricultural College of Pennsylvania, and by making liberal appropriations thereto; therefore,

SECTION 1. *Be it enacted by the Senate and House of Representative of the Commonwealth of Pennsylvania in General Assembly met, and it is hereby enacted by the authority of the same,* That the act of Congress, passed the second day of July, one thousand eight hundred and sixty-two entitled "An act donating lands of the several States and Territories which may provide colleges for the benefit of agriculture and the mechanic arts," be and the same is hereby accepted by the State of Pennsylvania, with all its provisions and conditions, and the faith of the State is hereby pledged to carry the same into effect.

SECTION 2. That the Surveyor General of the State of Pennsylvania is hereby authorized and required to do every act and thing necessary to entitle this State to its distributive share of land scrip, under the provisions of the said act of Congress, and when the said scrip is received by him, to dispose of the same, under such regulations as the board of commissioners hereafter appointed by this act shall prescribe.

SECTION 3. That the Governor, the Auditor General, and the Surveyor General are hereby constituted a board of commissioners, with full power and authority to make all needful rules and regulations respecting the manner in which the Surveyor General aforesaid shall dispose of the said land scrip, the investment of the proceeds thereof in the State stocks of this State, and apply interest arising therefrom as herein directed; and in general to do all and every act or acts necessary to carry into full effect the said act of Congress; *Provided,* That no investment shall be made in any other stocks than those of the United States or of this Commonwealth.

SECTION 4. That until otherwise ordered by the Legislature of Pennsylvania, the annual interest accruing from any investment of the funds acquired under the said act of Congress is hereby appropriated, and the said commissioners are directed to pay the same to the Agricultural College of Pennsylvania for the endowment, support, and maintenance of said institution, which college is now in full and successful operation, and where the leading object is, without excluding other scientific and classical studies, and including military tactics, to teach such branches of learning as are related to agriculture and the mechanic arts.

SECTION 5. That the said Agricultural College of Pennsylvania shall, on or before the first day of February of each year, make a report to the Legislature of the receipts and expenditures of the said institution for the preceding year.

APPROVED—The 1st day of April, A.D. 1863.
Andrew Gregg Curtin, Governor

NOTES

Prologue and Acknowledgments

1. Accounts vary, but it is highly likely that Frederick Watts was the first American to purchase the new McCormick Reaper, given his penchant for innovation and the wherewithal to afford the machine. Most accounts agree that the first one was sold in 1840. Helen Tritt, in *Local History: Agricultural Society in Its Infancy* (Carlisle, Pa.: Historical Association of Cumberland County, Pa., Hamilton Library. Read Before the Hamilton Library Association, Carlisle, Pa., February 21, 1913, and Published by the Historical Department, 3), says that Watts "purchased the first McCormick Reaper to be used in Pennsylvania"; Reuben Gold Thwaites, in *Cyrus Hall McCormick and the Reaper* (Madison: State Historical Society of Wisconsin, 1909, 243), says "two machines [were] sold in 1840, two others in 1841, seven in 1842" but claims that "the sales had wholly been in Virginia." Mitchell Wilson, in the *Encyclopedia Britannica*, says "he sold 2 reapers in 1841, 7 in 1842, 29 in 1853, and 50 the following year." See https://www.britannica.com/biography/Cyrus-McCormick. If only two had been sold in 1840, Watts was either the first or the second to buy the machine, "Cyrus McCormick," https://enwikipedia.org/wiki/Cyrus_McCormick.
2. Watts's McCormick Reaper demonstration compiled from four sources: Tritt, *Local History*, 3; Stevenson W. Fletcher, *Pennsylvania Agriculture and Country Life, 1840–1940* (Harrisburg, Pa.: Pennsylvania Historical and Museum Commission, 1955), 54, 145; Jerry Clouse and Kate Kauffman, "Watts' Folly," *Pennsylvania Heritage: Quarterly of the Pennsylvania Historical and Museum Commission* 15, no. 4 (1989): 13; Mark W. Podvia, "The Honorable Frederick Watts: Carlisle's Agricultural Reformer," *Penn State Environmental Law Review* 17, no. 3 (2009): 307–8.
3. Podvia, "Carlisle's Agricultural Reformer," 308.
4. Clouse and Kauffman, "Watts' Folly," 13.
5. Podvia, "Carlisle's Agricultural Reformer," 308.
6. "England: Closing of the Great Exhibition—The Balloon Hoax—Egyptian Railroad—Mr. McCormick's Reaping Machine," *New York Times*, November 5, 1851, https://timesmachine.nytimes.cotimesmachine/1851/11/05/297732542.pdf.
7. Sally McMurry, *Pennsylvania Farming: A History in Landscapes* (Pittsburgh: University of Pittsburgh Press, 2017), 26.

8. Fletcher, *Pennsylvania Agriculture, 1840–1940*, 145.
9. Lawrence L. Shenk, "Frederick Watts: Public Spirited Citizen," (master's thesis, Shippensburg State College, 1966), 13; Podvia, "Carlisle's Agricultural Reformer," 307.
10. Fletcher, *Pennsylvania Agriculture, 1840–1940*, 482.
11. Stevenson W. Fletcher, *Pennsylvania Agriculture and Country Life, 1640–1840* (Harrisburg: Pennsylvania Historical and Museum Commission, 1950), 1.
12. Michael Zuckerman, "The Making and Unmaking of the Pennsylvania Empire," in *Pennsylvania: A History of the Commonwealth*, ed. Randall M. Miller and William Pencak (University Park: Penn State University Press, 2002), 373.
13. Roger L. Williams, *Evan Pugh's Penn State: America's Model Agricultural College* (University Park: Penn State University Press, 2018).
14. Roger L. Williams, *The Origins of Federal Support for Higher Education: George W. Atherton and the Land-Grant College Movement* (University Park: Penn State University Press, 1991).

Chapter 1

1. Alfred Nevin, "Hon. Frederick Watts," in *Centennial Biography: Men of Mark of Cumberland Valley, Pa., 1776–1876* (Philadelphia: Fulton Publishing, 1876), 307–8.
2. I. Thornton Osmond, *Hon. Frederick Watts* (Carlisle, Pa.: Hamilton Library and Cumberland County Historical Society, 1930), 2. Read before the Hamilton Library and Cumberland County Historical Association on February 28, 1930.
3. The "Watts Exit" on U.S. 322 is three miles west of the Clark's Ferry Bridge across the Susquehanna. The exit is in Watts Township, Perry County, the township having been created in 1849 and named in memory of David Watts, the son of Frederick the elder and father of Frederick the younger. "Watts Township, Perry County, Pennsylvania," http://www.wattstownship.org/Pages/Home.aspx.
4. Osmond, *Hon. Frederick Watts*, 2.
5. Ibid., 3.
6. Charles Coleman Sellers, *Dickinson College: A History* (Middletown: Wesleyan University Press, 1973), 145, 484.
7. Thomas P. Slaughter, *The Whiskey Rebellion: Frontier Epilogue to the American Revolution* (New York: Oxford University Press, 1986), 96.
8. Osmond, *Hon. Frederick Watts*, 3.
9. Shenk, "Public Spirited Citizen," 13.
10. "Carlisle, Pennsylvania," Wikipedia, https://en.wikipedia.org/wiki/Carlisle,_Pennsylvania.
11. James Henry Morgan, *Dickinson College: The History of One Hundred and Fifty Years, 1783–1933* (Carlisle, Pa.: Dickinson College, 1933), 2.
12. Judith Ridner, *A Town In-Between: Carlisle, Pennsylvania, and the Early Mid-Atlantic Interior* (Philadelphia: University of Pennsylvania Press, 2010), 1–3.
13. Morgan, *Dickinson College*, 10–15.
14. Ibid., 147–48.
15. Osmond, *Hon. Frederick Watts*, 3–4.
16. Morgan, *Dickinson College*, 203–6.
17. Nevin, "Hon. Frederick Watts," 308. William Miles, Esq., an early pioneer, lawyer, developer, miller, and farmer in Erie County, was the father of Judge James Miles, Esq., one of the original trustees of the Farmers' High School. Both William and James are credited for "reclaiming from the wilderness a

large portion of the best lands of Erie County . . . having been brought into a good state of cultivation up to the year 1850." See Laura P. Sanford, *The History of Erie County from Its First Settlement* (Philadelphia: J. B. Lippincott, 1861 and 1894), 83, 262.

18. Nevin, "Hon. Frederick Watts," 308; Milton Embick Flower and Lenore Embick Flower, *This Is Carlisle: A History of a Pennsylvania Town* (Harrisburg, Pa.: J. Horace McFarland, 1944), 40.
19. Podvia, "Carlisle's Agricultural Reformer," 301.
20. Nevin, "Hon. Frederick Watts," 308–9.
21. Podvia, "Carlisle's Agricultural Reformer," 303; Nevin, "Hon. Frederick Watts," 308.
22. "Hon. Frederick Watts," obituary, *Carlisle (Pa.) Daily Herald*, August 19, 1889, 1.
23. Podvia, "Carlisle's Agricultural Reformer," 302.
24. Osmond, *Hon. Frederick Watts*, 4.
25. "Frederick Watts," obituary, *New York Times*, August 18, 1889, https://timesmachine.nytimes.com/timesmachine/1889/08/18/100967593.pdf.
26. Doris Kearns Goodwin, *Leadership in Turbulent Times* (New York: Simon & Schuster, 2018), 11.
27. H. W. Brands, *Heirs of the Founders: Henry Clay, John Calhoun, and Daniel Webster, the Second Generation of American Giants* (New York: Anchor Books, 2019), 236, 253–58, 367–68.
28. Jill Lepore, *These Truths: A History of the United States* (New York: W. W. Norton, 2018), 264.
29. Quoted in George F. Will, *The Conservative Sensibility* (Boston: Hachette, 2019), 514–15.
30. Podvia, "Carlisle's Agricultural Reformer," 305.
31. "Frederick Watts," obituary, *New York Times*.
32. Shenk, "Public Spirited Citizen," 14.
33. Osmond, *Hon. Frederick Watts*, 5.
34. Shenk, "Public Spirited Citizen," 6–7.
35. "History of Pine Grove Furnace State Park," Pennsylvania Department of Conservation and Natural Resources, https://www.dcnr.pa.gov/StateParks/FindAPark/PineGroveFurnaceStatePark/Pages/History.aspx.
36. "The Honorable Frederick Watts," obituary, *Carlisle (Pa.) Daily Herald*, August 19, 1889, 4–5.
37. Jerry A. Clouse and Kate Kauffman, "Watts' Folly," *Pennsylvania Heritage: Quarterly of the Pennsylvania Historical and Museum Commission* 15, no. 4 (1989): 13.
38. Sellers, *Dickinson College*, 177.
39. Morgan, *Dickinson College*, 220–22.
40. Shenk, "Public Spirited Citizen," 4.
41. Morgan, *Dickinson College*, 224.
42. Sellers, *Dickinson College*, 190–91.
43. Roger L. Geiger, *The History of American Higher Education: Learning and Culture from the Founding to World War II* (Princeton: Princeton University Press, 2015), 193–97; Morgan, *Dickinson College*, 227.
44. Sellers, *Dickinson College*, 198; Morgan, *Dickinson College*, 231–48.
45. Morgan, *Dickinson College*, 396–97.
46. Boyd Lee Spahr, quoted in Morgan, *Dickinson College*, viii.
47. Richard Hofstadter and Wilson Smith, eds., *American Higher Education: A Documentary History*, vol. 1 (Chicago: University of Chicago Press, 1961), 278.
48. Flower and Flower, *This Is Carlisle*, 45; Shenk, "Public Spirited Citizen," 8.
49. Flower and Flower, *This Is Carlisle*, 45.
50. Paul J. Westhaeffer, *History of the Cumberland Valley Railroad, 1835–1919*

(Washington, D.C.: Washington, D.C., Chapter, National Railway Historical Society, 1979), 30–32.
51. Nevin, "Hon. Frederick Watts," 308.
52. Westhaeffer, *Cumberland Valley Railroad*, 29.
53. Brands, *Heirs of the Founders*, 252.
54. Westhaeffer, *Cumberland Valley Railroad*, 9–33.
55. Frederick Watts to Robert C. Sterritt, March 2, 1849, Manuscript Collection, Cumberland County Historical Society, Carlisle, Pa., file 066-006.
56. Westhaeffer, *Cumberland Valley Railroad*, 33–37.
57. George H. Burgess and Miles C. Kennedy, *Centennial History of the Pennsylvania Railroad Company* (Philadelphia: Pennsylvania Railroad Company, 1949), 127; Shenk, "Public Spirited Citizen," 10–11.
58. Clouse and Kauffman, "Watts' Folly," 13.
59. Westhaeffer, *Cumberland Valley Railroad*, 29.
60. Shenk, "Public Spirited Citizen," 12.
61. Albert J. Churella, *The Pennsylvania Railroad*, vol. 1, *Building an Empire, 1846–1917* (Philadelphia: University of Pennsylvania Press, 2012), 186.
62. Westhaeffer, *Cumberland Valley Railroad*, 62.
63. Ibid., 115.
64. Ibid., 116–17.
65. Podvia, "Carlisle's Agricultural Reformer," 304.
66. "Union Meeting in Carlisle, Pa.," December 22, 1860, Manuscript Collection, Cumberland County Historical Society, Carlisle, Pa., miscellaneous publications, file P-006-003.
67. Osmond, *Hon. Frederick Watts*, 4–5.
68. Fletcher, *Pennsylvania Agriculture, 1640–1840*, 343.
69. Fletcher, *Pennsylvania Agriculture, 1840–1940*, 451.
70. Lord Kames (Henry Home), *The Gentleman Farmer: Being an Attempt to Improve Agriculture by Subjecting It to the Test of Rational Principles* (Edinburgh, 1776), xviii.
71. Frederick Watts, "Address to the Farmers and Citizens of Minnesota," Frederick Watts Collection 1870–87, Pennsylvania Historical and Museum Commission, Pennsylvania State Archives, MG 131.1.
72. Tritt, *Local History*, 1–2.
73. Tritt, *Local History*, 3–4.
74. Clouse and Kauffman, "Watts' Folly," 16.
75. Nancy Van Dolsen, *Cumberland County: An Architectural Survey* (Ephrata, Pa.: Science Press, 1990), 42.
76. Clouse and Kauffman, "Watts' Folly," 17.
77. Pennsylvania Historical and Museum Commission Marker, located along U.S. Route 11 west of Carlisle. The text reads, "On a 116-acre tract here stood the model farm created 1857–67 by this agricultural reformer. Watts was the first president of the Pennsylvania Agricultural Society, 1851; a founder of the Farmers' High School (now Penn State); and U.S. Commissioner of Agriculture, 1871–76. The farm remained until 1988. Its site selection, layout, and building designs reflected Watts's pioneering ideas on farm efficiency."
78. Sharon Basaraba, "A Guide to Longevity Throughout History," Verywell Health, https://www.verywellhealth.com/longevity-throughout-history-2224054.

Chapter 2

1. *Annual Report of the Transactions of the Pennsylvania State Agricultural Society,*

vol. 1, *1850–54* (Harrisburg, Pa.: A. Boyd Hamilton, 1854), 11.

2. Ibid.
3. Ibid., 12.
4. Bob Bitz, "A Review of the History of the New York State Agricultural Society," New York State Agricultural Society, July 2012, https://www.nysagsociety.org/history.
5. "Ohio Department of Agriculture," Ohio History Connection, http://www.ohiohistorycentral.org/w/Ohio_Department_of_Agriculture.
6. *Annual Report of the Agricultural Society*, 1:13.
7. Ibid., 1:13–14.
8. Brad Bauerly, "The Agro-Industrial State: Early Agrarian Influence on U.S. State Building," *Journal of Peasant Studies* 45, no. 3 (2018): 527–28, http://dx.doi.org/10.1080/03066150.2017.1284063.
9. Fletcher, *Pennsylvania Agriculture, 1640–1840*, 280.
10. Ibid., 145–46.
11. Ibid., 305.
12. Ibid., 285.
13. Ibid., 314, 286.
14. *Annual Report of the Agricultural Society*, 1:14.
15. "Historical Membership," Philadelphia Society for Promoting Agriculture, http://www.pspaonline.com/resources/historical-membership.
16. Fletcher, *Pennsylvania Agriculture, 1640–1840*, 347–50.
17. Simon Baatz, *"Venerate the Plough": A History of the Philadelphia Society for Promoting Agriculture, 1785–1985* (Philadelphia: Philadelphia Society for Promoting Agriculture, 1985), 3–4.
18. Ibid., 4, 6.
19. Ibid., 9–10.
20. Ibid., 12–13.
21. Ibid., 25, 15–16.
22. Ibid., 22.
23. Ibid., 58.
24. Philadelphia Society for Promoting Agriculture, http://www.pspaonline.com.
25. Joseph C. G. Kennedy, *Population of the United States in 1860: Compiled from the Original Returns of the Eighth Census* (Washington, D.C.: Government Printing Office, 1864), iv, vii.
26. Ariel Ron, "Movements in the Lobby: Agricultural Reform as a State-Building Social Movement" (paper presented to the Policy History Conference, Columbus, Ohio, June 2014), 19.
27. Ariel Ron, "From Social Movement to Political Player: The Antebellum Origins of the Agricultural Lobby" (paper presented to SHEAR Annual Meeting, St. Louis, Mo., July 2013), 2.
28. *Annual Report of the Agricultural Society*, 1:15–19.
29. Ibid., 1:25–27.
30. Fletcher, *Pennsylvania Agriculture, 1840–1940*, 482.
31. *Annual Report of the Agricultural Society*, 1:34.
32. Ibid., 1:34.
33. Ibid., 1:31.
34. For the historiographical consensus on the superiority of German farming, see Charles H. Glatfelter, *The Pennsylvania Germans: A Brief Account of Their Influence on Pennsylvania*, Pennsylvania History Studies 20 (University Park: Pennsylvania Historical Association, 2002), 8–9; Fletcher, *Pennsylvania Agriculture, 1640–1840*, 48–50; Wayland F. Dunaway, *A History of Pennsylvania* (New York: Prentice-Hall, 1935), 83–84.
35. McMurry, *Pennsylvania Farming*, 8–9.
36. Glatfelter, *Pennsylvania Germans*, viii.
37. *Annual Report of the Agricultural Society*, 1:369.
38. Ibid., 1:40–41.
39. Ibid., 1:53–55.

40. Ibid., 1:54.
41. Alfred C. True, *A History of Agricultural Education in the United States, 1785–1925*, U.S. Department of Agriculture, Misc. Pub. no. 36 (Washington, D.C.: Government Printing Office, 1929), 90–91.
42. Williams, *Origins of Federal Support*, 29.
43. *Annual Report of the Agricultural Society*, 1:60–100.
44. Ibid., 1:107–319.
45. Erwin W. Runkle, *The Pennsylvania State College, 1853–1932: Interpretation and Record* (State College: Pennsylvania State College, 1933; Nittany Valley Society, 2013), 32.
46. "Third Annual Exhibition of the Pennsylvania State Agricultural Society at Pittsburg," *Pennsylvania Farm Journal* 3, no. 8 (1853): 241.
47. *Annual Report of the Agricultural Society*, 1:371–72.
48. Ibid., 1:440–41.
49. Ibid., 1:371.
50. Ibid., 1:57–59.
51. *Annual Report of the Transactions of the Pennsylvania State Agricultural Society*, vol. 2 (Harrisburg, Pa.: A. Boyd Hamilton, 1855), 15.
52. Ibid., 85–329.
53. Ibid., 17.
54. Ibid., 15.
55. "CPI Inflation Calculator," Official Data Foundation, https://www.officialdata.org.
56. Nathan M. Sorber, *Land-Grant Colleges and Popular Revolt: The Origins of the Morrill Act and the Reform of Higher Education* (Ithaca: Cornell University Press, 2018), 13.
57. Ron, "From Social Movement to Political Player," 2.

Chapter 3

1. *Annual Report of the Agricultural Society*, 1:58.
2. Runkle, *Pennsylvania State College*, 42–43.
3. Ibid., 44.
4. J. S. Keller, "The Farmer's High School of Pennsylvania," *Pennsylvania Farm Journal* 3, no. 2 (1853): 109; Runkle, *Pennsylvania State College*, 44.
5. *Annual Report of the Agricultural Society*, 1:8.
6. Frederick Watts, "Education of Farmers," *Pennsylvania Farm Journal* 3, no. 2 (1853): 51.
7. *Annual Report of the Agricultural Society*, 1:10.
8. Ibid., 1:8–10.
9. "Bigler, William," *Biographical Directory of the United States Congress*, https://bioguideretro.congress.gov/Home/MemberDetails?memIndex=B000459.
10. *Annual Report of the Transactions of the Pennsylvania State Agricultural Society*, vol. 3, *For the Year 1855* (Harrisburg, Pa.: A. Boyd Hamilton, 1856), 319–20.
11. An Act to Incorporate the Farmers' High School of Pennsylvania, approved April 13, 1854, in *Annual Report of the Agricultural Society*, 1:479–81.
12. Frederick Watts, "The Pennsylvania Legislature and the Farmers' High School," *Pennsylvania Farm Journal* 4, no. 6 (1854): 170.
13. *Annual Report of the Agricultural Society*, 2:31.
14. Ibid., 2:31–32.
15. Ibid., 2:33.
16. Ibid., 2:33–34.
17. Ibid., 2:27.
18. "James Pollock," Pennsylvania Historical and Museum Commission, http://www.phmc.state.pa.us/portal/communities/governors/1790-1876/james-pollock.html.
19. Act of Incorporation of the Farmers' High School of Pennsylvania, March 1855, in *Annual Report of the Agricultural Society*, 2:12–14.

20. Williams, *Evan Pugh's Penn State*, 40.
21. "Petition of James Gowen, Esq., President of the Pennsylvania State Agricultural Society, in behalf of the Farmers' High School of Pennsylvania," in *Annual Report of the Agricultural Society*, 3:306.
22. "Circular to the Vice Presidents of the Pennsylvania State Agricultural Society from James Gowen, President of the Pennsylvania State Agricultural Society," in *Annual Report of the Agricultural Society*, 3:309.
23. "Act of Incorporation of the Farmers' High School," 2:12–14.
24. Minutes of the Board of Trustees, June 14, 1855, in Minutes of the Board of Trustees of the Pennsylvania State College, vol. 1, June 14, 1855 to June 25, 1890, Eberly Family Special Collections Library, Pennsylvania State University, 1.
25. Minutes of the Board of Trustees, July 17, 1855, in Minutes, 2–4.
26. *Annual Report of the Agricultural Society*, 3:17.
27. Minutes of the Board of Trustees, September 12, 1855, in Minutes, 4–9; Runkle, *Pennsylvania State College*, 48.
28. McMurry, *Pennsylvania Farming*, 25.
29. Runkle, *Pennsylvania State College*, 48.
30. James Irvin to the Executive Committee of the Pennsylvania State Agricultural Society, February 22, 1855, reproduced in Sylvester K. Stevens, *The Centre Furnace Story: A Return to Our Roots*, rev. and exp. Philip S. Klein (State College, Pa.: Centre County Historical Society, 1985), 48.
31. Stevens, *Centre Furnace Story*, 50.
32. Ibid., 52.
33. Minutes of the Board of Trustees, September 12, 1855, in Minutes, 8.
34. Leon J. Stout, "Why I Wouldn't Want to Be President" (paper presented to the State College [Pa.] Literary Club), May 7, 2001.
35. Williams, *Evan Pugh's Penn State*, 42.
36. Frederick Watts to Charles B. Trego, October 2, 1855, Frederick Watts Letters, Farmers' High School and Agricultural College of Pennsylvania Collection, Pennsylvania State University Archives (PSUA) 287, Special Collections Library, Pennsylvania State University [hereafter PSUA 287], Box 5, GST/D/1.21.
37. Charles Trego to Frederick Watts, October 4, 1855, quoted in Stout, "Why I Wouldn't Want to Be President."
38. Watts to Trego, October 8, 1855, Frederick Watts Letters, PSUA 287, Box 5, GST/D/1.21.
39. Trego to Watts, October 13, 1855, quoted in Stout, "Why I Wouldn't Want to be President."
40. Leon J. Stout, "The Penn State President Who Never Was," *Town and Gown*, April 1996, 23–25.
41. Williams, *Evan Pugh's Penn State*, 42.
42. *Annual Report of the Agricultural Society*, 3:302–5.
43. "Annual Address, Delivered before the Pennsylvania State Agricultural Society, at Its Fifth Annual Exhibition, at Harrisburg, on Friday, September 28, 1855, by the Hon. Frederick Watts," in *Annual Report of the Agricultural Society*, 3:78–85.
44. *Public Ledger* editorial, quoted in Runkle, *Pennsylvania State College*, 50–51.
45. "Annual Address, Delivered by the Hon. George W. Woodward, before the Pennsylvania State Agricultural Society, at its Sixth Annual Exhibition at Pittsburg, October 3, 1856," in *Annual Report of the Transactions of the Pennsylvania State Agricultural Society*, vol. 4, *For the Year 1856* (Harrisburg, Pa.: A. Boyd Hamilton, 1857), 94.

46. Frederick Watts, "Barn Speech," quoted in Runkle, *Pennsylvania State College*, 51.

Chapter 4

1. Runkle, *Pennsylvania State College*, 72.
2. Minutes of the Board of Trustees, January 4, 1856, in Minutes, 9.
3. Ibid., 10.
4. Frederick Watts, "First Annual Report of the Farmers' High School to James Gowen, president, Pennsylvania State Agricultural Society, December 3, 1856," in *Annual Report of the Agricultural Society*, 4:22–25. See also Runkle, *Pennsylvania State College*, 73.
5. Minutes of the Board of Trustees, October 6, 1856, in Minutes, 11–12.
6. Runkle, *Pennsylvania State College*, 73.
7. Ibid., 75–76.
8. Ibid., 77–78.
9. Wayland F. Dunaway, *History of the Pennsylvania State College* (Lancaster, Pa.: Lancaster Press, 1946), 19.
10. "Annual Address, Delivered by Edwin C. Wilson, Esq., before the Pennsylvania State Agricultural Society, at Its Seventh Annual Exhibition at Philadelphia, October, 2, 1857," in *Annual Report of the Transactions of the Pennsylvania State Agricultural Society*, vol. 5, *For the Years 1857–58* (Harrisburg, Pa.: A. Boyd Hamilton, 1859), 201.
11. "Panic of 1857," Wikipedia, https://en.wikipedia.org/wiki/Panic_of_1857.
12. Frederick Watts, "Annual Report of the Board of Trustees of the Farmers' High School of Pennsylvania, as Made to the Legislature, January 19, 1858," in *Annual Report of the Agricultural Society*, 5:28–31.
13. Runkle, *Pennsylvania State College*, 61–62.
14. Watts, "Annual Report," 30.
15. Ibid., 50–51.
16. Minutes of the Board of Trustees, June 16, 1858, in Minutes, 16.
17. Runkle, *Pennsylvania State College*, 73.
18. Dunaway, *History of the Pennsylvania State College*, 20.
19. Frederick Watts to Hugh N. McAllister, August 19, 1858, Frederick Watts Letters, PSUA 287, Box 5, GST/D/1.21.
20. Runkle, *Pennsylvania State College*, 74.
21. Minutes of the Board of Trustees, June 16, 1858, in Minutes, 17.
22. Minutes of the Board of Trustees, September 1, 1858, in Minutes, 18, 19.
23. *Annual Report of the Agricultural Society*, 5:293.
24. Ibid., 5:295.
25. Ibid., 5:288–89.
26. Ibid., 5:290.
27. Minutes of the Board of Trustees, December 8, 1858, in Minutes, 19–21.
28. Ibid.
29. "Annual Report of the Trustees of the Farmers' High School of Pennsylvania to the Honorable David Taggart, President of the Pennsylvania State Agricultural Society," in *Annual Report of the Agricultural Society*, 5:73–74.
30. Quoted in Dunaway, *History of the Pennsylvania State College*, 25.
31. Quoted in Runkle, *Pennsylvania State College*, 62.
32. Williams, *Evan Pugh's Penn State*, 42–45.
33. Runkle, *Pennsylvania State College*, 55.
34. Evan Pugh to Alfred W. Elwyn, undated but annotated as being sent "sometime before the summer of 1855," Evan Pugh Papers, 1822–64 [hereafter PP], PSUA 1261, Eberly Family Special Collections Library, Pennsylvania State University, Box 3, Folder 11.
35. Evan Pugh to Samuel W. Johnson, October 31, 1855, PP, PSUA 1261, Box 2, Folder 10.

36. Evan Pugh to Samuel W. Johnson, November 14, 1855, PP, PSUA 1261, Box 2, Folder 10.
37. Evan Pugh to William Darlington, May 13, 1858, William Darlington Collection, New York Historical Society.
38. Alfred Traverse, "Dr. Pugh's Herbarium," *Journal of the Botanical Research Institute of Texas* 7, no. 2 (2013): 755.
39. Evan Pugh to Frederick Watts, March 3, 1859, PP, PSUA 1261, Box 3, Folder 11.
40. Frederick Watts to Evan Pugh, April 10, 1859, PP, PSUA 1261, Box 5, Folder 23.
41. Frederick Watts to Hugh N. McAllister, July 2, 1859, Frederick Watts Letters, PSUA 287, Box 5, GST/D/1.21.
42. Frederick Watts to Hugh N. McAllister, July 8, 1859, and July 13, 1859, Frederick Watts Letters, PSUA 287, Box 5, GST/D/1.21.
43. Frederick Watts to William G. Waring, October 1, 1859, Frederick Watts Letters, PSUA 287, Box 6, GST/AR/1.11.

Chapter 5

1. Evan Pugh to Samuel W. Johnson, January 6, 1860, PP, PSUA 1261, Box 5, Folder 12.
2. Roger L. Geiger, "New Themes in the History of Nineteenth-Century Colleges," in *The American College in the Nineteenth Century*, ed. Roger L. Geiger (Nashville: Vanderbilt University Press, 2000), 132, 133.
3. Geiger, *History of American Higher Education*, 194.
4. Evan Pugh, *A Report upon a Plan for the Organization of Colleges and the Mechanic Arts, with especial reference to the organization of the Agricultural College of Pennsylvania in view of the endowment of this institution by the land scrip fund donated by Congress to the State of Pennsylvania* (Harrisburg, Pa.: Singerly and Myers, 1864), 34.
5. Geiger, *History of American Higher Education*, 262.
6. Williams, *Evan Pugh's Penn State*, 15.
7. Geiger, *History of American Higher Education*, 261.
8. Quoted in Julianna Chaszar, "Leading and Losing in the Agricultural Education Movement: Freeman G. Cary and the Farmers' College, 1846–1884," *History of Higher Education Annual* 18 (1998): 34.
9. Evan Pugh, *The Agricultural College of Pennsylvania; Embracing a Succinct History of Agricultural Education in Europe and America, together with the circumstances of the Origin, Rise and Progress of the Agricultural College of Pennsylvania [. . .] September 1862* (Philadelphia: William S. Young, 1862), 11, 12 [hereafter *Agricultural College of Pennsylvania, September 1862*].
10. Williams, *Evan Pugh's Penn State*, 87–88.
11. Ibid., 56–57; Runkle, *Pennsylvania State College*, 57.
12. Evan Pugh, *On the Mutual Relations of the Teacher and the Taught*, Inaugural Address 1860 (Philadelphia: William S. Young, 1860), 21–23.
13. Pugh, *Agricultural College of Pennsylvania, September 1862*, 45–48.
14. Pugh, *Catalogue of the Officers and Students for the Second Annual Session of the Farmers' High School of Pennsylvania* (Philadelphia: Bryson's Printing Rooms, 1860), 13.
15. Williams, *Evan Pugh's Penn State*, 67.
16. Pugh, *Catalogue of the Officers and Students*, 22.

17. Pugh, *An Address to the Cumberland County Agricultural Society at Their Fall Meeting, October 1860* (Carlisle, Pa.: The Society, 1860), 36–37.
18. Frederick Watts to Hugh N. McAllister, September 2, 1860, Frederick Watts Letters, PSUA 287, Box 6, GST/AR/1.11.
19. Minutes of the Board of Trustees, December 5, 1860, in Minutes, 26.
20. Williams, *Evan Pugh's Penn State*, 76.
21. Pugh, *Agricultural College of Pennsylvania, September 1862*, 41.
22. Frederick Watts to Evan Pugh, April 12, 1861, PP, PSUA 1261, Box 5, Folder 23.
23. Minutes of the Board of Trustees, May 1, 1861, and October 24, 1861, in Minutes, 27, 28.
24. Pugh, *Agricultural College of Pennsylvania, September 1862*, 43.
25. Williams, *Evan Pugh's Penn State*, 80–84.
26. Pugh, *Agricultural College of Pennsylvania, September 1862*, 44.
27. Frederick Watts to Evan Pugh, February 26, 1862, Frederick Watts Letters, PSUA 287, Box 6 GST/AR1.11.
28. Minutes of the Board of Trustees, May 6, 1862, in Minutes, 29.
29. Williams, *Evan Pugh's Penn State*, 93–97.
30. An Act Donating Public Lands to the Several States and Territories Which May Provide Colleges for the Benefit of Agriculture and the Mechanic Arts, Pub. L. 37-108, 12 Stat. 503 (1862).
31. Lepore, *These Truths*, 332, 333.
32. Ariel Ron, "The Hidden Development State: Land-Grant Policy and the Federal Government in the Nineteenth Century" (Working Paper, 2010), https://www.academia.edu/4217353.
33. Williams, *Evan Pugh's Penn State*, 111.
34. Geiger, *History of American Higher Education*, 281.
35. Margaret Tschan Riley, "Evan Pugh of Pennsylvania State University and the Morrill Land-Grant Act," *Pennsylvania History* 27, no. 4 (1960): 355.
36. Robert Bruce, *The Launching of Modern American Science, 1846–1876* (Ithaca: Cornell University Press, 1987), 302.
37. Earle D. Ross, *Democracy's College: The Land-Grant Movement in the Formative Stage* (Ames: Iowa State College Press, 1942), 55.
38. Asa E. Martin, "Pennsylvania's Land-Grant Under the Morrill Act of 1862," *Pennsylvania History* 9, no. 2 (1942): 93.
39. Williams, *Evan Pugh's Penn State*, 116.
40. Pugh, *Report*, 34.
41. Williams, *Evan Pugh's Penn State*, 118–19.
42. Minutes of the Board of Trustees, September 2, 1862, in Minutes, 30.
43. Evan Pugh to Hugh N. McAllister, January 17, 1863, PP, PSUA 1261, Box 5, Folder 29.
44. Evan Pugh to Hugh N. McAllister, January 29, 1863, PP, PSUA 1261, Box 5, Folder 29.
45. Williams, *Evan Pugh's Penn State*, 120–21.
46. *The Legislative Record Containing the Debates and Proceedings of the Pennsylvania Legislature for the Session of 1864*, by George Bergner (Harrisburg, Pa.: "Telegraph" Steam Book and Job Office, 1864), 771.
47. Evan Pugh to Hugh N. McAllister, March 23, 1863, PP, PSUA 1261, Box 5, Folder 29.
48. An Act to Accept the Grant of Public Lands by the United States to the Several States, for the Endowment of Agricultural Colleges, P.L. 213, no. 227 (signed into law April 1, 1863).
49. Williams, *Evan Pugh's Penn State*, 123–35.

50. Minutes of the Board of Trustees, September 2, 1863, and December 1863 (no precise date provided), in Minutes, 33.
51. Minutes of the Board of Trustees, January 6, 1864, in Minutes, 34.
52. Ross, *Democracy's College*, 73, 239.
53. Pugh, *Report*, 7.
54. Ibid., 31–32.
55. Ibid., 33–35.
56. Evan Pugh, *A Statement made by Dr. E. Pugh, of the Agricultural College of Pennsylvania, at a special meeting of the Judiciary Committee at Harrisburg, convened March 3rd, 1864, in reference to the proposition to deprive this College of its Endowment,"* 2–8. PP, PSUA 1261, Box 5 (folder unknown).
57. Augustus O. Hiester to Evan Pugh, November 24, 1863, PP, PSUA 1261, Box 5, Folder 35.
58. Daniel Kaine to Evan Pugh, November 27, 1863, PP, PSUA 1261, Box 5, Folder 35.
59. Quoted in Runkle, *Pennsylvania State College*, 125.
60. *Legislative Record, 1864*, 920–21.
61. Williams, *Evan Pugh's Penn State*, 150–55.
62. Evan Pugh's response to H.B. 809, his last written words, April 22, 1864, with an annotation by C. Alfred Smith, Class of 1861, "student and closest friend of Dr. Pugh," PP, PSUA 1261, Box 4, Folder 16.
63. Williams, *Evan Pugh's Penn State*, 156–60.
64. *Legislative Record, 1864*, 1045.

Chapter 6

1. "Resolution upon the Death of President Pugh," by students of the Agricultural College of Pennsylvania, April 30, 1864, PP, PSUA 1261, Box 5, Folder 28.
2. Alfred L. Elwyn, Evan Pugh obituary, undated, PP, PSUA 1261, Box 5, Folder 48.
3. Evan Pugh obituary, *American Journal of Science and Arts* 38 (September 1864), PP, PSUA 1261, Box 5, Folder 48.
4. Frederick Watts to Hugh N. McAllister, May 4, 1864, Frederick Watts Letters, PSUA 287, Box 6, GST/AR/1.11.
5. Minutes of the Board of Trustees, June 15, 1864, 35.
6. Williams, *Evan Pugh's Penn State*, 99.
7. Ibid., 83.
8. Charles A. Browne, "European Experiences of an Early American Agricultural Chemist—Dr. Evan Pugh (1828–1864)," *Journal of Chemical Education* 7, no. 3 (1930): 517.
9. Alan I. Marcus, *Agricultural Science and the Quest for Legitimacy: Farmers, Agricultural Colleges, and Experiment Stations, 1870–1890* (Ames: Iowa State University Press, 1985), 20.
10. Frederick Watts to Hugh N. McAllister, May 12, 1864, Frederick Watts Letters, PSUA 287, Box 6, GST/AR/1.11.
11. Frederick Watts to Samuel W. Johnson, May 10, 1864, Frederick Watts Letters, PSUA 287, Box 6, GST/AR/1.11.
12. Hugh N. McAllister to Samuel W. Johnson, May 6, 1864, Hugh McAllister Letters, PSUA, Box 6, GST/AR.1.11.
13. Samuel W. Johnson to Hugh N. McAllister, May 12, 1864, PP, PSUA 1261, Box 5, Folder 47.
14. Thomas B. Osborne, *Biographical Memoir of Samuel William Johnson, 1830–*1909 (Washington, D.C.: National Academy of Sciences, 1911), 205–9.
15. Frederick Watts to Hugh N. McAllister, May 4, 1864, Frederick Watts Letters, PSUA 287, Box 6, GST/AR/1.11.

16. Minutes of the Board of Trustees, June 15, 1864.
17. Sellers, *Dickinson College*, 228.
18. Runkle, *Pennsylvania State College*, 141.
19. Quoted in Morgan, *Dickinson College*, 286.
20. "History," Girard College, https://www.girardcollege.edu/about/history.
21. Minutes of the Board of Trustees, June 15, 1864, in Minutes, 36.
22. Minutes of the Board of Trustees, July 14, 1864, in Minutes, 37.
23. Peter L. Moran and Roger L. Williams, "Saving the Land Grant for the Agricultural College of Pennsylvania," in *The Land-Grant Colleges and the Reshaping of American Higher Education*, ed. Roger L. Geiger and Nathan M. Sorber, Perspectives on the History of Higher Education 30 (New Brunswick, N.J.: Transaction, 2013), 116–18.
24. Minutes of the Board of Trustees, June 15, 1864, in Minutes, 36.
25. Caldwell, quoted in Kristen A. Yarmey, *Labors and Legacies: The Chemists of Penn State, 1855–1947* (University Park: Pennsylvania State University Department of Chemistry, 2006), 39–40.
26. Ibid., 44.
27. Michael Bezilla, *Penn State: An Illustrated History* (University Park: Penn State University Press, 1985), 15–16.
28. Runkle, *Pennsylvania State College*, 150–51.
29. Minutes of the Board of Trustees, February 8, 1866, 47.
30. Runkle, *Pennsylvania State College*, 147.
31. Williams, *Evan Pugh's Penn State*, 168.
32. Leon Stout, "A Look at Some of Penn State's First First Ladies," *Town and Gown*, 60.
33. Dunaway, *History of the Pennsylvania State College*, 65.
34. Minutes of the Board of Trustees, February 8, 1866, in Minutes, 43.
35. *Agricultural College of Pennsylvania Memorial to the Senate and House of Representatives, in relation to the Endowment of the College, and the Establishment of Experimental Farms in connection therewith,* undated, but early 1866, GVH/Administrative/History/General, PSUA.
36. *A supplement to the act to accept the grant of public lands by the United States to the several States, for the endowment of Agricultural Colleges, passed the first day of April, one thousand eight hundred and sixty-three,* Farmers' High School and Agricultural College of Pennsylvania Collection, Code of Laws and Statutes, Box 4, Book 6, GST/AM/1.11, PSUA 287.
37. Minutes of the Board of Trustees, September 4–5, 1866, in Minutes, 51.
38. Runkle, *Pennsylvania State College*, 152.
39. Minutes of the Board of Trustees, December 20, 1866, in Minutes, 56.
40. Williams, *Evan Pugh's Penn State*, 177.
41. An act relating to the Agricultural College of Pennsylvania, and to the establishment of experimental farms in connection therewith, Farmers' High School and Agricultural College of Pennsylvania Collection, Code of Laws and Statutes, PSUA 287, Box 4, Book 6, GST/AM/1.11.
42. Williams, *Evan Pugh's Penn State*, 176–77.
43. Ibid., 178.
44. Minutes of the Board of Trustees, March 13, 1867, in Minutes, 61.
45. Frederick Watts to George W. Tate, January 1, 1868, Frederick Watts Letters, PSUA 287, Box 5 GST/D/1.21.

46. Bezilla, *Penn State*, 17.
47. Ibid.
48. Minutes of the Board of Trustees, May 14, 1868, in Minutes, 78.
49. Michael Bezilla, *The College of Agriculture at Penn State: A Tradition of Excellence* (University Park: Penn State University Press, 1987), 24.
50. Dunaway, *History of the Pennsylvania State College*, 70.
51. Minutes of the Board of Trustees, May 27, 1868, in Minutes, 81.
52. William Walker to Hugh N. McAllister, July 15, 1868, Farmers' High School and Agricultural College of Pennsylvania Collection, PSUA 287, Box 5 GST/D/1.21.
53. Roy J. Passmore to Hugh N. McAllister, June 4, 1868, Farmers' High School and Agricultural College of Pennsylvania Collection, PSUA 287, Box 5 GST/D/1.21.
54. Minutes of the Board of Trustees, September 1, 1868, in Minutes, 81,82.
55. Minutes of the Board of Trustees, November 20, 1868, and December 10, 1868, in Minutes, 85.
56. David Wilson to Hugh N. McAllister, May 25, 1868, Farmers' High School and Agricultural College of Pennsylvania Collection (PSUA 287), Box 7, GST/AR/1.12.
57. Waterman Thomas Hewitt, *Cornell University: A History*, vol. 1 (New York: University Publishing Society, 1905), 97.
58. Andrew D. White, *Autobiography of Andrew Dickson White*, vol. 1 (New York: Century, 1905), 369, 436.
59. Morris Bishop, *A History of Cornell* (Ithaca: Cornell University Press, 1962), 279.
60. Williams, *Evan Pugh's Penn State*, 168.
61. Minutes of the Board of Trustees, January 23, 1868, in Minutes, 76.
62. Robert Landis Mohr, *Thomas Henry Burrowes, 1805–1871* (Philadelphia: University of Pennsylvania Press, 1946), 204–5.
63. J. Lacey Darlington to Hugh N. McAllister, December 28, 1868, Farmers' High School and Agricultural College of Pennsylvania Collection (PSUA 287), Box 7, GST/AR 1.12.
64. Minutes of the Board of Trustees, October 29, 1868, in Minutes, 84.
65. Minutes of the Board of Trustees, November 20, 1868, in Minutes, 85.
66. Minutes of the Board of Trustees, December 10, 1868, in Minutes, 86.
67. Bezilla, *Penn State*, 18.
68. Bezilla, *College of Agriculture*, 25.
69. Ibid.
70. A. J. Hamilton to Hugh N. McAllister, February 20, 1871, Box 5, GST/D/1.21. Farmers' High School and Agricultural College of Pennsylvania Collection (PSUA 287).
71. *First Annual Report of the Superintendent of the Eastern Pennsylvania Experimental Farm* (West Chester: Hickman & Hammer, Printers, 1869), 3–4. General Vertical Files/Administration/History/General (PSUA 287).
72. J. Lacey Darlington to Hugh N. McAllister, December 28, 1868, Farmers' High School and Agricultural College of Pennsylvania Collection (PSUA 287).
73. J. Lacey Darlington to Frederick Watts, January 20, 1868, Farmers' High School and Agricultural College of Pennsylvania Collection, PSUA 287, Box 7, GST/AM.1.14.
74. Minutes of the Board of Trustees, November 17, 1869.
75. Frederick Watts to Hugh N. McAllister, September 2, 1870, Frederick Watts Letters, PSUA 287, Box 5 GST/D/1.21.
76. Bezilla, *College of Agriculture*, 28.

77. Ibid., 39.
78. Ibid., 47.
79. Catalogue of the Agricultural College of Pennsylvania, 1872 (Philadelphia: Jas. B. Rodgers, 1872), 4.
80. Frederick Watts to Hugh N. McAllister, July 1, 1871, Frederick Watts Letters, PSUA 287, Box 5 GST/D/1.21.
81. Frederick Watts to Hugh N. McAllister, July 24, 1871, Frederick Watts Letters, PSUA 287, Box 5, GST/D/1.21.

Chapter 7

1. Minutes of the Board of Trustees of the Agricultural College of Pennsylvania, March 10, 1871.
2. Minutes of the Board of Trustees, March 21, 1871, in Minutes, 114.
3. Runkle, *Pennsylvania State College*, 171.
4. Hillsdale College, https://en.wikipedia.org/wiki/Hillsdale_College.
5. Frederick Watts to Hugh N. McAllister, July 1, 1871, Frederick Watts Letters, PSUA 287, Box 5, GST/D/1.21.
6. Minutes of the Board of Trustees, July 26, 1871, in Minutes, 116.
7. C. Alfred Smith, "Evan Pugh, Ph.D., F.C.S. Memorial Address, June 25, 1890." Delivered on the occasion of the presentation of a portrait of Dr. Pugh to the Pennsylvania State College, June 25, 1890, Box 5, Folder 51, Pugh Papers (PSUA 1261).
8. Runkle, *Pennsylvania State College*, 172.
9. Bezilla, *Penn State*, 22.
10. Minutes of the Board of Trustees, September 5, 1871, in Minutes, 117.
11. Carol Sonenklar, *We Are a Strong, Articulate Voice: A History of Women at Penn State* (University Park: Penn State University Press, 2006), 5.
12. Ibid., 7.
13. Runkle, *Pennsylvania State College*, 172.
14. *Catalogue of the Pennsylvania State College*, 1878–79, 8–13.
15. Nancy Weiss Malkiel, "'Keep the Damned Women Out': Fifty Years of Coeducation at American Colleges," *Chronicle of Higher Education: Chronicle Review*, January 25, 2019, B17–B19. Yale and Princeton led the way, going coeducational in 1969 and triggering a stampede by many of their elite counterparts to do likewise over the next five years.
16. Runkle, *Pennsylvania State College*, 173.
17. An Act directing the sale of the bonds composing the Agricultural College land scrip fund, and authorizing the issue of a new bond in lieu thereof, and abolishing the board of commissioners created by act of April first, one thousand, eight hundred and sixty-three, Farmers' High School and Agricultural College of Pennsylvania Collection, Code of Laws and Statutes, Box 4, Book 6, PSUA 287 GST/AM/1.11.
18. Runkle, *Pennsylvania State College*, 173.
19. Williams, *Evan Pugh's Penn State*, 152.
20. Frederick Watts to James Calder, May 12, 1873. Presidents' Office Records, PSUA 1250, Box 1, Folder 3, James Calder, business affairs, 1871–74.
21. Minutes of the Board of Trustees, July 23, 1873, in Minutes, 129.
22. Minutes of the Board of Trustees. July 29, 1874, in Minutes, 137.
23. Bezilla, *Penn State*, 21.
24. Runkle, *Pennsylvania State College*, 169.
25. Ibid., 175, 176.
26. Bezilla, *Penn State*, 23.
27. *Catalogue of the Agricultural College of Pennsylvania, 1872* (Philadelphia: Jas. B. Rodgers, 1872), 12.
28. Frederick Watts to James Calder, August 21, 1872. Presidents' Office

Records, PSUA 1250, Box 1, Folder 3, James Calder, business affairs, 1871–74.

29. *Catalogue of the Pennsylvania State College, 1873–74* (Philadelphia: Jas. B. Rodgers, 1874), 12.
30. *Catalogue of the Pennsylvania State College, 1875–76* (Harrisburg, Pa.: Patriot Publishing Company, 1876), 14.
31. *Catalogue of the Pennsylvania State College, 1879–80* (Harrisburg, Pa.: Lane S. Hart, Printer, 1880), 13.
32. *Catalogue of the Pennsylvania State College, 1882–83* (State College, Centre County, Penna., 1883), 29.
33. Bezilla, *Penn State*, 24.
34. Action of Patrons of Husbandry, Centre Hall, Pennsylvania, September 24, 1877, as printed in *Catalogue of the Pennsylvania State College, 1877–78* (Harrisburg: Lane S. Hart, Printer, 1878), 23.
35. Pennsylvania State Patrons of Husbandry, December 10, 1878, as printed in the *Catalogue of the Pennsylvania State College, 1878–79* (Harrisburg, Pa.: Lane S. Hart, Printer, 1879), 22–24.
36. Bezilla, *Penn State*, 24–25.
37. Ibid., 25.
38. Williams, *Evan Pugh's Penn State*, 172.
39. Quoted in Runkle, *Pennsylvania State College*, 196.
40. Dunaway, *History of the Pennsylvania State College*, 95.
41. Runkle, *Pennsylvania State College*, 198.
42. Ibid., 206.
43. Williams, *Origins of Federal Support*, 66–74.
44. Ibid., 75–78.
45. Lepore, *These Truths*, 335.
46. Sorber, *Land-Grant Colleges*, 84.
47. Ibid., 87.
48. Sorber, *Land-Grant Colleges*, 99–116.
49. Marcus, *Agricultural Science*, 38.
50. Williams, *Origins of Federal Support*, 92.
51. Ibid., 97–116.
52. Williams, *Origins of Federal Support*, 117–22.
53. Lepore, *These Truths*, 335.

Chapter 8

1. "Life Expectancy in the 1800s Not As Bad As Reported," https://gcanyon.wordpress.com/2009/06/25/life-expectancy-in-the-1800s-not-as-bad-as-reported.
2. Podvia, "Carlisle's Agricultural Reformer," 321n125.
3. An Act to Establish a Department of Agriculture, approved May 15, 1862, https://www.nal.usda.gov/act-establish-department-agriculture.
4. Frank P. Evans, "Reminiscences covering personal characteristics of several Executive Heads of the United States Department of Agriculture, 1871 to 1906," 1900, U.S. Department of Agriculture, National Agricultural Library, https://archive.org/details/reminiscencescov00evan.
5. Bauerly, "Agro-Industrial State," 536.
6. Fletcher, *Pennsylvania Agriculture, 1840–1940*, 387, 388.
7. *Report of the Commissioner of Agriculture for the Year 1870* (Washington, D.C.: Government Printing Office, 1871), 7.
8. Marcus, *Agricultural Science*, 132.
9. T. Swann Harding, *Two Blades of Grass: A History of Scientific Development in the U.S. Department of Agriculture* (Norman: University of Oklahoma Press, 1947), 29.
10. Evans, "Reminiscences."
11. An Act to Establish a Department of Agriculture, approved May 15, 1862, https://www.nal.usda.gov/act-establish-department-agriculture.
12. Podvia, "Carlisle's Agricultural Reformer," 325.

13. Untitled, *Daily Critic*, Washington, D.C., April 13, 1874, cited in Podvia, "Carlisle's Agricultural Reformer," 325.
14. An Act Donating Public Lands to the Several States and Territories Which May Provide Colleges for the Benefit of Agriculture and Mechanic Arts, Section 5.
15. *Report of the Commissioner of Agriculture for the Year 1874* (Washington, D.C.: Government Printing Office, 1875), 5, 6.
16. Cited in True, *Agricultural Education in the United States*, 192, 193.
17. Ibid., 193.
18. Bezilla, *College of Agriculture*, 26.
19. True, *Agricultural Education in the United States*, 193–95.
20. Proceedings of the National Agricultural Convention Held at Washington, D.C., February 15, 16, and 17, 1872. Senate, 42nd Congress, 2nd Session, Mis. Doc. No. 164 (Washington, D.C.: Government Printing Office, 1872), 4.
21. Ibid., 3.
22. Ibid., 17, 18.
23. Ibid., 18, 19.
24. Ibid., 57.
25. Ibid., 58.
26. Marcus, *Agricultural Science*, 134.
27. Ibid., 20.
28. *Proceedings*, 62.
29. Williams, *Origins of Federal Support*, 108–16.
30. Marcus, *Agricultural Science*, 136.
31. Frederick Watts, Department of Agriculture Circular, May 25, 1872, addressed to John Hamilton, Agricultural College, Centre County, Pa., Centre County Historical Society, Thompson and Related Families Collection, Box 12. John Hamilton collection, Folder 2.
32. Frederick Watts, Department of Agriculture Circular, October 15, 1872, addressed to Rev. James Calder, D.D., Agricultural Post Office, Pa. Centre County Historical Society, Thompson and Related Families Collection, Box 12. John Hamilton collection, Folder 2.
33. Williams, *Origins of Federal Support*, 80.
34. Ibid., 197–222.
35. Williams, *Origins of Federal Support*, 138–49.
36. *Report of the Commissioner of Agriculture for the Year 1871* (Washington, D.C.: Government Printing Office, 1872), 3.
37. Ibid., 3.
38. Ibid., 306–35.
39. Ibid., 345, 336.
40. Ibid., 344.
41. *Report of the Commissioner of Agriculture for the Year 1872* (Washington, D.C.: Government Printing Office, 1873), 396.
42. Pugh, *Report*, 15.
43. *Report of the Commissioner of Agriculture for the Year 1873* (Washington, D.C.: Government Printing Office, 1874), 321.
44. Ibid., 350.
45. *Report of the Commissioner of Agriculture for the Year 1874* (Washington, D.C.: Government Printing Office, 1875), 312.
46. *Report of the Commissioner of Agriculture for the Year 1875* (Washington, D.C.: Government Printing Office, 1876), 429.
47. Williams, *Evan Pugh's Penn State*, 107.
48. *Report of the Commissioner of Agriculture for the Year 1875* (Washington, D.C.: Government Printing Office, 1876), 517–20.
49. Fletcher, *Pennsylvania Agriculture, 1840–1940*, 482.
50. *Report of the Commissioner of Agriculture for the Year 1876* (Washington,

D.C.: Government Printing Office, 1877), 326.
51. *Catalogue of the Pennsylvania State College 1878–79* (Harrisburg, Pa.: Lane S. Hart, Printer, 1879), 44, 45.
52. Marcus, *Agricultural Science*, 146.
53. An Act to Establish a Department of Agriculture, approved May 15, 1862, https://www.nal.usda.gov/act-establish-department-agriculture.
54. *Report of the Commissioner of Agriculture for the Year 1871* (Washington, D.C.: Government Printing Office, 1872), 2.
55. Shenk, "Public Spirited Citizen," 31.
56. *Report of the Commissioner,* 1872, 6.
57. *Report of the Commissioner,* 1871, 4.
58. Frederick Watts to John Hamilton, June 17, 1872. Centre County Historical Society, Thompson and Related Families Collection, Box 12. John Hamilton collection, Folder 2.
59. *Report of the Commissioner*, 1876, 14.
60. *Report of the Commissioner*, 1875, 8, 9.
61. Ibid., 7, 8.
62. *Report of the Commissioner*, 1872, 7.
63. *Report of the Commissioner*, 1877, 18.
64. Shenk, "Public Spirited Citizen," 32.
65. *Report of the Commissioner*, 1871, 3, 4.
66. *Report of the Commissioner*, 1872, 6.
67. *Report of the Commissioner*, 1873, 6.
68. *Report of the Commissioner*, 1875, 9.
69. Shenk, "Public Spirited Citizen," 34.
70. *Report of the Commissioner*, 1872, 4.
71. Gladys L. Baker, Wayne D. Rasmussen, Vivian Wiser, and Jane M. Porter, *A Century of Service: The First 100 Years of the United States Department of Agriculture* (Washington, D.C.: U.S. Department of Agriculture, 1963), 19.
72. Ibid., 20.
73. *Report of the Commissioner*, 1873, 13.
74. *Report of the Commissioner*, 1874, 11–12.
75. Ibid., 11–12.
76. Shenk, "Public Spirited Citizen," 40.
77. *Report of the Commissioner*, 1876, 12.
78. *Report of the Commissioner*, 1871, 10.
79. Baker et al., *Century of Service*, 20.
80. *Report of the Commissioner*, 1873, 10.
81. *Report of the Commissioner*, 1876, 8.
82. "Franklin B. Hough," https://foresthistory.org/research-explore/us-forest-service-history/people/chiefs/franklin-b-hough.
83. Chuck Lyons, *1874: The Year of the Locust*, http://www.historynet.com/1874-the-year-of-the-locust.htm.
84. *Report of the Commissioner*, 1874, 8.
85. *Report of the Commissioner*, 1875, 8.
86. Ibid., 7.
87. Stephanie Grauman Wolf, "Centennial Exhibition (1876)," *Encyclopedia of Greater Philadelphia*, 2013, https://philadelphiaencyclopedia.org/archive/centennial.
88. Ibid.; "Exhibition Facts," Centennial Exhibition Digital Collection, Free Library of Philadelphia, 2001, http://libwww.library.phila.gov/CenCol/exh-org.htm.
89. "Exhibition Facts."
90. *Report of the Commissioner*, 1876, 7.
91. 1876 United States Presidential Election, Wikipedia, https://en.wikipedia.org/wiki/1876_United_States_presidential_election.
92. Untitled, *Daily Critic*, March 10, 1877, 2, cited in Podvia, "Carlisle's Agricultural Reformer," 325.
93. *Report of the Commissioner, 1876*, 15.
94. Shenk, "Public Spirited Citizen," 45.

Epilogue

1. Shenk, "Public Spirited Citizen," 55–56.
2. Thomas I. Mairs, "Frederick Watts," in *Some Pennsylvania Pioneers in Agricultural Science*, The Pennsylvania State College Studies in Agriculture, No. 1, College Series No. 2 (State College, Pa.: Pennsylvania State College, 1928), 177.

3. "The Hon. Frederick Watts, 1801–1889," *Carlisle (Pa.) Daily Herald*, August 19, 1889, 1.
4. *Resolution of the Cumberland County Bar*, August 20, 1889, reproduced in Shenk, "Public Spirited Citizen," appendix.
5. Nevin, "Hon. Frederick Watts," 308–9.
6. Osmond, *Hon. Frederick Watts*, 9.
7. Saul Bellow, *Ravelstein* (New York: Viking Penguin, 2000), 161.
8. David Hackett Fischer, *Albion's Seed: Four British Folkways in America* (New York: Oxford University Press, 1989), 4.
9. Frederick Watts, untitled manuscript for speech delivered to the Cumberland County Agricultural Society, September 1870. Watts, Frederick, Collection, 1870–1887, Pennsylvania Historical and Museum Commission, Pennsylvania State Archives, MG #131.1.
10. Pennsylvania Farm Show, https://www.farmshow.pa.gov/about/Pages/default.aspx.
11. Pennsylvania Agriculture, https://www.agriculture.pa.gov/about/pa_agriculture_industry/Pages/default.aspx.
12. Northeast States Ranking 2018, https://www.nass.usda.gov/Statistics_by_State/Regional_Office/Northeastern/includes/Publications/Rankings/Northeast%20States%20Ranking%202018.pdf.
13. Center for World University Rankings, https://cwur.org/2018-19.php.
14. "Penn State Tops NSF Rankings for Breadth of Research Expertise," https://news.psu.edu/story/608532/2020/02/18/research/penn-state-tops-nsf-rankings-breadth-research-expertise.
15. *2018 President's Report on Philanthropy and Endowments*, 24–29, https://issuu.com/givetopsu/docs/2018_2019_presidentsreport?fr=sOTFlNzQoMjI1NQ.
16. Williams, *Origins of Federal Support*, 115.

BIBLIOGRAPHY

Collections

Cromer, Abbie. Papers, 1950–53. Eberly Family Special Collections Library, Pennsylvania State University. MGN 23 AX/CATO/MS/00077.

Darlington, William. Collection. New York Historical Society.

Farmers' High School and Agricultural College of Pennsylvania Collection, PSUA 287, Special Collections Library, Pennsylvania State University.

Manuscript Collection, Cumberland County Historical Society, Carlisle, Pa.

McAllister, Hugh. Letters, 1857–74. Farmers' High School and Agricultural College of Pennsylvania Collection. Pennsylvania State University Archives (PSUA) 287, Eberly Family Special Collections Library, Pennsylvania State University, Box 6, GST/AR.1.11.

Minutes of the Board of Trustees of the Pennsylvania State College. Vol. 1: June 14, 1855, to June 25, 1890. Eberly Family Special Collections Library, Pennsylvania State University.

Pugh, Evan. Papers, 1822–64. Pennsylvania State University Archives 1261. Eberly Family Special Collections Library, Pennsylvania State University.

Thompson and Related Families Collection. Centre County Historical Society, State College, Pa.

Waring, William G. Papers. 1851–71. Eberly Family Special Collections Library, Pennsylvania State University.

Waring Family Papers. Eberly Family Special Collections Library, Pennsylvania State University, MGN 107, Box 3, GST/A/1.26.

Watts, Frederick. Collection, 1870–87. Pennsylvania Historical and Museum Commission, Pennsylvania State Archives, MG 131.1.

Watts, Frederick. Letters, 1857–74. Farmers' High School and Agricultural College of Pennsylvania Collection. Pennsylvania State University Archives (PSUA) 287, Eberly Family Special Collections Library, Pennsylvania State University, Box 5, GST/0/1.21.

Published Sources

An Act Directing the Sale of the Bonds Composing the Agricultural College Land Scrip Fund, and Authorizing the Issue of a New Bond in Lieu Thereof, and Abolishing the Board of Commissioners Created by Act of April First, One Thousand, Eight Hundred and Sixty-Three.

Farmers' High School and Agricultural College of Pennsylvania Collection. Pennsylvania State University Archives 287, Code of Laws and Statutes, Box 4, Book 6 GST/AM/1.11.

An Act Donating Public Lands to the Several States and Territories which May Provide Colleges for the Benefit of Agriculture and the Mechanic Arts. Pub. L. 37–108, 12 Stat. 503 (1862).

An Act of Incorporation of the Farmers' High School of Pennsylvania, March 1855. In *Annual Report of the Transactions of the Pennsylvania State Agricultural Society*, vol. 2, 12–14.

An Act Relating to the Agricultural College of Pennsylvania, and to the Establishment of Experimental Farms in Connection Therewith. Farmers' High School and Agricultural College of Pennsylvania Collection. Pennsylvania State University Archives 287, Code of Laws and Statutes, Box 4, Book 6, GST/AM/1.11.

An Act to Accept the Grant of Public Lands by the United States to the Several States, for the Endowment of Agricultural Colleges. P.L. 213, no. 227 (April 1, 1863).

An Act to Establish a Department of Agriculture, Approved May 15, 1862. https://www.nal.usda.gov/act-establish-department-agriculture.

An Act to Incorporate the Farmers' High School of Pennsylvania, approved April 13, 1854. In *Annual Report of the Transactions of the Pennsylvania State Agricultural Society*, vol. 1, *1850–54*, 479–81.

Agricultural College of Pennsylvania Memorial to the Senate and House of Representatives, in Relation to the Endowment of the College, and the Establishment of Experimental Farms in Connection Therewith. Undated, early 1866. Pennsylvania State University Archives, GVH/Administrative/History/General.

Annual Report of the Transactions of the Pennsylvania State Agricultural Society. 12 vols. Harrisburg, Pa.: A. Boyd Hamilton, 1854–77.

Baatz, Simon. *"Venerate the Plough": A History of the Philadelphia Society for Promoting Agriculture, 1785–1985*. Philadelphia: Philadelphia Society for Promoting Agriculture, 1985.

Baker, Gladys L., Wayne D. Rasmussen, Vivian Wiser, and Jane M. Porter. *A Century of Service: The First 100 Years of the United States Department of Agriculture*. Washington, D.C.: U.S. Department of Agriculture, 1963.

Basaraba, Sharon. "A Guide to Longevity Throughout History." Verywell Health, April 24, 2020. https://www.verywellhealth.com/longevity-throughout-history-2224054.

Bauerly, Brad. "The Agro-Industrial State: Early Agrarian Influence on US State Building." *Journal of Peasant Studies* 45 (2018): 525–44. http://dx.doi.org/10.1080/03066150.2017.1284063.

Bellow, Saul. *Ravelstein*. New York: Viking Penguin, 2000.

Bergner, George. *The Legislative Record Containing the Debates and Proceedings of the Pennsylvania Legislature for the Session of 1864*. Harrisburg, Pa.: "Telegraph" Steam Book and Job Office, 1864.

Bezilla, Michael. *The College of Agriculture at Penn State: A Tradition of*

Excellence. University Park: Penn State University Press, 1987.
———. *Penn State: An Illustrated History*. University Park: Penn State University Press, 1985.
"Bigler, William." *Biographical Directory of the United States Congress*. https://bioguideretro.congress.gov/Home/MemberDetails?memIndex=B000459.
Bishop, Morris. *A History of Cornell*. Ithaca: Cornell University Press, 1962.
Bitz, Bob. "A Review of the History of the New York State Agricultural Society." New York State Agricultural Society, July 2012. https://www.nysagsociety.org/history.
Brands, H. W. *Heirs of the Founders: Henry Clay, John Calhoun, and Daniel Webster, the Second Generation of American Giants*. New York: Anchor Books, 2019.
Browne, Charles A. "European Experiences of an Early American Agricultural Chemist—Dr. Evan Pugh (1828–1864)." *Journal of Chemical Education* 7, no. 3 (1930): 499–517.
Bruce, Robert. *The Launching of Modern American Science, 1846–1876*. Ithaca: Cornell University Press, 1987.
Burgess, George H., and Miles C. Kennedy. *Centennial History of the Pennsylvania Railroad Company*. Philadelphia: Pennsylvania Railroad Company, 1949.
Catalogue of the Agricultural College of Pennsylvania, 1872. Philadelphia: Jas. B. Rodgers, 1872.
Catalogue of the Pennsylvania State College, 1873–74. Philadelphia: Jas. B. Rodgers, 1874.
Catalogue of the Pennsylvania State College, 1875–76. Harrisburg, Pa.: Patriot Publishing, 1876.
Catalogue of the Pennsylvania State College, 1877–78. Harrisburg, Pa.: Lane S. Hart, Printer, 1878.
Catalogue of the Pennsylvania State College, 1878–79. Harrisburg, Pa.: Lane S. Hart, Printer, 1879.
Catalogue of the Pennsylvania State College, 1879–80. Harrisburg, Pa.: Lane S. Hart, Printer, 1880.
Catalogue of the Pennsylvania State College, 1882–83. State College, Pa., 1883.
Chaszar, Julianna. "Leading and Losing in the Agricultural Education Movement: Freeman G. Cary and the Farmers' College, 1846–1884." *History of Higher Education Annual* 18 (1998): 25–46.
Churella, Albert J. *The Pennsylvania Railroad*. Vol. 1, *Building and Empire, 1846–1917*. Philadelphia: University of Pennsylvania Press, 2012.
Clouse, Jerry A., and Patrick J. Donmoyer, eds. *Farming on the Ridges and in the Valleys of Perry County*. Kutztown, Pa.: Historic Barn and Farm Foundation of Pennsylvania, 2019.
Clouse, Jerry A., and Kate Kauffman. "Watts' Folly." *Pennsylvania Heritage: Quarterly of the Pennsylvania Historical and Museum Commission* 15, no. 4 (1989): 12 17.
Dolsen, Nancy Van. *Cumberland County: An Architectural Survey*. Ephrata, Pa.: Science Press, 1990.
Dunaway, Wayland F. *A History of Pennsylvania*. New York: Prentice-Hall, 1935.
———. *History of the Pennsylvania State College*. Lancaster, Pa.: Lancaster Press, 1946.
Elwyn, Alfred L. Evan Pugh obituary. Undated. Pennsylvania State University Archives 1261, Pugh Papers, undated, Box 5, Folder 48.

"England: Closing of the Great Exhibition—The Balloon Hoax—Egyptian Railroad—Mr. McCormick's Reaping Machine." *New York Times*, November 5, 1851. https://timesmachine.nytimes.cotimesmachine/1851/11/05/297732542.pdf.

Evan Pugh obituary. *American Journal of Science and Arts* 38 (September 1864). Pennsylvania State University Archives 1261, Pugh Papers, Box 5, Folder 48.

Evans, Frank P. "Reminiscences Covering Personal Characteristics of Several Executive Heads of the United States Department of Agriculture, 1871 to 1906." USDA National Agricultural Library, 1900. Internet Archive. https://archive.org/details/reminiscencescovooevan.

Exhibition Facts. Centennial Exhibition Digital Collection, Free Library of Philadelphia, 2001. http://libwww.library.phila.gov/CenCol/exh-org.htm.

First Annual Report of the Superintendent of the Eastern Pennsylvania Experimental Farm. West Chester, Pa.: Hickman & Hammer, Printers, 1869. Pennsylvania State University Archives 287, General Vertical Files/Administration/History/General.

Fischer, David Hackett. *Albion's Seed: Four British Folkways in America*. New York: Oxford University Press, 1989.

Fletcher, Stevenson W. *Pennsylvania Agriculture and Country Life, 1640–1840*. Harrisburg, Pa.: Pennsylvania Historical and Museum Commission, 1950.

———. *Pennsylvania Agriculture and Country Life, 1840–1940*. Harrisburg, Pa.: Pennsylvania Historical and Museum Commission, 1955.

Flower, Milton Embick, and Lenore Embick Flower. *This Is Carlisle: A History of a Pennsylvania Town*. Harrisburg, Pa.: J. Horace McFarland, 1944.

"Franklin B. Hough." Forest History Society. https://foresthistory.org/research-explore/us-forest-service-history/people/chiefs/franklin-b-hough.

Geiger, Roger L. *The History of American Higher Education: Learning and Culture from the Founding to World War II*. Princeton: Princeton University Press, 2015.

———, ed. "The Land-Grant Act and American Higher Education: Context and Consequences." Special issue. *History of Higher Education Annual* 18 (1998).

———. "New Themes in the History of Nineteenth-Century Colleges." In *The American College in the Nineteenth Century*, edited by Roger L. Geiger, 132–33. Nashville: Vanderbilt University Press, 2000.

Geiger, Roger L., and Nathan M. Sorber, eds. *The Land-Grant Colleges and the Reshaping of American Higher Education*. Perspectives on the History of Higher Education, vol. 30. New Brunswick, N.J.: Transaction, 2013.

Glatfelter, Charles H. *The Pennsylvania Germans: A Brief Account of Their Influence on Pennsylvania*. Pennsylvania History Studies 20. University Park: Pennsylvania Historical Association, 2002.

Goodwin, Doris Kearns. *Leadership in Turbulent Times*. New York: Simon & Schuster, 2018.

———. *Team of Rivals: The Political Genius of Abraham Lincoln*. New York: Simon & Schuster, 2005.

Harding, T. Swann. *Two Blades of Grass: A History of Scientific Development in the U.S. Department of Agriculture.* Norman: University of Oklahoma Press, 1947.

Hewitt, Waterman Thomas. *Cornell University: A History*, vol. 1. New York: University Publishing Society, 1905.

"History of Pine Grove Furnace State Park." Pennsylvania Department of Conservation and Natural Resources. https://www.dcnr.pa.gov/StateParks/FindAPark/PineGroveFurnaceStatePark/Pages/History.aspx.

Hofstadter, Richard, and Wilson Smith, eds. *American Higher Education: A Documentary History*, vol. 1. Chicago: University of Chicago Press, 1961.

"James Pollock." Pennsylvania Historical and Museum Commission. http://www.phmc.state.pa.us/portal/communities/governors/1790-1876/james-pollock.html.

Kames, Lord (Henry Home). *The Gentleman Farmer: Being an Attempt to Improve Agriculture by Subjecting It to the Test of Rational Principles.* Edinburgh, 1776.

Keller, J. S. "The Farmer's High School of Pennsylvania." *Pennsylvania Farm Journal* 3. no. 2 (1853): 109.

Kennedy, Joseph C. G. *Population of the United States in 1860: Compiled from the Original Returns of the Eighth Census.* Washington, D.C.: Government Printing Office, 1864.

Lepore, Jill. *These Truths: A History of the United States.* New York: W. W. Norton, 2018.

"Life Expectancy in the 1800s Not As Bad As Reported." Geoff Canyon's Appeal to Authority (blog), June 25, 2009. https://gcanyon.wordpress.com/2009/06/25/life-expectancy-in-the-1800s-not-as-bad-as-reported.

Lyons, Chuck. "1874: The Year of the Locust." *History Net.* http://www.historynet.com/1874-the-year-of-the-locust.htm.

Mairs, Thomas I. "Frederick Watts." In *Some Pennsylvania Pioneers in Agricultural Science.* College Series 2, 170–78. State College, Pa.: Pennsylvania State College Studies in Agriculture, 1928.

Malkiel, Nancy Weiss. "'Keep the Damned Women Out': Fifty Years of Coeducation at American Colleges." *Chronicle of Higher Education: Chronicle Review*, January 25, 2019.

Marcus, Alan I. *Agricultural Science and the Quest for Legitimacy: Farmers, Agricultural Colleges, and Experiment Stations, 1870–1890.* Ames: Iowa State University Press, 1985.

Martin, Asa E. "Pennsylvania's Land-Grant Under the Morrill Act of 1862." *Pennsylvania History* 9, no. 2 (1942): 85–117.

McMurry, Sally. *Pennsylvania Farming: A History in Landscapes.* Pittsburgh: University of Pittsburgh Press, 2017.

Memorial of the Committee of the Board of Trustees of the Farmers' High School of Pennsylvania to the Honorable the Senate and House of Representatives of the Commonwealth of Pennsylvania in General Assembly met. In *Fourth Annual Report of the Transactions of the Pennsylvania State Agricultural Society for the Year 1856.* Harrisburg, Pa.: A. Boyd Hamilton, 1857, 104–10.

Mohr, Robert Landis. *Thomas Henry Burrowes, 1805–1871*. Philadelphia: University of Pennsylvania Press, 1946.

Moran, Peter L., and Roger L. Williams. "Saving the Land Grant for the Agricultural College of Pennsylvania." In *The Land-Grant Colleges and the Reshaping of American Higher Education*, edited by Roger L. Geiger and Nathan M. Sorber, 105–29. Perspectives on the History of Higher Education, vol. 30. New Brunswick, N.J.: Transaction, 2013.

Morgan, James Henry. *Dickinson College: The History of One Hundred and Fifty Years, 1783–1933*. Carlisle, Pa.: Dickinson College, 1933.

Nevin, Alfred. "Hon. Frederick Watts." In *Centennial Biography: Men of Mark of Cumberland Valley, Pa., 1776–1876*, 307–9. Philadelphia: Fulton Publishing, 1876.

"Northeast States Ranking 2018." https://www.nass.usda.gov/Statistics_by_State/Regional_Office/NortheasternincludesPublicationsRankingsNortheast%20States%20Ranking%202018.pdf.

"Ohio Department of Agriculture." Ohio History Connection. http://www.ohiohistorycentral.org/w/Ohio_Department_of_Agriculture.

Osborne, Thomas B. *Biographical Memoir of Samuel William Johnson, 1830–1909*. Washington, D.C.: National Academy of Sciences, 1911.

Osmond, I. Thornton. *Hon. Frederick Watts*. Carlisle, Pa.: Hamilton Library and Cumberland County Historical Society, 1930.

Pacchioli, David. "Penn State Tops NSF Rankings for Breadth of Research Expertise." Penn State News, February 18, 2020. https://news.psu.edu/story/608532/2020/02/18/research/penn-state-tops-nsf-rankings-breadth-research-expertise.

"Pennsylvania Agriculture." Pennsylvania Department of Agriculture. https://www.agriculture.pa.gov/about/pa_agriculture_industry/Pages/default.aspx.

Pennsylvania Farm Journal, vols. 3 and 4, 1853 and 1854. West Chester, Pa.

"Pennsylvania Farm Show." https://www.farmshow.pa.gov/pafarmshow/Pages/default.aspx.

Podvia, Mark W. "The Honorable Frederick Watts: Carlisle's Agricultural Reformer." *Penn State Environmental Law Review* 17, no. 3 (2009): 299–328.

Proceedings of the National Agricultural Convention Held at Washington, D.C., February 15, 16, and 17, 1872. Senate, 42nd Congress, 2nd Session, Misc. Doc. No. 164. Washington, D.C.: Government Printing Office, 1872.

Pugh, Evan. *An Address to the Cumberland County Agricultural Society at Their Fall Meeting, October 1860*. Carlisle, Pa.: The Society, 1860.

———. *The Agricultural College of Pennsylvania; Embracing a Succinct History of Agricultural Education in Europe and America, together with the circumstances of the Origin, Rise and Progress of the Agricultural College of Pennsylvania [. . .] September 1862*. Philadelphia: William S. Young, 1862.

———. *Catalogue of the Officers and Students for the Second Annual Session of the Farmers' High School of Pennsylvania*. Philadelphia: Bryson's Printing Rooms, 1860.

———. *On the Mutual Relations of the Teacher and the Taught*. Inaugural

Address 1860. Philadelphia: William S. Young, 1860.

———. *A Report Upon a Plan for the Organization of Colleges of Agriculture and the Mechanic Arts, with special reference to the organization of the Agricultural College of Pennsylvania in view of the endowment of this institution by the land scrip fund donated by Congress to the State of Pennsylvania.* Harrisburg, Pa.: Singerly and Myers, 1864.

———. Response to H.B. 809, his last written words, April 22, 1864, with an annotation by C. Alfred Smith, Class of 1861, "student and closest friend of Dr. Pugh." Unpublished. Pennsylvania State University Archives 1261, Pugh Papers, Box 4, Folder 16.

———. "A Statement made by Dr. E. Pugh, of the Agricultural College of Pennsylvania, at a special meeting of the Judiciary Committee at Harrisburg, convened March 3rd, 1864, in reference to the proposition to deprive this College of its Endowment." Pennsylvania State University Archives 1261, Pugh Papers.

Report of the Commissioner of Agriculture for the Year 1870. Washington, D.C.: Government Printing Office, 1871.

Report of the Commissioner of Agriculture for the Year 1871. Washington, D.C.: Government Printing Office, 1872.

Report of the Commissioner of Agriculture for the Year 1872. Washington, D.C.: Government Printing Office, 1873.

Report of the Commissioner of Agriculture for the Year 1873. Washington, D.C.: Government Printing Office, 1874.

Report of the Commissioner of Agriculture for the Year 1874. Washington, D.C.: Government Printing Office, 1875.

Report of the Commissioner of Agriculture for the Year 1875. Washington, D.C.: Government Printing Office, 1876.

Report of the Commissioner of Agriculture for the Year 1876. Washington, D.C.: Government Printing Office, 1877.

Report of the Commissioner of Agriculture for the Year 1877. Washington, D.C.: Government Printing Office, 1878.

"Resolution upon the Death of President Pugh." By students of the Agricultural College of Pennsylvania, April 30, 1864. Pennsylvania State University Archives 1261, Pugh Papers, Box 5, Folder 28.

Ridner, Judith. *A Town In-Between: Carlisle, Pennsylvania, and the Early Mid-Atlantic Interior.* Philadelphia: University of Pennsylvania Press, 2010.

Riley, Margaret Tschan. "Evan Pugh of Pennsylvania State University and the Morrill Land-Grant Act." *Pennsylvania History* 27, no. 4 (1960): 339–60

Ron, Ariel. "From Social Movement to Political Player: The Antebellum Origins of the Agricultural Lobby." Paper presented to SHEAR Annual Meeting, St. Louis, Mo., July 2013.

———. "The Hidden Development State: Land Grant Policy and the Federal Government in the Nineteenth Century." Working paper, 2010. https://www.academia.edu/4217353.

———. "Movements in the Lobby: Agricultural Reform as a State-Building Social Movement." Paper presented to the Policy History Conference, Columbus, Ohio, June 2014.

———. "Scientific Agriculture and the Agricultural State: Farmers, Capitalism, and Government in the Late Nineteenth Century."

Journal of the Gilded Age and Progressive Era 15 (2016): 294–309.

———. "Summoning the State: Northern Farmers and the Transformation of American Politics in the Mid-Nineteenth Century." *Journal of American History* 103, no. 2 (2016): 1–38.

Ross, Earle D. *Democracy's College: The Land-Grant Movement in the Formative Stage*. Ames: Iowa State College Press, 1942.

Runkle, Erwin W. *The Pennsylvania State College, 1853–1932: Interpretation and Record*. State College: Pennsylvania State College, 1933; Nittany Valley Society, 2013.

Sanford, Laura P. *The History of Erie County from Its First Settlement*. Philadelphia: J. B. Lippincott, 1861 and 1894.

Sellers, Charles Coleman. *Dickinson College: A History*. Middletown: Wesleyan University Press, 1973.

Shenk, Lawrence L. "Frederick Watts: Public Spirited Citizen." Master's thesis, Shippensburg State College, 1966.

Slaughter, Thomas P. *The Whiskey Rebellion: Frontier Epilogue to the American Revolution*. Oxford: Oxford University Press, 1986.

Smith, C. Alfred. "Evan Pugh, Ph.D., F.C.S. Memorial Address, June 25, 1890." Delivered on the occasion of the presentation of a portrait of Dr. Pugh to the Pennsylvania State College, June 25, 1890. Pennsylvania State University Archives 1261, Pugh Papers, Box 5, Folder 51.

Sonenklar, Carol. *We Are a Strong, Articulate Voice: A History of Women at Penn State*. University Park: Penn State University Press, 2006.

Sorber, Nathan M. *Land-Grant Colleges and Popular Revolt: The Origins of the Morrill Act and the Reform of Higher Education*. Ithaca: Cornell University Press, 2018.

Spero, Patrick. *Frontier Country: The Politics of War in Early Pennsylvania*. Philadelphia: University of Pennsylvania Press, 2016.

Stevens, Sylvester K. *The Centre Furnace Story: A Return to Our Roots*. Revised and expanded by Philip S. Klein. State College, Pa.: Centre County Historical Society, 1985.

Stout, Leon J. "A Look at Some of Penn State's First First Ladies." *Town & Gown*, September 1997.

———. "The Penn State President Who Never Was." *Town and Gown*, April 1996, 23–25.

———. "Why I Wouldn't Want to Be President." Paper presented to the State College (Pa.) Literary Club, May 7, 2001.

A Supplement to the Act to Accept the Grant of Public Lands by the United States to the Several States, for the Endowment of Agricultural Colleges, Passed the First Day of April, One Thousand Eight Hundred and Sixty-Three. Farmers' High School and Agricultural College of Pennsylvania Collection. Pennsylvania State University Archives 287, Code of Laws and Statutes, Box 4, Book 6, GST/AM/1.11.

"Third Annual Exhibition of the Pennsylvania State Agricultural Society at Pittsburg." *Pennsylvania Farm Journal* 3, no. 8 (1853): 241–49.

Thwaites, Reuben Gold. *Cyrus Hall McCormick and the Reaper*. Madison: State Historical Society of Wisconsin, 1909.

Traverse, Alfred. "Dr. Pugh's Herbarium." *Journal of the Botanical Research*

Institute of Texas 7, no. 2 (2013): 751–64.

Tritt, Helen. *Local History: Agricultural Society in Its Infancy*. Carlisle, Pa.: Historical Association of Cumberland County, Hamilton Library, 1913.

True, Alfred C. *A History of Agricultural Education in the United States, 1785–1925*. U.S. Department of Agriculture, Misc. Pub. no. 36. Washington, D.C.: Government Printing Office, 1929.

2019 President's Report on Philanthropy and Endowments, Penn State University Development, 1–36. https://issuu.com/givetopsu/docs/2018_2019_presidentsreport.

Watts, Frederick. "Annual Address, Delivered before the Pennsylvania State Agricultural Society, at Its Fifth Annual Exhibition, at Harrisburg, on Friday, September 28, 1855, by the Hon. Frederick Watts." In *Annual Report of the Agricultural Society*, vol. 3, *For the Year 1855*, 78–85.

———."Annual Report of the Board of Trustees of the Farmers' High School of Pennsylvania, as Made to the Legislature, January 19, 1858." In *Annual Report of the Transactions of the Pennsylvania State Agricultural Society*, vol. 5, *For the Years 1857–58*, 28–31.

———. "Education of Farmers." *Pennsylvania Farm Journal* 3, no. 2 (1853): 51.

———. "First Annual Report of the Farmers High School to James Gowen, President, Pennsylvania State Agricultural Society, December 3, 1856." In *Annual Report of the Transactions of the Pennsylvania State Agricultural Society*, vol. 4, *For the Year 1856*, 22–25.

———. "The Pennsylvania Legislature and the Farmers' High School." *Pennsylvania Farm Journal* 4, no. 6 (1854): 170.

Westhaeffer, Paul J. *History of the Cumberland Valley Railroad, 1835–1919*. Washington, D.C.: Washington, D.C., Chapter, National Railway Historical Society, 1979.

White, Andrew D. *Autobiography of Andrew Dickson White*, vol. 1. New York: Century, 1905.

Will, George F. *The Conservative Sensibility*. New York: Hachette, 2019.

Williams, Roger L. *Evan Pugh's Penn State: America's Model Agricultural College*. University Park: Penn State University Press, 2018.

———. *The Origins of Federal Support for Higher Education: George W. Atherton and the Land-Grant College Movement*. University Park: Pennsylvania State University Press, 1991.

Wilson, Edwin C. "Annual Address, Delivered by Edwin C. Wilson, Esq., before the Pennsylvania State Agricultural Society, at Its Seventh Annual Exhibition at Philadelphia, October, 2, 1857," in *Annual Report of the Transactions of the Pennsylvania State Agricultural Society*, vol. 5, *For the Years 1857–58* (Harrisburg, Pa.: A. Boyd Hamilton, 1859), 193–214.

Wolf, Stephanie Grauman. "Centennial Exhibition (1876)." *Encyclopedia of Greater Philadelphia*, 2013. https://philadelphiaencyclopedia.org/archive/centennial.

Woodward, George F. "Annual Address, Delivered by the Hon. George W.

Woodward, before the Pennsylvania State Agricultural Society, at Its Sixth Annual Exhibition at Pittsburg, October 3, 1856." In *Annual Report of the Transactions of the Pennsylvania State Agricultural Society*, vol. 4, *For the Year 1856* (Harrisburg, Pa.: A. Boyd Hamilton, 1857), 90–104.

Yarmey, Kristen A. *Labors and Legacies: The Chemists of Penn State, 1855–1947*. University Park: Pennsylvania State University Department of Chemistry, 2006.

Zuckerman, Michael. "The Making and Unmaking of the Pennsylvania Empire." In *Pennsylvania: A History of the Commonwealth*, edited by Randall M. Miller and William Pencak, 371–85. University Park: Penn State University Press, 2002.

INDEX